SOLDIER *of*
SOUTHWESTERN
VIRGINIA

SOLDIER *of* SOUTHWESTERN VIRGINIA

THE CIVIL WAR LETTERS OF
CAPTAIN JOHN PRESTON SHEFFEY

Edited by James I. Robertson, Jr.

*Published in Cooperation
with the Virginia Center for
Civil War Studies*

LOUISIANA STATE UNIVERSITY PRESS
BATON ROUGE

Frontispiece: "Pres" Sheffey, in his Confederate uniform, probably early in the war

Designer: Amanda McDonald Scallan
Typeface: Minion
Typesetter: Coghill Composition Co., Inc.
Printer and binder: Thomson-Shore, Inc.

Library of Congress Cataloging-in-Publication Data

Sheffey, John Preston.
    Soldier of southwestern Virginia : the Civil War letters of Captain John
    Preston Sheffey / edited by James I. Robertson, Jr.
        p.   cm.
    Includes bibliographical references and index.
    ISBN 0-8071-3013-3 (hardcover : alk. paper)
    1. Sheffey, John Preston—Correspondence.   2. Confederate States of
America. Army. Virginia Cavalry Regiment, 8th.   3. Virginia—History—Civil
War, 1861–1865—Personal narratives.   4. United States—History—Civil War,
1861–1865—Personal narratives, Confederate.   5.
Soldiers—Virginia—Marion—Correspondence.   6. Marion (Va.)—Biography.
I. Robertson, James I.   II. Title.
E581.68th . S54   2004
973.7′455′092—dc22   2004010854

SECOND PRINTING, 2005

CONTENTS

ACKNOWLEDGMENTS

Fundamental credit for this book goes to the descendants of Pres and Josie Sheffey. They preserved the captain's letters, gathered together other writings on the couple, amassed newspaper clippings, and thus created a valuable collection of Civil War–era material. Ultimately, Betty Blair Stewart, Caroline Parrish Seager, and Martha Copenhaver, all of Marion, became custodians of the papers. Joan Tracy Armstrong of Marion, together with Copenhaver, first transcribed Sheffey's wartime correspondence. The three descendants of the captain could not have been more supportive in the production of this volume. A major regret will always be that Caroline Seager did not live to see the work to its conclusion.

Sheffey's letters appear in print a year sooner than might have been the case because of the pioneering editorial work of Prof. Robert Seager II. An in-law and historian in his own right (a biography of John Tyler being his best-known work), Seager organized the letters, made new transcriptions, provided some beginning annotation—especially useful where Sheffey family members are concerned—and wrote vignettes on a half-dozen battles and events mentioned in the letters. His groundbreaking efforts were many and time saving.

Sara Eye, my graduate teaching assistant for a year, agreed to serve also as chief research aide on this project. She patiently pored through census returns, helped in the always-present search to identify Sheffey's literary references, struggled with my editorial scribbles, and prepared the final draft of the manuscript. Much of this book is a testimony to Eye's talent as a researcher and editor.

Marilyn L. Norstedt, reference/bibliographic librarian at Virginia Tech, answered even the most obscure query with her characteristic promptness and thoroughness.

Joe and Betty Gillespie were gracious hosts as well as painstaking researchers in their Wytheville area.

George Skoch demonstrated anew why he is one of the best Civil War mapmakers in the business. ˙

Sylvia Frank Rodrigue of Louisiana State University Press shared our early enthusiasm for the Sheffey letters and, with the care inherent in a great editor, nursed the project to its completion. Deep appreciation goes to managing editor Lee Campbell Sioles, who accompanied the manuscript through copy editing and publication with the ease of a true professional.

To each of the following, whose individual contributions added much to the text, go profound thanks: Beth R. Brown, Patricia Cooper, Charles Crockett, James Finck, Don Francis, Dr. J. Stephen Hudgins, Prof. James C. Klotter, Cathy Carlson Reynolds, Elizabeth G. Robertson, James I. Robertson III, Carole Wassum Rosenbaum, Thomas E. Sebrell II, Prof. Paul M. Sorrentino, and James E. Talbert.

Although Sheffey's education and knowledge were extraordinary for the time, his writing style left something to be desired. Certain grammatical improvements have been made for this publication. Necessary punctuation is in place. Long sentences with multiple clauses have been broken down into two or more sentences. In an apparent effort not to waste space, Sheffey did little paragraphing. That has been corrected, as have misspellings of proper names.

The royalties from this book will be used for the establishment at Virginia Tech of the John Preston Sheffey Graduate Scholarship for the Study of Civil War History. I think Pres Sheffey would like that.

SOLDIER *of* SOUTHWESTERN VIRGINIA

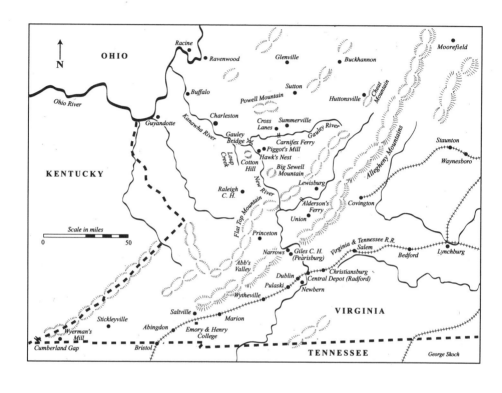

INTRODUCTION

Disappointingly little has been written on southwestern Virginia in the Civil War. Although most of the area consisted of sparsely settled mountainous terrain, the land held vast deposits of coal, lead, and salt. Such natural resources can be the difference between victory and defeat in war, and thus southwestern Virginia was indispensable to any long-range success the Confederate States of America might have. The struggle between North and South was also the world's first railroad war, and snaking through the valleys of the region was the principal line in Virginia, the Virginia and Tennessee Railroad, completed in 1852. The fact that the Virginia and Tennessee was the only railroad connecting the Confederate capital at Richmond with the western theater gave it almost inestimable military importance. All of these factors made southwestern Virginia's importance to the South as much of material as of manpower.

The region was too vast and too mountainous, its communities too scattered and too isolated, to be sufficiently neutralized by Union military efforts. For example, the small town of Marion was idyllic in appearance, with seemingly little to make it of any military value. Yet it was alongside the Virginia and Tennessee Railroad; twenty miles to the west were the brine ponds of Saltville; forty miles to the east were the lead mines at Austinville; and Camp Jackson, the principal rendezvous point for Confederate recruits in southwestern Virginia, was twenty-five miles away at Wytheville. Federal offensives throughout that part of the Old Dominion consisted mainly of hit-and-run raids. Confederate defensive efforts necessarily became centered around detachments posted at strategic spots to block enemy seizure of the railroad, salt works, and lead mines.

John Preston Sheffey was a member of one such Southern unit guarding the region's resources. Descended from Virginia pioneers, he inherited an abiding love for his native state. Any regret he felt about his Confederate service was due to his inability to see more actual fighting in defense of his homeland.

The Sheffeys were relative newcomers to southwestern Virginia. In the late

1770s two brothers of German ancestry left Maryland and came to these mountains. The elder, Daniel Sheffey, settled in Wythe County and studied law under Alexander Smyth (for whom the adjoining county would be named). Daniel later moved northward to Staunton in Augusta County, where he became a successful attorney, state legislator, and member of Congress.

The other brother, Henry Sheffey, also settled in the mountain wilderness. He acquired considerable land and farming interests in the Cripple Creek region of Washington County. In time he married Margaret White, the sister of Col. James White, a man of powerful ability and standing in the county. From that union came a son, appropriately named James White Sheffey. After Margaret's sudden death, Colonel White assumed responsibility for three of her sons. One was eight-year-old James White Sheffey. The lad grew up in his uncle's care, then studied law under several attorneys at the county seat of Abingdon. At the age of twenty-one, James was admitted to the bar. His uncle and namesake entrusted him with legal work pertaining to the nearby salt ponds and lead mines in which Colonel White had heavy investments. James Sheffey's law career prospered.

In September 1835 the young lawyer married Ellen Preston, a descendant of pioneer statesman William Preston of Smithfield. Her mother had been a Preston as well. Ellen had thirteen brothers and sisters. To say that her links with the dominant Preston clan were strong would be an understatement.

Shortly after their marriage, James and Ellen Sheffey moved to the Smyth County seat of Marion. Their union would produce eleven children, only seven of whom survived infancy. The second child, and only son, was born on December 12, 1837. He was christened John Preston Sheffey and known throughout his life to friends as "Pres."

The boy prospered in a well-to-do, highly intellectual environment. His father's broad knowledge and his mother's inherent culture were constant gifts to the children. Pres Sheffey's first education came from private tutoring in Marion. He then entered nearby Emory & Henry College and graduated at the head of the class of 1857. His favorite teacher at the college was ancient-languages professor William E. Peters, who twice became Sheffey's brother-in-law—Peters first married Margaret Sheffey, who died in 1869, and four years later wed Mary Sheffey.

Following graduation from college, Pres spent two years in law studies at the University of Virginia; admission to the Virginia bar came easily. He followed a natural course by joining his father's law firm in Marion. By then

James White Sheffey had become one of Smyth County's leading attorneys as well as an extensive landholder. The father-son legal practice flourished for the next eighteen months.

With 1861 came the imminent threat of war. James Sheffey was elected Smyth County's representative to the Virginia State Convention. Its primary duty was to recommend whether Virginia remain in an unsettled Union or secede and join other Southern states in a new nation. Sheffey was a political moderate who doubted the wisdom of secession. Yet he voted in favor of disunion after Pres. Abraham Lincoln's call for troops to coerce the South into submission.

Meanwhile, Pres Sheffey was also active. An ardent secessionist, the young man spoke often at political rallies. He also was instrumental in organizing a local company of horsemen. The unit adopted the name "Smyth Dragoons" and was among the first Virginia units to volunteer for service in the Confederate States of America.

The Dragoons actually had a choice of duties in the war's first weeks. The men could proceed to Lynchburg for attachment to the main army forming in the state, could become part of guerrilla forces then organizing in the mountain region, or could serve with Brig. Gen. John B. Floyd, a former governor of Virginia and secretary of war under Pres. James Buchanan, in the threatened western counties of Virginia. Sheffey wanted the excitement of being in a guerrilla company. Yet since both Floyd and his wife were cousins of Sheffey's mother, the young recruit was not overly disappointed when the Dragoons voted to become part of Floyd's command.

Their decision proved fortuitous. Sheffey's company would become part of the 8th Virginia Cavalry Regiment. Seldom were all ten companies together. Few of them served in the Army of Northern Virginia. The regiment never fought as a whole in any of the major battles of the Civil War and thus escaped the crippling combat losses that befell most mounted Confederate units. For the three years that Sheffey was in the field, the 8th Virginia Cavalry's service was in eastern West Virginia, southwestern Virginia, eastern Tennessee, and the Shenandoah Valley. That is a major reason for the value of Sheffey's wartime letters to Josephine Spiller, the young woman who became his wife.

In highly literate fashion Sheffey describes the Civil War in overlooked—if not forgotten—areas. Few writers have given much attention to the southwestern Virginia and eastern West Virginia theaters. Yet tens of thousands of men North and South fought there, large numbers suffered there, and thousands died there. Their pains and deaths were no less real than what comrades endured at Second Manassas, Antietam, Gettysburg, and other major battle sites. Furthermore, what took place on the western perimeter of Virginia was far more critical to the outcome of the Civil War than is generally realized.

Pres Sheffey left for war with two major goals in his life: to defend his beloved Virginia and to marry Josephine Spiller. The quest for Spiller was probably his most arduous campaign. "Josie" Spiller was two and a half years younger than Sheffey. She was born March 31, 1840, at Wytheville and was one of eight siblings. Her mother, Susan Crockett (1809–83), came from a large and prominent Wythe County family. Her father, William Hickman Spiller, was born in 1800 in Danville, Virginia. He moved to Wytheville and bought a partnership in a mercantile business. In steady fashion Spiller acquired general stores in both Wytheville and Marion as well as extensive real estate in the two adjoining counties. Josie graduated from William D. Roedel's Seminary for Girls, a Wytheville academy known for high standards of scholarship.

In 1855 James Austin Graham, a member of an affluent Wythe County family, shot and killed William Spiller in a local hotel. Graham had sought in vain to marry one of the Spiller daughters and blamed the father for his failure. James White Sheffey was prosecuting attorney in the ensuing trial. For the first time in Virginia jurisprudence, the defendant was adjudged "not guilty by reason of temporary insanity." Graham was committed permanently to the state insane asylum.

Apparently Pres Sheffey met and briefly courted Josie Spiller in 1857. He was an upperclassman at Emory & Henry, and she was elected "Queen of Love and Beauty" in an annual pageant at Wytheville. Sheffey was immediately smitten; Spiller was more reserved. In March 1861 Pres reopened contact with Josie by means of a long, practiced, highly intellectual letter. He wrote in part, "Like the ghosts of pleasant dreams, the memories of my boyhood and youth, of my college-days and university-days gather round me, but no reminiscences of the past do I better love to recall than the memory of that correspondence, short-lived & ill-fated though it proved to be." Sheffey signed the letter: "As ever your sincere friend." When Josie made a quick and positive response, Pres sent an essay-length letter in return. A long-distance romance thus began. So did civil war a month later.

Within weeks, Sheffey was asking for a quick wedding. He wanted to marry Spiller before he left for military duty, but she was understandably hesitant, repeatedly asking for time to consider the matter. In May Lieutenant Sheffey and his cavalry company left Marion for further training at Camp Jackson on the outskirts of Wytheville. During the next two months, the couple became much better acquainted. But a wedding date remained somewhere in the future.

In the last week of July, Sheffey and the Smyth Dragoons departed for war. He was then twenty-three years old, five feet seven inches tall, with hazel eyes, sandy hair, and a light complexion. He was also hopelessly in love. In his next letter to Josie, he stated, "my thoughts revert as they have done constantly since my departure from Wytheville to you and the good old town which has so long been dearer to me than any other spot on earth because it was your home." He closed with the assertion: "I think I will be quite successful in making myself a soldier. With your love to urge me & sustain me, I could accomplish anything." That was not quite so, for Sheffey was under the command of General Floyd. Wherever the militarily untutored Floyd went, disaster followed.

Early that summer Federal forces in northwestern Virginia defeated the main Confederate army in the region at Corrick's Ford. The Northern advance through extreme western Virginia pressed on until its commander, Maj. Gen. George B. McClellan, left for Washington to take command of what would become the Army of the Potomac. Hoping to seize the initiative, Confederate authorities directed Floyd's brigade to rendezvous at Lewisburg with Brig. Gen. Henry A. Wise's legion, then retreating eastward through the Kanawha Valley from Charleston.

The possibility of Floyd and Wise working together was nonexistent. Both men were appointed generals because of political prominence, not military acumen. Both were ex-governors, autocratic, tempestuous, and jealous of competition. Floyd was the senior in rank and in overall command. Wise displayed a consistent reluctance to obey Floyd's orders. Floyd viewed his subordinate as the root cause of all the military problems he faced. Even Union general Jacob Cox, who took over from McClellan, declared after the war that if Wise "had been half as troublesome to me as he was to Floyd, I should indeed have had a hot time of it." As it was, the Federals had a relatively easy time with the two Confederate prima donnas.

Sheffey naturally sided with Floyd on every issue. After all, Floyd's mother was the granddaughter of William Preston, just as was Sheffey's mother. Allegiance to Floyd was familial.

The Marion lieutenant's first contacts with the enemy came on August 26 at Cross Lanes and on September 2 at Hawks Nest. Both engagements were only skirmishes, but to Sheffey they were monumental encounters. That he survived his initial meeting with the Federals gave him a momentarily macabre sense of humor: "One of the [wounded] Yankees lived more than a day with his brains shot out, conclusive evidence that they can get along almost as well without [brains] as with them." A week later at Carnifex Ferry, Sheffey got his first full taste of battle, from which he emerged a real soldier.

Sheffey spent much of the autumn begging his fiancée to write more often. Frequently he voiced frustrations that the Floyd-Wise combine could not get any military objective accomplished—even after Gen. Robert E. Lee came west to assist. Sheffey saw limited action in skirmishes at Sewell Mountain, Armstrong Creek, Loup Creek, and Guyandotte. At the same time, sickness and disease that would kill two soldiers for every one man slain in battle had engulfed the southwestern Virginia units. Encampment became as dangerous as an engagement.

The situation improved but little in the first half of 1862. Josie's letter writing was sporadic. At one point Sheffey moaned: "The days lengthen into weeks, the long weeks into months, and still you will not write. . . . I . . . will surrender myself to the Yankees or incurable blues within a fortnight if you don't write." What made the loneliness so unbearable, he added as winter descended, was that "[w]e live here like Greenlanders . . . , warming our frozen bodies with fats and oils, and shivering like Switzerlanders in the midst of glaciers and peaks covered with ice and snow."

Winter encampment near Princeton followed. The 8th Virginia Cavalry's chief duty was to guard one of the major approaches a possible Union strike force might use against the Virginia and Tennessee Railroad. Sheffey participated in clashes at Giles Court House, Princeton, and especially the battle of Lewisburg in May 1862. Although he escaped injury, the young Virginian was not a happy soldier. His regiment had become part of the fifteen-hundred-man "Army of New River" commanded by Brig. Gen. Henry Heth, an officer he did not respect. Furthermore, even though Sheffey was appointed captain of his company that spring, he did not enjoy good relations with either the colonel or the lieutenant colonel of the 8th Virginia Cavalry.

In mid-May 1862 his patience with Josie came to a momentary end. Sheffey declared that they should either marry or call off the engagement. She apparently asked him to visit her to discuss their future. He obtained leave and traveled to Wytheville, but it seems the couple came to no conclusions. Sheffey then took a different tack; his first letter after returning to camp was sprinkled with reports of the attractive young ladies he was meeting in the town where the 8th Virginia Cavalry was stationed.

Later in the summer, just before the twin Confederate disasters at Antietam and Perryville, Sheffey left on his most memorable campaign of the entire war. Union strength in western Virginia steadily declined as troops left to reinforce McClellan's Army of the Potomac. General Lee suggested that the cavalry in that region exploit this force reduction by conducting widespread raids against Union posts to create confusion and possibly even reoccupy the vital Kanawha Valley.

Brig. Gen. Albert Jenkins would be in command of the movements. With five hundred horsemen (most from Sheffey's regiment), Jenkins undertook a five-hundred-mile ride through all of the Union-held counties of western Virginia. "Jenkins's Raid" involved a circular sweep that ranged as far north as Weston. From there the cavalry galloped west, crossed the Ohio River, and became the first force to raise the Confederate flag on Ohio soil. The Southerners then recrossed the river and rode east toward Charleston. Any gains from this expedition were more psychological than material, and the victory was short lived; but it was a dramatic and dashing success at a time when the South needed a boost in morale. Sheffey was part of it, and he wrote extensively about it.

Afterward it was back to dreary patrol duty along the frontier. Sheffey's previous posts on such assignments had been Monroe, Mercer, and Greenbrier Counties. Now he shifted closer to home. The 8th Virginia Cavalry guarded the Virginia and Tennessee Railroad at Newbern and Central Depot (present-day Radford) before returning to the picket posts at Lewisburg. Sheffey also came to know the leading Confederate generals in the department: Samuel Jones, John Echols, John McCausland, and Gabriel C. Wharton. Echols and Wharton became his close friends.

In addition, Sheffey finally succeeded in winning a wife. In a number of letters to Josephine Spiller, he continued describing the beautiful and unattached ladies he was meeting at his various military stations. If this was not an ongoing effort to exert marital pressure on his fiancée, it gave every indication of being so. In any event, on June 9, 1863, Pres and Josie were married in Wytheville.

After returning to duty in Greenbrier County, Sheffey wrote his bride on June 20: "I have been congratulated, to an *enormous degree*. I do not think that a young man forced away from a wife, who is dearer to him than every thing else on earth, is an object of congratulation." Sheffey sought long, hard, but in vain to have Josie join him in camp. Meanwhile, isolated from the major military theaters, he could only speculate on the big picture of the war. For the first time Sheffey began to feel pangs of anxiety about the Confederacy's future; comments on skirmishes, friends, and compatriots became more serious. It was as if marriage had both aged and sobered him.

Then, almost without warning, the enemy appeared in Sheffey's own neighborhood. On July 17–18 some thirteen hundred Union cavalrymen attempted to cut the Virginia and Tennessee Railroad by a heavy raid on Wytheville. A sharp fight occurred, producing at least one hundred Union casualties. The raiders retaliated by burning several public buildings and looting a number of private homes. Sheffey spent days agonizing over the safety of his wife. Josie was not harmed. In fact, her mother, Susan Crockett Spiller, gave aid and shelter to a wounded Union colonel, who would reciprocate the kindness in time to her son-in-law.

Well into the autumn of 1863, Sheffey and his regiment were on patrol in Greenbrier (by now part of the new state of West Virginia) and Tazewell Counties. Confederates were continually moving to counter Union probes aimed at the railroad and the vital works at Saltville. Even Sheffey's father went on duty with home guards to meet the enemy threats. The young captain suffered personal hardships also during this period. First, he was unable to have his wife join him in camp near Lewisburg, despite his best efforts. Second, he contracted an eye infection that incapacitated him to varying degrees for months. But Sheffey tried to remain optimistic. At one point in October he wrote home: "The news from [General] Lee is glorious. Bragg also is said to be fighting & Vallandigham is reported to have been elected Gov. of Ohio." None of these reports was true. This showed the general fallacy of the "news" that drifted across the mountains.

Sheffey was nevertheless an extraordinarily observant soldier. His letters mention many residents of the counties where he was posted. And if his reports were sometimes nothing more than rumors exaggerated to a higher level, he at least reflected the musings and the morale in camp.

Mid-October 1863 brought orders for the 8th Virginia Cavalry to proceed to Abingdon to become part of a mounted brigade commanded by Brig. Gen. William E. "Grumble" Jones. But until the following spring, Sheffey's sole responsibility was serving as judge advocate on a departmental court-martial that met in the far southwestern Virginia counties of Lee and Scott. Boredom was the overriding emotion of those weeks, though the duty at least kept him indoors and away from a cold camp in the field.

For five weeks in April and May 1864, Sheffey was near Wytheville and his wife. This long gap in the correspondence is regrettable, for it was the time when Lt. Gen. U. S. Grant began his multifront campaign to crush not only Lee but also the entire Confederacy once and for all.

Late in May the 8th Virginia Cavalry and its sister units galloped northward to defend the threatened Shenandoah Valley. Sheffey and his comrades arrived after the June 5 battle at Piedmont, where the Federals routed the outmanned Southern cavalry and killed General Jones. Yet Sheffey did see action at Lynchburg; Hanging Rock (near present-day Salem); Leetown, West Virginia; and Frederick, Maryland, during the first stages of Lt. Gen. Jubal Early's raid on Washington.

Sheffey expressed mixed feelings about Maryland. He told Josie: "A more beautiful country never gladdened the eye of man. The horn of plenty had been outpoured upon the fields. . . . But the people, the people, the villainous Dutch with their outlandish lingo! What a pity that they should hold so fair a land!"

Following the raid (and a side trip to Chambersburg, Pennsylvania), the Confederate cavalry were resting in camp near Moorefield, West Virginia, when on August 7, Union horsemen swooped down in a surprise dawn attack. Among those wounded was the 21st Virginia Cavalry's Col. William E. Peters, Sheffey's brother-in-law; among those taken prisoner was Captain Sheffey. The captured officer spent the next six months in Prison No. 1, Camp Chase Military Prison at Columbus, Ohio. A former training base for Buckeye recruits, Camp Chase in 1862 became an enclosed-barracks compound surrounded by high wooden fences and guard towers. Its highest population total came in January 1865, when more than nine thousand prisoners of war were incarcerated there.

Camp Chase was nowhere near the hell-hole that prisons such as Andersonville and Elmira became. In fact, the officer section of Camp Chase seems to have been quite endurable. Sheffey's major complaint was loneliness. As he wrote Josie in November 1864, "The weary time drags very slowly away at best, but when many days elapse without bringing me a letter from you, it becomes still more intolerable." Other than a smallpox vaccination that became infected, Sheffey underwent few physical discomforts at Camp Chase.

His confinement ended in February 1865 after North and South resumed a policy of prisoner exchange. Sheffey was transferred to the military prison at Point Lookout, Maryland, and exchanged for a captured Union officer of equal rank. In all likelihood he was back in southwestern Virginia prior to Lee's surrender at Appomattox and the end of the war.

The more than ninety letters in the John Preston Sheffey Papers, now deposited in the Special Collections division of the Virginia Tech library, are a wonderful mixture of love and war. Sheffey's observations of people and events in the border counties on either side of the Virginia–West Virginia line have no parallel in printed works. He even describes actions so isolated that they are mentioned only in passing in the mammoth *Official Records of the Union and Confederate Armies.* The collection that follows provides an unprecedented picture of sociomilitary affairs in southwestern Virginia.

{ CHAPTER 1 }

War Clouds and Love Showers

As winter became spring in 1861, Pres Sheffey should have been busy. His father was Smyth County's representative to a convention meeting in Richmond that would determine whether Virginia remained in the Union or joined her Southern sisters. The elder Sheffey was a cautious moderate on the secession question until the bombardment of Fort Sumter and Abraham Lincoln's call for troops to coerce the South into submission. He then cast his vote with the majority for secession.

Meanwhile, Pres Sheffey operated the father-son law practice alone in Marion. Legal work must have been minimal at the time, for the twenty-three-year-old reopened a correspondence begun in 1858 with Josephine Spiller. She was three years younger than Sheffey and lived with her widowed mother in Wytheville, a day's ride from Marion.

The young attorney wrote three letters of courtship, each long and literate, in an attempt to gain Spiller's favor. When the young lady responded encouragingly, Sheffey fell completely in love. But civil war exploded across the nation shortly afterward. Sheffey's ardor toward war was only slightly less than his love for Spiller. He helped organize a local company of horsemen, which adopted the name "Smyth Dragoons," and Sheffey became its second lieutenant.

He sought desperately to marry Spiller before leaving for war, but she was not so anxious. Sheffey begged for a late-April wedding; she preferred to wait until mid-June. The more involved he became with war matters, the more frustrated he became with matters of the heart.

Marion, Va., MARCH 14, 1861

Miss Josie,

I take advantage of the privileges of an old correspondent and old friend to send you by this evening's mail, a copy of our village paper which as it contains several productions from the now overflowing pens of the young

Josephine Spiller, the Wytheville, Virginia, lady whom Sheffey courted for six years.

men of Smyth [County] is more than usually interesting to our own people and, if you love politics, may possibly serve to amuse you for a few moments.

The first article is the production of Mr. John S. Pendleton, Jr., at present a resident of Richmond and is sufficiently secession[ist] to suit the tastes of Wm. L. Yancey himself.[1] "The World's Ingratitude" is from the pen of Mr. A. F. St. John,[2] a young Smyth-ite, a student at E & H College who though not related to the "Henry St. John Gentlemen" of the olden time immortalized by Jno. Esten Cooke,[3] appears to be equally a lover and favorite

1. John Strother Pendleton later served as assistant surgeon in the 63d Virginia Infantry and surgeon of the 45th Virginia Infantry Battalion. Alabama's William Lowndes Yancey, known as the "Prince of Fire-Eaters," devoted his energies throughout the 1850s to secession and an independent Southern nation.

2. Andrew F. St. John became an officer in Sheffey's company of the 8th Virginia Cavalry.

3. John Esten Cooke was one of Virginia's most voluminous writers. His novel *Henry St. John, Gentleman,* appeared in 1859 and was the seventh of thirty-one works of fiction by the Winchester native.

of the ladies. He has frequently appeared before in the columns of the *Marion Visitor* over the signature of "Alpha." A better article is headed "A Trip to Sandy" and was written by Mr. Andrew P. Cole,[4] a young lawyer of Marion and native of Smyth who is gifted with a good deal of humor, dry wit and good sound sense and will some day make his mark.

The synopsis of the *Franklin Plan* of adjustment embodied in the Editorial, and enclosed in pencil brackets is from my own pen, as are also the article signed "Ike," and the six first resolutions adopted at our patriotic ultra-Southern meeting here last Saturday [March 9]; but as I have appeared in the columns of the Marion Visitor and elsewhere so frequently and under so many different signatures, they are not so interesting as the articles from the aforesaid young gentlemen.

We had a very enthusiastic secession meeting here last Saturday and much "rhetorical flourish."[5] A condensed account of the proceedings may be found in the paper I send you. I had prepared a Preamble and Resolutions, which members of the Committee have informed me would have been adopted without material alteration or objection had not Mr. Watson been appointed upon the Committee. They consequently had to be mutilated to suit his less Southern tastes. To the series adopted he made no objection when the vote was taken in the meeting, yet he comes out now with a card denying that he endorses them. He will be answered in a card next week by the five other members of the Committee.[6]

But I forget. I am going beyond my assumed privileges and trespassing too far upon your patience. I indeed very frequently regret that I do not still occupy the privileged position of one of your correspondents, but I threw away foolishly those privileges again. Like the ghosts of pleasant dreams, the memories of my boyhood and youth, of my college-days and university-days gather around me, but no reminiscences of the past do I better love to recall

4. Cole enlisted in the Smyth Dragoons with the first wave of volunteers and served in the 8th Virginia Cavalry until his discharge on December 15, 1863. In the postwar years he was successively commonwealth attorney for Smyth County and judge of the county court.

5. At that time, secessionists across the state were holding county meetings to generate public support for Virginia leaving the Union. The full text of the Smyth County resolutions is in Virginia State Library, comp., *Proceedings of the Virginia State Convention of 1861*, 4 vols. (Richmond, Va., 1965), 1:586–88.

6. The resolutions committee consisted of William Farer, W. F. Hurst, Edward A. Scott, W. D. Strother, and Edward S. Watson. Sheffey did not feel that Watson, a Marion dry-goods merchant, shared the secessionist ardor of his colleagues.

than the memory of that correspondence, short-lived & ill-fated though it proved to be.

You will therefore forgive the *presumption* if you so deem it, of this missive with which I have pleasantly whiled away a little of the leisure of an idle hour.

As ever your sincere friend,

Jno. Preston Sheffey

MARCH 23, 1861

Miss Josie,

I received and read with much pleasure your letter of the 17th inst. and regret that I have no better excuse to offer for again throwing myself upon your kind indulgence, than my own irresistible inclination.

A letter from you written in the familiar characters of *lang* syne, carries me back upon the wings of memory to the same old time idolatry and dreamy worship of long ago; and as I read, I forget the stern pride and worldly ambition that hourly grow upon me and become again the visionary boy, all heart, all happiness, indweller between the two right worlds of Poetry and Love. Bright worlds indeed are they, but they are worlds in the past to me. The future is indeed gilded by that false glimmer Hope, but it is the Hope only of the glittering baubles, Wealth and Fame. God willing, I will yet win both of them, but they have nothing to do with Heart or Happiness. They, the latter, belong to the past, and like the old man who sees before him only the hearse, the ghostly tombstone and the grassy mound, I also am too prone to live in the world that has passed away.

But enough of that! The great gulf you have fixed between yourself and me, you told me long ago (I say "long ago" for it seems a lonely, weary age) would be *forever* impassable. I am not one of those whose love is like the ephemera of the Ganges or the Nile,[7] which is born with the rising, to die with the setting sun, and I shall perhaps *never* cease to regret your decision; but I am too well aware that any attempt on my part to bridge the abyss would be worse than useless.

Not as a real "love-letter" therefore is the missive intended, though a superficial observer of the preceding sentences might so perhaps regard it.

Its object like the first is altogether political. I cannot quite gather from your letter whether you are a secessionist or a partial lover of this unholy

7. Sheffey refers poetically to the ebb and flow of the largest rivers in India and Egypt.

union with our enemies. I cannot believe the latter. The ladies of Eastern and Southwestern Virginia are almost universally secessionists. You say well, that "let the result be as it may, you will hail with joy the restoration of our former commercial and social happiness and prosperity; more than all, our dignity as one of the great nations of the Earth."

With all my heart I endorse the sentiment, provided it does not mean a reconstruction. That, moreover, is forever impossible. The mutual hatred of the North & South now is too deep, too irradicable. Such a reunion, further, like the present union of the Border States and the Republicans, would be too degrading, too disgraceful, to be endured by the proud slaveocracy of the gallant South. Would the seceded States enter into it? Never! Never! Can we do without them?

Let us try it and we shall see. Without them, we would not have the slightest voice in the government. We would make ourselves thoroughly ridiculous if we were to attempt to run a candidate or even to *vote* in the next Presidential election. We would wear forever the badge of our self-imposed inferiority as we do now. Better, far, that we should never attain to prosperity again. Better, far better, that we should live the life of the famished wolf, gaunt starveling though he be, yet free and wild in his native mountains, than like the well fed cub bear for a single day upon our creased necks and ignoble badge of our fawning servility. "Where Liberty dwells, there is my Country,"[8] and I am no longer a Virginian when her Judas Iscariots shall have succeeded in betraying her to the enemies of the South. We can never attain "our former commercial and social happiness and prosperity" or to "our dignity among the great nations of the Earth" except as two separate and distinct peoples.

Virginia has but one destiny and that is with the South. The young men and the rest of the true Southrons of Virginia have said it, and if the Old Fogies do refuse to us for a while the thing which is nearest and dearest to our hearts, the time will nevertheless come when we will decree a triumph to the glorious Southern Cause, and beat the Southern reveille over their ignoble graves. What right have Messrs. Rives and Summers and Robert Ridgeway,[9] with all the rest of the old line Whigs and Douglas Democrats who under the specious guise of "Unionism," the silver veil of the Hideous Mo-

8. This was the motto of American Revolution patriot James Otis.
9. Diplomat William Cabell Rives of Albemarle County, delegate George William Summers of Kanawha County, and *Richmond Daily Whig* editor Robert Ridgeway were among Virginians pleading for moderation that spring.

kanna[10] are still tied to their ancient idols, what right have they, because of their uncompromising hatred of the Breckinridge[11] slave-ocrats of the South, to tie us down to a doom of hopeless poverty and everlasting deprivation? That such is the fate they are seeking to bring upon us has been proven by the recent brilliant arguments of Randolph and Holcombe in the Virginia Convention.[12]

I send you by today's mail a copy of the Richmond Dispatch which you have not perhaps seen, containing a condensed report of my old Professor James Holcombe of the University [of Virginia] in the Convention of the 21st inst.

I will receive the full report in a few days and will send it to you also.

The proceedings at the Public Meeting in Wytheville[13] and at the supper given to Mr. Wm. H. Cook[14] prove that Wythe County stands side by side and shoulder with Smyth and Pulaski and glorious old Tazewell. And still the ball rolls on. The revulsions in faith of the followers of Ridgeway and the credulous geologists and antiquarians generally who look with a love akin to idolatry upon the gray old fossils that daily exhibit themselves to their worshippers in the Virginia Convention. The triumphant acquittal and vindication of Gov. Floyd[15] has also injured, not a little, the cause of his unscrupulous calumniators. The Voice of the People goes up in thunderstorms to the Convention commanding their servants to obey their will, and the men there who recently said they would "go nowhere" and "do nothing"

10. In the first of the four tales of Thomas Moore's poem *Lalla Rookh,* Hakem ben Haschem (whom Sheffey here calls "Mokanna") was a prophet who wore a veil to conceal his extreme ugliness.

11. John Cabell Breckinridge of Kentucky, the former vice president of the United States, had been the presidential candidate of Southern Democrats in the four-man election of 1860.

12. George Wythe Randolph of Richmond and James P. Holcombe of Albemarle County were outspoken secessionists.

13. The Wythe County petitions for secession, dated March 14, 1861, are in *Proceedings of the Virginia State Convention,* 1:657–60.

14. William H. Cook was a prominent Wytheville attorney. He later commanded the Wythe Rifles in the 51st Virginia Infantry.

15. John B. Floyd, like Sheffey, had blood ties to the influential Preston family of southwestern Virginia. Following a term as Virginia governor, Floyd became Pres. James Buchanan's secretary of war. He was widely accused in the North of transferring large amounts of government ordnance to the Southern states. The reports were exaggerated; Floyd appears to have been guilty of his old habit of slipshod administration. He resigned from the cabinet over the issue of reinforcing Federal forts in the South.

have at last actually come over far enough to stand with the friends of the Border State Conference.[16]

How passing strange that Citizens of Virginia should seem so blinded to what is plainly and palpably the highest honor and her best interests? It can only be accounted for on the ground of their hatred for the party on the other side, or some bargain with the Republicans to sell Virginia for a share in the spoils of future Republican victories. It cannot be blindness except according to the old saw that "none are so blind as those who *won't* see."

For but a few weeks ago sixty-nine Republicans in Congress voted in effect for interference with slavery in the states. The masses in the North are now plainly *worse* than their political leaders. The Republican elections, since the election of Lincoln, instead of showing the prophecied reaction indicate an alarming increase of strength. Each gale that comes from the North brings to our ears the clanking of fresh chains, the news of more brilliant orations, the joyous shouts over more decided Republican triumphs. The next gale that comes from the South may "bring to our ears, the clash of resounding arms."[17]

At Charleston the Floating Battery is moored within two hundred yards of [Fort] Sumter,[18] and at Pensacola the Confederate Troops are prepared and eager for the conflict. Let it begin, and straightway from the whole infuriated North, the curses of millions of fanatics will come to us, and soon upon the soil of Virginia, we shall hear the measured tread of legions of armed men, and over the old Mother still "lying supinely on her back and hugging the delusive phantom of Hope"[19] the dear, disgraced old "Star-spangled Banner," itself will wave, mocking her imbecility and triumphing in her subjugation.

We have nothing else to hope for. The shoemaker [Henry] Wilson and the base demagogue [Charles] Sumner are in the chairs where sat but yester-

16. One tactic of delay by Virginia moderates at the state convention were several motions to summon a conference of the Border States, including Virginia, Maryland, Kentucky, and Tennessee, to discuss common problems and collective solutions.

17. In his famous "Give Me Liberty" speech, Patrick Henry had shouted, "The next gale that sweeps from the north will bring to our ears the clash of resounding arms!"

18. Confederate general P. G. T. Beauregard had more than a mere battery aimed at the small Federal garrison at Fort Sumter. During the bombardment that occurred in mid-April, Confederate cannon fired over four thousand rounds at the incomplete fort.

19. In Samuel Johnson's philosophical romance *Rasselas* appear the lines, "Ye who listen with credulity to the whispers of fancy, and pursue with eagerness the phantoms of hope . . . attend to the history of Rasselas, Prince of Abyssinia."

day the glorious [Rufus] Choate and the sublime [Daniel] Webster. The notorious [David] Wilmot too has come up from Pennsylvania, and the blood
thirsty [Zachariah] Chandler hails from Michigan to fill the place of the
noble old [Lewis] Cass. Upon the throne of the Caesars sits the Catiline[20] of
this conspiracy: Abraham Lincoln in the Chair of George Washington. There
Jefferson sat in the earlier and better days; there Madison and Monroe and
the grand old hero of the Hermitage. How fallen the sceptre! The Rail Splitter
has caught the mantle, and aided by Wm. H. Seward, the Apollyon of the
Republican Party[21]—"the power behind the throne greater than the throne
itself"—promulgates his imperial edicts from the desecrated seats of those
demigods of fame with as much sang-froid as if he were himself Pope Pius,
the ninth,[22] and his own tongue and pen were armed with all the thunders of
the Vatican.

Can we submit? No! The women of the land say No! The high-toned and
brave cannot submit. The Spartan mothers of the South have placed the
sword in the hands of their darling sons and told them to "go and fight for
their country," and so will those in Virginia who are Mothers in Israel. Our
sisters and our sweethearts, I mean the sweethearts of those of us who are
young enough and fortunate enough (I am neither) to have such unnecessary
hearts, will cheer us on to the conflict, and I for one will not weep over its
coming. It will put Virginia all right upon the "Great Issue" and that is a
consummation devoutly to be wished.

Forgive me for wearying you with this long letter. I sincerely hope you
will not read one tenth part of it.

APRIL 8, 1861

Miss Josie,

I am very—very grateful to you for the two kindly and beautiful letters you
have written to me. But I feel that I have as it were stolen them from you, that

---

20. Catiline was a Roman patrician who headed a conspiracy to overthrow the empire and
obtain power for himself and his followers. The plot failed when Cicero revealed it to authorities.

21. The "Rail Splitter" was a nickname given to Abraham Lincoln. His secretary of state
was the cunning William H. Seward of New York. To Sheffey, Seward was Apollyon, who in
mythology was king of hell and angel of the bottomless pit.

22. Pius IX had the longest pontificate in history (1846–78). He turned the papacy sharply
from liberalism to conservatism. During his reign appeared the declaration of the doctrine of
the Immaculate Conception.

I have drawn you into this correspondence, *almost,* if not altogether against your consent. I wish it were not so. But I will do nothing calculated in the slightest degree to offend you. I have therefore apologized for the two letters I have written; and I ought to ask your forgiveness for this one in almost every sentence, for it is thoroughly uncalled for by anything I can find in either of yours. They are brief, but beautiful and I shall treasure them up to remind me as I journey on alone and wearily through the vale of years, how much I have lost, and how bitter is the lot to which you have doomed me.

I wish I could continue this correspondence, but it would perhaps be improper for me even to ask it, and I am too well aware that it would only end speedily as did that former short-lived ill-fated one, to the beginning of which I look back with so much pleasure and to whose finale I recur with so much of sadness and pain. I could not be admitted into the inner sanctuary of your friendship and yet endure to remain a miserable hopeless outcast as I am from your love. Some parts of this confessional, you may perhaps regard as silly and unmanly, but I will make it nevertheless, like the doomed criminals of old time, holding on by the horns of the altar. You know when a chance was given them for life, they fled to the temples and no one dared to slay them while they held by the horns of the altar.

Stoical and immovable in aught else when I choose to be, I am yet helpless before this strange passion which was born in my boyhood and has grown and strengthened as the long years flew away. I have fled before it and I have sought to crush it. In *la belle monde,* with the loving, the lovely and gay around me, I have tried to forget it. In laborious toil I have sought to destroy its memory. Night after night, pouring over musty volumes, I have seen the midnight taper die in its socket, until tired Nature twice or thrice has yielded in the conflict. I have wandered off after other idols and have sought in vain to build up a love that might overtop and strangle this. But like the ghost of Banquo, it "will not down."[23]

Still it arises mockingly, now shaking its "gory locks" at me as if to "say I did it" but oftener, all spirituelle and beautiful it comes to the dresser of today, as it came to the dreaming boy long years ago. His Uriel the Angel of the Sun in its loveliness; it is Azrael the spirit of Death in the desolation that follows where it comes.[24] Can it never—never come as the healing angel

23. In *Macbeth,* Banquo was a general in the king's army. An untrusting Macbeth had him murdered. Later Banquo's ghost appeared and served as a foil to the ambitious Macbeth.

24. Uriel appears in John Milton's *Paradise Lost;* he was one of seven angels who stood nearest to God's throne and was the most perceptive member of the group. Azrael, in Jewish and Islamic mythology, is the angel of death and one of the four highest angels of the throne of God.

bending upon its white wings of love to soothe the woes and sorrows it has caused? Never! Like the laws of the Medes and Persians, your decrees cannot be changed. Is it so? Are you indeed changeless forever? Can no circumstances induce you to revoke that decision so cruel? I fear not.

Those fatal sentences which I still preserve were too firm, too decided. But even the icebergs that so often appear to be changelessly fixed in the cold Arctic, can melt at times and tear themselves loose from their centurial moorings. And why cannot you relent—you who are yourself the embodiment of "heart and happiness," and whose kindliness of heart looks forth through every sentence of your beautiful letters. There is nothing honorable and possible I would not dare, to gain your love. There are few things I would not try to be, to merit it.

I have proven the sincerity of my own, and am the same today that I was two-three-four years ago. I have seen you indeed but once or twice in the interval, but it was because I could *not trust myself* because I was trying to escape from the influence of that haunting passion, if possible to crush it and free myself from its hopeless thralldom. I have failed. The love of my boyhood is the hopeless love of my early manhood. It will be the companion of all the long years that are yet to come. Should I ever link my destinies with those of another, I would forewarn her of the "uncanny ghost," the ever present, shadowy rival she would have to encounter.

For your assurance that "successful in whatever pursuit in life I will ever have your warmest congratulations," I am deeply grateful, as also am I for the wish that "heart and happiness may be linked with the realization of my every dream of ambition." I appreciate its beauty and long for its fulfillment, but you perceive from what I have written that its fulfillment is impossible unless—unless you yourself revoke the decision you made more than two years ago and allow me to come back again to "happiness and thee."

Your views of Politics and of the Law are just and meet with my full concurrence. My own highest ambition for the present is to make myself as nearly as possible a *thorough lawyer.* That indeed requires the *lucubrationes viginiti annorum,* and even the lucubrations of twenty years sometimes fail to effect it; but I will early attain an advantageous standpoint, if diligence and assiduity can accomplish anything. But while like yourself I regard the law as the more noble science and profession, I do so simply because the science of Politics has been the most abused. Followed by such men as Webster, Clay and Calhoun, it was a glorious profession; expounded by them it was a sublime science. But the Triumvirs passed away, and after them came the Demagogues, the ignorant, conceited fanatical Tribunes of the People; until Demagogism and Politics have become convertible and almost synonymous terms.

But a new and startling era is upon us. The people are casting about them now, not for the men who are most eager and willing, but for those who are most able to guide them aright. They have put vanward in the Southern Confederacy men able and willing to lead the gallant States onward, conquering and to conquer. Only in the North and in the Border States is Demagogism still triumphant, and here certainly its power is declining. It will die out in the land to be resurrected, it is to be hoped no more forever, as soon as the Virginia Convention shall have run its tedious course.

The ignominy which the tyrannical majority in that convention have brought upon that body and the state, will not be forgiven or forgotten, and I wish devoutly that the gallant band there which is true to the South would leave for their homes, that the rest, if they could get a quorum, might work out their nefarious plans and thereby accomplish their own inevitable & merited destruction. Then will the good men and true of Va. go forth to battle with the Philistines, and if the Sauls will not don their armor and meet the Champions, we will find ten thousand Davids, fresh from the hills where they have watched their father's flocks, who with faith in God and the Right, and the Southern Cross, will meet the vaunting braves and vanquish them even though they be Goliaths of Gath.[25]

Demagogues then must go to the wall, and the science of Politics will emerge from the cesspools of iniquity to which it has so long been steeping, and will rise again, pure immaculate, to its former glory and sublimity. We will find Washingtons & Jeffersons, Madisons and Monroes, Calhouns, Clays, and Jacksons in Virginia to take the place of Martins, the McMullens, the Wilsons which have so long burthened us as with an incubus.[26] If I have read aright the signs of the times, such is the epoch which has been already inaugurated; and I regard it as the part of patriotism itself for every man, woman and child in Virginia to be as thoroughly versed as possible in the politics of the day.

Our History is being written and it is to be a Chronicle of stirring times

25. Goliath, a giant from Gath, fell victim to young David's marksmanship with a sling. 1 Samuel 17.

26. Former congressmen Elbert S. Martin and Fayette McMullen, plus Harrison County's Benjamin Wilson, a delegate to the Virginia State Convention, doubted the wisdom of secession while urging patience until the convention could recommend action.

and stirring events, of tumults and carnage, of "Gorgons Hydras and Chimeras dire."[27] If the news which comes to us today be reliable, we shall soon hear the "noise of the Captains and the shouting," the shrill fife, the winding clarion,

> The deep thunder peal on peal afar
> And near the beat of the enlivening drum
> xxxxxxxxxxxxxxxxxxxxxxxxxxxxxxxxxxxx
> While throng the citizens with terror dumb
> Or whispering with white lips "The foe, they come, they come."[28]

In conclusion, I appeal to you by all pure and holy things to revoke your decision of the past and remove the ban you have placed upon me; to write to me soon again and frequently and allow me to write to you, and to accept now, tried and proven as it is, the love you rejected when I was a schoolboy and which is again laid at your feet with fear and trembling. I entertain for you the highest respect and the sincerest affection. You cannot doubt it. I dare not hope for a favorable answer. I have no right to hope for it. I am a hopeless, sorrowful, miserable man. But the world does not know it. To you only do I unveil my heart. I do not admit the prying rabble into its sacred *Penetralia*. I do not allow profane eyes to read its treasured secrets.

In all other respects, the present and future like the past are bright before me. I have begun life under the most favorable auspices, and in my profession I have been thus far successful beyond my most sanguine expectations. I have indeed, like my father before me and every other man who is deemed worthy of being stricken by the poisoned shafts of Envy and Malice, some few secret and unscrupulous enemies, but like him I will yet ride scornfully over them and trample them into the dust. They do not trouble me, and if I only had the "heart and happiness" which you alone can give, bright indeed would be the "realization of every dream of ambition."

27. In classical mythology three Gorgons existed, with serpents on their heads instead of hair; they were considered such hideous monsters that all who looked at them were turned to stone. Chimera was another ugly creature described by Homer as having a goat's body, a lion's head, and a dragon's tail. Hydra was a nine-headed serpent; when any of its heads was cut off, two new ones replaced it.

28. These lines are from Lord Byron's poem *Childe Harold's Pilgrimage*. The narrative tells of a hero who travels through Europe. Haunted by sins from his past, Harold attempts to shun humanity. The phrase "noise of the Captains and the shouting," preceding Byron's lines, is from Psalms 39:25.

You know that I am your true friend under all circumstances. Whatever therefore be this, your second decision upon this subject, I shall bow to it with deference. If favorable, I should be in Wytheville, I assure you, as speedily as possible. If otherwise, I would avoid that delightful little place, as I would the abode of a pestilence.

Trusting to Him Who doeth All things well, I commend this letter to you, and await your decision, feeling that upon the cast of this die depends my only chance for happiness in the years which are to come.

Marion, Va., APRIL 23–24, 1861

Mavourneen,[29]

I went to the Rye Valley yesterday, made a speech to an enthusiastic crowd and raised a perfect furore. It is impossible that such a people should ever be subdued. I secured a number of recruits for our company of dragoons, raised forty two dollars for our flag, and procured 17 names for a home guard at Sugar Grove in the upper end of the valley. The ball is effectually in motion. I and two gentlemen who were with me put the ladies to work to get money for us, and they will get it. A great many of the people are poor there, but the blood of the Revolution of 76 is in their veins, and those who can give no treasure will pour out their blood like water in defence of Virginia. In the Home Guard we enrolled the names of three grayheaded veterans, soldiers of 1812, venerable men who have come down to us from a remarkable generation. The men of their day were men indeed, and the men of today will prove themselves worthy sons of their glorious sires.

Today we organized the company of "Smyth Dragoons." I was elected Second Lieutenant, the only office to which I aspired, a post of high honor in such a Company. Our dress uniform will be black cassimere pants with yellow stripe, black cloth jockey coats for the men, frock coats for the officers, helmets with black plumes, sword-proof for the men, and felt hats with larger black plumes for the officers.[30] The commissioned officers, Captn., 1st and 2nd Lieutenants, only have epaulets. John Thompson is our Captain, a son

29. Sheffey explains the origin of this nickname in his letter to Josephine Spiller of April 29, 1861, reproduced below.

30. Some of the Smyth Dragoons may actually have worn such an elaborate uniform, though not for long in the rigors of army life. Everyday clothes would mark the attire of most Confederates. See James I. Robertson Jr., *Soldiers Blue and Gray* (Columbia, S.C., 1988), 14–17.

of Major Henry B. Thompson, and a descendant of Old Rees Bowen of the Olden time—men of known and tried blood.[31] He will keep the promise of his youth and the faith of his fathers.

We parted as you know with our gallant "Blues" today,[32] but we told them when we bade them farewell that the clatter of our horses hoofs would soon be heard upon the plains of the battle, that we would be with them and their motto "God and Liberty" should be ours also. Brave boys are they! The tears and lamentations of their wives, their sisters, [and] their mothers almost un-manned them; but they nerved themselves, and went off rejoicing like Roman Conquerors returning from the battle.

John Gibboney[33] came to Marion last night and offered to enroll his men in our company as he has but thirty. We will probably unite—unless our company increases to over 70 men. We want to go to the field with a round hundred.

I will very probably be in Wytheville on a flying trip tomorrow night—principally because I can't stay away from you, and partly because I have some other business in Wytheville. I will return to Marion on the midnight train. Every hour that I am away from you seems an age to me. I probably write too often to you, but. . . .

The mail was sent out a few minutes too soon or you would have received the foregoing hasty and blotted scrawl last evening. I am compelled to do every thing now in the utmost haste and to leave "ten thousand" necessary things undone. I received your letter this morning, informing me of the departure of your gallant company and the reception of the Smyth Blues by your citizens. We have cause to be proud of our brave men.

Why should we sorrow! Virginia, mindful of the blood that flows in her old veins, mindful of her historic fame, proud of the prestige of her past, has shaken off her lethargic slumbers and under the very heel of the tyrant awakes and arises to glory again. With banners waving, and the measured tread of legions of armed men, she marches like a giantess to the conflict,

31. Able and popular John Henry Thompson was captain of the Smyth Dragoons until he was wounded on November 10, 1861, in a skirmish at Guyandotte in western Virginia. Thompson later served in the Virginia General Assembly. His forebear, Rees Bowen of Smyth County, died a hero's death at the 1780 battle of King's Mountain.

32. The Smyth Blues became Company D of the 4th Virginia Infantry. This regiment attained high fame under legendary general Thomas J. "Stonewall" Jackson. See James I. Robertson Jr., *The Stonewall Brigade* (Baton Rouge, 1963).

33. John H. Gibboney failed to recruit a full company. He was later a captain in the Quartermaster Department.

and all her brave sons now like the sons of Old Sparta[34] will remember how glorious a thing it is to die for their country. Each of our Southwestern lads will know no fear and brave as the Scotch Lochiel,[35] "untainted by flight or by chains,

> While the kindling of life in his bosom remains
> Will victor exult, or in death be laid low
> With his back to the field and his feet to the foe
> And leaving in battle no blot on his name
> Look proudly to heaven from a death-bed of Fame.[36]

Rather therefore should we rejoice in the destiny that awaits them and the opportunity afforded them. I flatter myself that my letters are welcome, and if so, they cannot be too frequent. I have had invitations to address the people in different parts of the county in order to induce them to organize—but I have had my hands entirely too full of other matters now. The people are organizing. The blood is up. Volunteer companies are forming all over the County. Smyth will willingly furnish many more than her quota. The time has come for action, not for words, and the people will come to the mark.

But I must close or my letter will not get into the mail. Nellie sends her love.[37] You do not know how much we *all* love you. I wish you would consent to become my wife before the next eight days of April have passed away, and would come and spend part of your time, at least while I am gone, with my mother and sisters. They love me with an affection that is unbounded and will welcome you to their hearts with the same illimitable love. Such a step would perhaps require some haste, but you have determined upon your destiny, and I would be better able to look directly to your welfare. The cars are coming. Do you like to be called pet names. If so, God bless you, my darling.

Marion, Va., APRIL 29TH, 1861

Mavourneen,

You perceive what a favorite this sweetest of all words the wish "my darling" is with me. No word in any dialect has the liquid more charmingly

34. Sparta was one of the leading city-states of ancient Greece. Its citizens were noted for frugality, stern discipline, and courage.

35. Lochiel is the title of the head of the clan Campbell.

36. These lines are from the poem "Lochiel's Warning," by early-nineteenth-century Scottish poet Thomas Campbell.

37. Ellen White Sheffey was Pres Sheffey's sister.

joined together or expressed a sweeter sentiment than this double word "Ma Vourneen." Tom Moore, sweetest poet of the beautiful Erin, or "Erin Mavourneen," as Kavenagh calls his mother-land,[38] loved it before me, and since I first heard the old song about the sweet Kathleen, I too have loved it as the embodiment of the sweet and beautiful. I spoke of it long ago in the second or third letter I ever wrote to you, and since then I have not thought or dreamed of it without thinking or dreaming also of one dearer to me than the darling Kathleen ever could have been to the love-lorn poet who sung so charmingly of her. Long ago, without your permission, I dedicated to you this sweetest of all words and now it is yours by undisputed right. You will find it engraved in the ring I have ordered if that lazy jeweler under Shockoe Hill[39] can ever tear himself away from the busy scenes around him long enough to send it to me.

This strain has a slight savor of sentiment, and I would not indulge in it if I did not know your assertion to the contrary notwithstanding that you are as sentimental as I am myself. No one could think and dream of the "mellow moon-light" as you do without a considerable sprinkling of sentiment in her composition. (Ha, ha!) I love sentiment, because you are the mainspring of it all. Without love, sentiment would be a very dull institution. "Who loves, raves, Tim Youth's frenzy." I hope like "John Anderson my Jo," it will be the frenzy of my old age also.

To him whose heart has yielded itself entirely to its sweet idolatry, the world of sentiment is a fairy land—a world of music and poetry and dreams, of visions and castles in the air. Like Aladdin with his wonderful lamp, he rears at will his gorgeous palaces with spacious halls and tessellated floors with towers and spires gleaming in the sun. Too often as he draws near, the bright mirage vanishes into thin air, the towers topple, the walls crumble, and he finds himself ere he is aware, like the Roman upon the site of the fallen Carthage, in the midst of ruins and desolation. Have you not seen your brightest hopes decay? I have seen mine. I have mourned over the failure of cherished projects, and now that they are building again, I long for their realization, and tremble at the thought that the brightness before me might prove unreal, that the Hand of Destiny might at one fell stroke sweep it all away and leave me desolate, indeed ruined at last, and broken in spirit and in heart.

38. Thomas Moore and Morgan Peter Kavanaugh were Irish poets of the early nineteenth century.
39. Shockoe Slip is part of downtown Richmond, Virginia.

I am glad you always look upon the bright side. You must teach me. I thought years ago that I loved you as well as any one could be loved, but in all seriousness if anything were to befall you now, God only knows what would become of me. I heard that hollow cough last night in perfect terror and have come to the conclusion that I am growing as foolish as Prof. Peters is about his Maggie.[40]

As to your decisions, they are always just and reasonable.[41] I have no particular objection to waiting until June, since it is your pleasure though I shall count the days and the hours as they fly slowly away. I learned from gentlemen on the cars last night that there is no probability of cavalry being needed for months. Thompson and I will go on preparing our troop, but nothing short of a call for cavalry or an invasion of Virginia will force me away from you. "None but the brave deserve the fair," says the poet,[42] and I know you would not have me falter for a moment whenever it becomes my duty to go. In the meantime, I can accomplish much more good at home than I could if I were in the barracks at Richmond eating bean-soup with the Blues and Grays.[43]

I have been today aiding in the organization of committees for the relief of the families of the volunteers who have gone from the County—a very important matter—as the daily wages of many of the volunteers were the only support of their families.

I have a good deal of work to do within the next week or two, and do not know when I can come to Wytheville again. But I will write constantly and will come as soon as possible. You may rest assured that like the Irish man's parrot, I shall "kape up a divil of a thinking" about you all the time. I saw a very intelligent old lady today who is much given to butchering the King's English. She says that this fight with Abe Lincoln she "respects will be a sight wuss nor the Resolutionary War." I thought if all the volunteers had to determine like myself between their love and their patriotism, this war would be more of a Resolutionary War than the former.

But enough. Keep out of the moon-light while you have such a cough. I

40. Sheffey is referring to his brother-in-law and Emory & Henry College professor, William E. Peters. "Maggie" was Margaret Sheffey Peters.
41. Although Sheffey had argued for an April 30 wedding with Josie Spiller, she opted at the time for a mid-June ceremony.
42. This quotation is from John Dryden, "Alexander's Feast" (1796).
43. Volunteers from an adjacent county formed the Wythe Grays, Company A of the 4th Virginia Infantry.

will try and do star-gazing enough for both of us. During the last few weeks I have learned all about the stormy Arcturus and the sweet influences of the Pleiades. Guy Mannering never was such an Astrologer as I will become in a month or two.[44] I would be the equal of the Chaldees[45] and the superior of that fellow in Rasselas, I have forgotten his name, that acquaintance of Imlac,[46] the poet who imagined he could learn everything from the stars. He was crazy. Poe was much more sensible when he wrote that

> The stars never rise
> But I feel the bright eyes
> Of my beautiful Annabel Lee
> And the moon never beams
> Without bringing me dreams
> Of my beautiful Annabel Lee.

He never loved his Annabel half so well as I do mine. But good bye, Mavourneen. I do not like to quit for I love to write to you, but the letter will not get into the mail if I do not hurry. One of my younger sisters composed a short poem once, a stanza of which I recollect I recite it to you:

> Think of me fondly, dearest
> At morning, at noon and at night
> To think of thee *always,* darling
> It is my greatest and truest delight.

If I had composed it I would have written *"gloriousest"* instead of *"truest,"* though the sentiment expressed by "truest" is as "true as preaching."

Marion, MAY 1ST, 1861

Mavourneen,

I have but a moment's time to write. Have been very busy all day. Election for 1st Lieutenant of Smyth Dragoons came off this evening. I told you I

44. Sheffey is alluding to Sir Walter Scott's characters in the 1815 novel *Guy Mannering* and to such star formations as the Pleiades. Arcturus is the brightest star in the N celestial sphere.

45. The Chaldeans were Semitic people related to the Babylonians whose culture was heavily dependent on astrology.

46. In Johnson's 1759 book, *Rasselas, Prince of Abyssinia,* Rasselas makes his rambles through the countryside with his close companion, the poet and traveler Imlac.

would get the office, but gave up my claims. Profr. W. E. Peters and Maggie came down from E & H C[ollege] evening before last. I proposed to him this morning that if he would become a member of the Smyth Dragoons, *he* should have the First Lieutenancy. He did so, and was unanimously elected. Nothing now can prevent our becoming a splendid company. Mag cried a little, but her patriotism at last got the better of her love, if such a thing be possible.

Advertisement from [William H.] Richardson, Adjutant Genl., dated yesterday came to us today instructing cavalry companies to be ready to march. Captn. Thompson and Lieutenants Peters and Sheffey will lead as gallant a band as can be found in the South West. We will try and make it as good as any in the Old Dominion.

Four Hundred and Fifty Alabama, Kentucky and, I believe, Tennessee Troops passed eastward this morning. I suppose the citizens of Wytheville assembled at the Depot to greet them as did the "*gude men & wives*" of gallant little Smyth. I was there, and had a very pleasant confab with Lieutenant Weedon of the Alabama Company, an old acquaintance of mine.[47] The soldiers, many of them, are fine-looking men. Bronzed, muscular, sinewy, it will not take such men long to strike terror into the Yankee heart. The Alabamians are from around Mobile, the Kentuckians from near Louisville.

My father started home from Richmond this morning.[48] He will be here tomorrow. I received your ring from Richmond by last mail. I will bring it to you in a few days if I can get off. Besides a good deal of other work, I expect henceforth for several days, to drill all day and study Gilham's Manual of Tactics[49] all night more or less. We will find great difficulty in procuring arms and uniforms. Our agents inform us that no cloth can be procured in Richmond. We will be compelled to apparel ourselves in Thomas Jeans. It will perhaps be better than any thing else for service. So might it be. Gay border lads we'll be, any how.

47. John Weeden was a second lieutenant in the Mobile Cadets, which became Company A of the 3d Alabama. For the formation and Virginia trip of this unit, see "A Sketch of 12 Months Service in the Mobile Rifle Co.," *Alabama Historical Quarterly* 25 (1963): 149–52.

48. With the work of the Virginia State Convention all but completed, Smyth County delegate James White Sheffey returned to Marion.

49. William Gilham had a distinguished career as professor of infantry tactics and commandant of cadets at the Virginia Military Institute. Although he wrote *Authorized Cavalry Tactics, U.S.A.: Manual of Instruction* . . . (Philadelphia, 1861), Gilham became more famous for his *Manual of Instruction for the Volunteers and Militia of the Confederate States* (Richmond, Va., 1861).

A member of [the] Smyth Blues writing to his father in Marion says that he and four others occupy Cattle Stall No. 94 in the Fair Ground. Delectable! Several of the young men are reported quite ill. They'll soon get used to it. I do not like the life of the footmen. Too much camp duty. Give us our saddles and gallant steeds, and we'll find green woods for our merry men—like Marian & Robin Hood in the olden time. The merry green wood and a ranger's life for me! Such is the life before us. We will be called to the border like the "Highland Chills" in the days of Vich Ian Vohr.[50] Apart from the dull towns and dusty walks of men, the lives of those of us, who leave no hearts behind them, will be exceedingly delightful. But mine will be always "with my darling away," and I shall be, oh how sorrowful.

Abingdon, MAY 16, 1861

My dear Josie,

I take the liberty of dropping the handle to your name because it sounds so formal and distant, your name is a beautiful one—the sweetest in the language to my ear. It needs no "Miss" or "Empress" to make it musical. Like yourself, "when unadorned, adorned the most,"[51] it is sweetest without any ornament. Will you not give me also the name by which Frank[52] called you before he left—the name by which I have been known among those who loved me since my earliest recollection? I will become more attached to it than ever, when you have learned to know me by none other than simply Pres.

I have received no letter from you for so long a time, that I sometimes fear you do not think of me very often, but such thoughts do not linger. They distress me so much if I indulge them for a moment that I drive them away speedily. I know that you love me, for you have told me so and in my own heart, you have so long been set up as the standard of all that is good and pure and beautiful, that I am happy in the faith and hope that your love will be as unwavering and abiding as my own. Without your love, life would be

50. In Sir Walter Scott's novel *Waverly,* Mac-Ibor Vich Ian Vohr of Glennaquoich was a young Highland chieftain who was in the Jacobite forces opposing English rule. The Jacobites fought many battles, often in dreadful weather. Vich Ian Vohr was eventually convicted of high treason and executed.

51. The lines "For loveliness / Needs not the foreign aid of ornament, / But is when unadorned adorned the most" are from James Thomson's *The Seasons: Autumn* (1730).

52. Frank Spiller was Josephine's brother.

worthless to me—and I long for the hour to draw nigh when I can feel and know that nothing but death can come between me and thee. I wish it were so now.

I sometimes think that I am the victim of a strange destiny. In my boyhood, before I had seen you, I was not happy for there was nothing in the world around me that I could love with my whole soul. And when you would not love me—but I have told you how miserable I was, and you did not believe me, because you saw that I laughed and was merry with the votaries of Pleasure. It is often the case that those who laugh loudest and seem merriest are saddest at heart, especially if they are too proud to unseal the secret book and let the prying throng into the sacred secrets that are written there. I sought for happiness "under green shades, by fountains shrill amidst the nymphs and sirens, fruits and flowers," but it was not there; and then I followed it up the steep, rough hill "climbed through sunshine, snow and showers" and still the bright phantom eluded me, for you were not there.

It was the old butterfly chase over again, and when at times I fancied I had secured the long sought prize, the glittering bauble, spoiled of its gaudy hues, died fluttering in my grasp. At last when I found that you cared something for me, that you would love me, oh how happy I was—but again the phantom escapes me, for in a few more days we must part, to meet perhaps no more forever.

Several days have now elapsed since the Smyth Dragoons received their orders to march into service, and we are preparing as swiftly as possible to obey the order. We will set out for Lynchburg next Wednesday or Thursday. Prof. Peters and I have been here for some time and have learned the cavalry drill pretty well. We have also learned much of the infantry tactics and will be soon prepared to drill our troop thoroughly in both.

I have deliberated much with regard to the course before us, and am satisfied that an immediate marriage will conduce to the happiness of both of us. If we are not married during the next week, the probability is that we will not be married for years. Perhaps the uncertainty of human life, and the fortunes of war, may prevent me from accomplishing at all the cherished object of my life. I am satisfied that it would have been wiser, if we had married on the 30th of April as I proposed, but you objected and I was content because you had promised to marry me whenever I should be called away.

If you keep that promise, it will prevent the infinite unhappiness of both of us. I will not probably be ordered for some time upon any expedition out of Virginia, and will have frequent opportunities to be with you, as my wife, but no soldier can get a furlough to go and see his sweetheart. We will in all probability be stationed at Lynchburg for a month or two, and you can, if you are willing, be with me there. Maggie [Peters] will be there, and I have many friends there who will make your time pass pleasantly away. If you will marry me and go with me, you will be with Maggie all the time, and will find her one of the best women and dearest of friends.

Lieut. Peters and I will leave here for Marion tomorrow morning. I will be in Wytheville Saturday night or Sunday night. I have much to think about, and in this matter we must think fast and act accordingly. The hour for cavalry drill arrived; Lady Davis, my beautiful charger all saddled and bridled, is at the door and I must close. Listen to the suggestions of one who loves you infinitely better than all the world beside, act for yourself and I know you will act wisely and well. With a further assurance of my unalterable affection I am as ever your devoted friend.

P.S. Back from Cavalry drill, your letter has reached me, and I am as happy as a man can be. I am glad you enjoyed yourself so much on your trip to Pulaski. Glad you met McMahon,[53] a clever whole-souled fellow. Belongs to the Church Militant and the Smyth Dragoons. Has fought long and well with the sword of the Spirit. Will try now what virtue there is in more carnal weapons. Says he is a good fencer and we will try and find him plenty of opportunities for practice. I have written hastily and with a very bad pen but bad writing is excusable in a soldier.

The company of Mounted Rifles here, under Capt. Jones[54]—a magnificent company—are very anxious that the Smyth Dragoons should be thrown with them. That, however, can only be done by immediate application to General Lee.[55] Meanwhile, we must obey the order of Col. Langhorne and march.[56]

53. J. J. McMahan, a Presbyterian cleric, entered Confederate service as chaplain of the 51st Virginia Infantry, another unit recruited in southwestern Virginia.

54. Glade Spring's William E. Jones led the Washington Mounted Rifles, a company that became part of the 1st Virginia Cavalry.

55. On April 23, 1861, former U.S. Army colonel Robert E. Lee accepted command of the armed forces of Virginia. Lee spent the weeks thereafter mobilizing all available troops into regiments and battalions.

56. Lt. Col. Daniel A. Langhorne was in charge of mustering into service the units raised in the southwest quadrant of Virginia. U.S. War Department, *War of the Rebellion: A Compilation of the Official Records of the Union and Confederate Armies,* 128 vols. (Washington, 1880–1901), ser. 1, 2:807. Cited hereafter as *Official Records;* unless otherwise stated, all references are to series 1.

Marion, Va., MAY 28, 1861

My darling,

Do you not love to be called *darling?* How sweet a word it is! So musical! So expressive!

I received your note this morning and have lent a moment to reply to it before going to the drill ground. While it has filled my own heart with inexpressable sadness, I have already learned to have no wish that is not yours—to desire nothing that will not contribute in the highest degree to your happiness. I do not like the sound of the expression "*indefinite* postponement." It sounds like a prelude to something that would be sadder still, and the cherished idea of domestic happiness, "the only bliss" Cowper [wrote], "which has survived the Fall," becomes again an attenuated phantom, the mere shadow of something that is afar off in the untravelled future.

I cannot tell you how much I regret your wish. We would have almost as much sunshine as shadow if the arrangement for the 19th of June were allowed to stand. I would never be very far away from you, and as a trooper constantly ordered from one part of the country to another, I would frequently be thrown near to you. Unless we are triumphantly victorious at the start, this war will not confine itself to the banks of the Potomac and the shores of the Chesapeake. It will follow us into our own mountains, and when it does, I will be here.

A proposition was made yesterday by Gov. Floyd[57] to our Company to attach itself to his brigade and be mustered into service immediately. If we accept his proposition instead of going to Lynchburg, we will be stationed at Marion for some time to come. I do not see the force of the argument that it would be more difficult to part after marriage than before. If so, it would be only another reason why I should desire it.

My highest earthly desire through the long years has been to gain your unlimited love. I know nothing of baser motives which prompt men to marry. The idea that when I go away "we will not meet again for months," and I see you have scratched out the word "years" and written "months"

57. John B. Floyd had returned to southwestern Virginia after his resignation from President Buchanan's cabinet. On May 14, 1861, Confederate president Jefferson Davis wired Floyd, "Can you get in a brigade of your mountain riflemen with their own tried weapons?" He replied, "I can raise the brigade and will begin immediately." A week later Floyd was appointed a brigadier general, with the primary responsibility of protecting the Virginia and Tennessee Railroad in southwestern Virginia. Ibid., 838, 909.

instead, is I think, erroneous. We would meet often, and the pleasure of meeting would more than compensate for all the pains of separation. No man can be always at home, except the dull plodders at some dull calling, and the soldier as a general thing is not much oftener away from his dear ones than the successful lawyer or physician. I cannot believe that it is your intention to defer our marriage until this war is ended, yet I can see nothing else in an indefinite postponement. But I have divested my love for you of everything which looked towards self and will leave the matter to you. Whatever you may determine will meet with my concurrence. Love to all.

Marion, Va., MAY 30, 1861

Miss Josie,

By an almost unanimous vote of the troop, the Smyth Dragoons today entered the Floyd Brigade.[58] Col. Radford informed us this morning through Mr. Gilmore that he would be glad to receive us into his guerrilla regiment and this was my first choice, but I am satisfied with the vote of the company.[59] The matter was in the hands of the officers, but we very properly left it to the vote of the men.

We will, of course, not go to Lynchburg, and will not obey the orders of Col. Early[60] or Lieut. Col. Langhorne.

I cannot look into the future and do not know what disposition will be made of us. Under Genl. Floyd, I will have better chances for promotion than anyone else, as my mother is nearly related to him and his wife has always been her favorite cousin.[61]

I was told by Dr. Clark of Mt. Airy[62] today that we would very probably

58. The company's decision to join Floyd's brigade was momentous, for it kept the Smyth Dragoons in western Virginia for four years and out of the major fighting in the central and eastern regions of the state.

59. Richard Carlton Walker Radford of Bedford was then organizing what became the 2d Virginia Cavalry. Prominent Marion citizen James H. Gilmore was in charge of procuring supplies and equipment for Sheffey's company. See Joan Tracy Armstrong, *History of Smyth County, Virginia,* 2 vols. (Marion, Va., 1986), 2:105.

60. Jubal Anderson Early had been Franklin County's representative to the Virginia State Convention and had strongly opposed secession. He began his rise to lieutenant general in the Confederate army by organizing the 24th Virginia Infantry at Lynchburg.

61. General Floyd's wife, Sally Buchanan Preston, was a cousin of Sheffey's mother. This linked both Floyd and Sheffey to William Preston, patriarch of the family and possibly the most influential figure in the settlement of southwestern Virginia.

62. According to the 1860 census, Dr. Hobson H. Clark was in his mid-twenties and relatively new to the area. He became examining physician for many of the recruits who reported

be ordered to rendezvous at Wytheville. If so, how long we will stay there I cannot tell. Please do not determine to defer our marriage until I see you. I will, of course, not insist upon anything which I cannot gain with your full consent. This indefinite postponement amounts to an absolute punishment of me, because I have done my duty. "Duty" has been always my moniter, and I have always obeyed its calls hard or burthensome. I know you will not think less of me because I obey the dictates of Honor and Duty, and hold myself ready to obey all the calls of my country. I know your own character, I think, too well to believe that your patriotism also will not bear you through every ordeal through which you may be called to pass.

Next to love of God, the love of our country is the noblest of all the emotions, and I thank Him today, who rules our destinies, that I am ready to make every necessary sacrifice to offer up heart, happiness, life, everything but my honor, if need be, upon the altar of our common cause. These are right sentiments; the sentiments of the noble men and women of every age, the sentiments of all the gallant Southrons who have gone to defend the grave of Washington. In after times, it will be a matter of pride with every man in Virginia and the South, who can say "I aided in gaining the independence of the Confederate States of America." It is the duty of the women of today and, God bless them, they are doing their duty throughout Virginia and the entire South to say to their husbands & sweethearts "Go and God speed ye," feeling like Mrs. Hagy of Washington[63] that they had rather be the widows of brave men than the wives of cowards.

These are the sentiments of the women of Virginia and the South, and the precepts and examples of those who think and act differently are not suited to the time. It is a privilege to make sacrifices now to the great cause in which we are engaged. It is the same cause which has immortalized the names of Cincinnatus[64] and the later Rienze, the last of the Tribunes of Kosciusko, the Pole,[65] of "the patriot Tell and Bruce of Bannockburn" of Emmet, the Irishman,[66] and of the great American demigod, George Washington; and shall

---

to the Wytheville area. See J. L. Scott, *45th Virginia Infantry* (Lynchburg, Va., 1989), 5. Mount Airy is now Rural Retreat, Virginia.

63. This is probably a reference to a member of the prominent Hagy family in adjacent Washington County, Virginia.

64. A former Roman consul, Cincinnatus left his farm to become dictator around the 500–430 BC period. He delivered his country from danger and then returned to his plow.

65. Cola di Rienzi, who was the last of the ten Roman magistrates representing the plebeian populace, assumed the title Tribune of Liberty, Peace, and Justice.

66. Just as William Tell is the Swiss national hero, Robert Bruce is the same for Scotland. Robert Emmet was an Irish patriot executed at the age of twenty-five for treason.

not we now be proud to emulate their illustrious examples? Believing like the young David that the God of the Israelites is on our side and trusting in Him, I know I shall do my whole duty.

Why then will you not unite your fortunes to mine now? If it be up to Him Who doeth all things well, and ask Him to nerve us through the trial, then I shall be better and braver because I have something to live for, something dearer than all those who are dear to me, to fight for. I cannot tell how eagerly I have looked forward to the hour when I could call you "mine." There is nothing wrong in that. It is the highest compliment a true man can pay to a true woman.

Our Union upon the 19th would be attended by no sacrifice whatever. You would have your choice of home and your circle of friends, relatives, and dear ones would be very widely enlarged. I will have to say "Please" as the little girls say to me sometimes, and I do not see how you can stand "Please" from one who loves you so much.

As Genl. Floyd has not yet made up his brigade, the probability is that we will be stationed here in Western Va. for a long time, perhaps two or three months. If I am ordered off before the 19th or if there is any probability of my having to go within two or three days afterwards, I will be resigned to my fate and will not ask you to marry me until my return. In all these things, let it be just as you think best.

I have infinite amount of work to do now, and cannot get to Wytheville to see you for a week or so. I hope you will write to me. Our company is daily increasing and the men are learning the drill very fast. We will have opportunities of my moving the company very fast now in every respect.

This pen is getting so abominable that I can write no more and I certainly have written enough to weary you very much.

I will keep you fully informed of our movements and of everything calculated to interest you concerning us. Goodbye.

Marion, Smyth Co., Va.
JUNE 2ND, 1861

Mavourneen,

This Sabbath day is so peaceful and beautiful, so calm and bright, that I am almost tempted to write you an old-fashioned sentimental love-letter, but the coming cars will force me to resist the temptation. Besides, I could only reiterate what I have so often told you. Few men can say with truth, as I can, that though I have paid court to several, I have loved but once. That has been all the time since I first saw you. My life since then has been a strange dream, filled full of sadness. I sometimes wish I could blot out from my memory the years that have passed since I left the University [of Virginia]. They fill up the pleiade of a dream as horrible to me as the Inferno of Dante. How incomparably brighter are the years that stretch away in the future before me! Fierce indeed are the storm clouds that impend over them, but, with your love to sustain me, I know I shall never fear to breast the wave and battle with the storm. I never yet knew what it was to fear, but that was because the future had nothing in store for me that could approximate the good old idea of happiness. Now when you have learned to think something of me, and the future except for our political troubles would have been so bright, I am forced to own up to an occasional faltering. Yet to me the future is brighter than it ever was before, and I will walk the waters trustingly, assured that nothing but happiness will await me when this inhuman war shall end.

I will be in Wytheville Tuesday night at nine o'clock if I can possibly get off from here. I will return that same night. A week without seeing you seems an age to me. I know not what I shall do when I am called away into active service. There is every probability now that we will be quartered here or at Wytheville for some months, and I cannot tell you how much I hope that you will not defer our marriage. I have loved you so long and, which may sound silly to you but is nevertheless true, have suffered so much through the years when I looked upon you as lost to me forever, that I have now, morning, noon and night, but one desire, and that is to be able to call you mine, mine forever, as in heart at least, I have, it seems to me, *always* been *yours*.

If there is any earthly objection to this consummation of our engagement on the 19th, which I can remove, I will pledge myself to do it. The objection that it would be more painful for us to part after marriage than before would be a valid one if it were our object never to love each other well enough to feel sorrow at separation. It is, I think, the desire of both of us that the affection each has expressed for the other should grow and increase and strengthen, and if we are true to our God, our country, ourselves and each other as we will try to be, our hearts like our love will grow stronger every hour and we will always be able to bear the trials which may necessarily be imposed upon us.

Our troop will be mustered into service tomorrow by John W. Johnston.[67]

---

67. John W. Johnston was an officer of the circuit court in Marion.

The pay, which is an important matter to some of our men who are poor and have large families, commenced day before yesterday.

We gave up our barracks entirely last night to the Washington Mounted Rifles who are on their way to Richmond, and will stay in Wytheville tonight. A fine body of men!

The cars are coming & I must get this into the mail. Goodbye.

CHAPTER 2

EN ROUTE TO CARNIFEX FERRY

Pres Sheffey and his compatriots left Marion early in June 1861 for Wytheville and further military training. On June 14 a correspondent for the *Lynchburg Virginian* wrote from Wytheville: "A splendid cavalry company . . . called [the] Smyth Dragoons arrived here a few days ago and have created quite a sensation. The men are from the first rank of Smyth Gentlemen and are as finelooking a body of men as can be found in the State. . . . The horses of this company are well selected, and cannot be surpassed by any other company in the South."

The eight-week gap here in Sheffey's letters to his fiancée, and the sentiments expressed at the outset of his July 26 letter, are evidence that he and Josephine Spiller were together in Wytheville for much of that period. Her original agreement to a mid-June wedding passed with the time. The couple obviously had reached some understanding about their future together, for Sheffey's letters now become more factual and less emotional—except for the long period through which he went awaiting a letter from Spiller.

A month of training and impatience ended on July 26, when the Dragoons departed Wytheville with Brig. Gen. John B. Floyd's small brigade of mountain volunteers. Two weeks earlier Union forces in northwestern Virginia had defeated the main Confederate host at Corrick's Ford. The Federal advance continued, then faltered when its commander, Maj. Gen. George B. McClellan, was summoned to Washington to take charge of the principal army in the East. Confederate authorities moved to take advantage of this lull by directing Floyd's brigade to move north from Wytheville to Lewisburg and there join Brig. Gen. Henry A. Wise's legion, which was retreating through the Kanawha Valley from Charleston.

But Floyd and Wise could not cooperate. Both were political generals and military novices, with domineering, emotional, and petty personalities. Floyd was senior in rank and therefore assumed command of the combined force, but Wise displayed a consistent reluctance to take orders. By early September, Wise wrote of his relations with his fellow brigadier, "I feel if we remain together, we will unite in more wars than one." That situation did not bode well for Southern efforts at regaining control of the northwestern counties of Virginia.

At Lewisburg the Smyth Dragoons and two other cavalry companies became part of a temporary battalion under Maj. Charles E. Thorburn. That alignment changed when Floyd advanced to meet the enemy, the three cavalry companies being temporarily attached to the 50th Virginia Infantry.

Sheffey's first encounters with the enemy came on August 26 at Cross Lanes and September 2 at Hawks Nest. Although these were only skirmishes, to the highly observant Sheffey they were significant engagements. He thus produced minute-by-minute details of each action. The Marion native's first real battle came on September 10 at Carnifex Ferry. That four-hour fight turned him into a real soldier.

With a politician's eye, Sheffey could not help but take sides in the infamous Floyd-Wise squabble—Floyd was a kinsman.

Shannon's,[1] *Bank of Walker's Creek*
Giles Co., JULY 28TH, 1861

My dear Josie,

A second night in camp, my thoughts revert as they have done constantly since my departure from Wytheville to you and the good old town which has so long been dearer to me than any other spot on earth because it was your home. We camped yesterday a few miles east of the Revd. Geo. Painter's[2] in Pulaski, upon the land, I believe of Mr. John Sayers,[3] with all of whom you are well acquainted.

I met yesterday at Mr. Painter's two lady friends, the sight of whom called upon some delightful old time memories. Miss Ewing[4] and Mrs. Sophie F. Crockett.[5] I had not seen either for many years. Mrs. Crockett sent me this

1. Thomas Shannon was an elderly, wealthy farmer listed in the 1860 census as residing in the Staffordsville district of Giles County.

2. George Painter, sixty-five years old in 1860, was an "Old School" Presbyterian minister in Pulaski County. He also taught a boarding school.

3. One of the largest landowners in the area, John Thompson Sayers had farms in both Wythe and Pulaski Counties.

4. Caroline Ewing was one of six students then studying at Reverend Painter's school. She was in her mid-twenties at the time of Sheffey's letter.

5. The former Sophia F. Tate was the wife of Wythe County's James Montgomery Crockett. She was also a cousin-in-law to Josephine Spiller.

morning a wagon-load of the nicest imaginable eatables, for myself and friends. As I was upon the march when I came across the aforesaid vehicle, I had time to appropriate very little to my own use, but I believe the soldiers behind me made good use of the opportunity. I was very grateful to her for her kindness, and I hope when you see her you will thank her for me. If I knew her Post Office, I would write her a note in acknowledgment. Soldiers know how to appreciate such kindnesses.

I am getting along delightfully, lacking only your presence to make me perfectly happy.

We will move forward about twenty miles tomorrow, perhaps further. I will take advantage of every available opportunity to keep you informed of our movement. I am writing upon a camp chest without any of the appliances, but I can trust to your love to excuse whatever may look like negligence. We overtook the infantry of the 2nd Regiment[6] this evening and are encamped close to them.

I can write no more now as I am "officer of the day" for the next twenty four hours & have much to see after. I think I will be quite successful in making myself a soldier. With your love to urge me & sustain me, I could accomplish anything. I am satisfied that I will be able to bear a great deal of exposure and an indefinite amount of fatigue if such an expression be admissible. If you write within the next five days, direct to Sweet Springs, Monroe Co., Va.

My best love to all.

Camp Bee near Red Sweet Springs, Alleghany Co., Va.
AUGUST 3RD, 1861

My dear Josie,

I wrote to you last, I believe from Camp Bartow on the land of Hugh Tiffany, Esq., Monroe Co.[7] The names of the camps, you will perceive from my letters, change with every stopping point. The camp we are now in is the second Camp Bee, and the headquarters of the Brigade.

The day after I last wrote to you we marched from Camp Bartow to Camp Smith, named in honor of Genl. Kirby Smith, on the land of a man named

---

6. The 2d Regiment in Floyd's brigade was officially the 50th Virginia Infantry.

7. In the 1860 census Hugh Tiffany was listed as a fifty-eight-year-old farmer with three children and two laborers. His home was in the Peterstown district of Monroe County.

Campbell. Our march to that point was very fatiguing. The Dragoons were rear-guard and I was left in command. You may imagine my feelings as the hot sun came down and the wagons one after another stuck in the mud or balked on the steep hill sides. Twenty-three miles we marched that day, over the worst roads in the world. The infantry which were before us all day and camped two miles to our rear that night seemed to be much wearied, and I brought one or two of their men whom they seemed to have left upon the wayside into camp on horseback. The poor fellows have a hard time of it on these long marches, but they seem to enjoy themselves fully nevertheless.

The next morning we left Camp Smith at Campbell's, for the Sweet Springs, in the midst of a drizzling rain. Two or three of the Dragoons broke out that morning with the measles.[8] They were put into the wagons, not withstanding the heavy loads already in them. To have forced men with measles to ride horseback through such a rain would have been murder in the first degree. The windows of heaven were opened, and the rain came down in torrents. Many of us were drenched, but we are rapidly getting used to that. We passed the Sweet Springs, thirteen miles from Camp Smith, about 12 o'clock.

The old sweet is a beautiful place, the most beautiful I have yet seen in Virginia. It ought to be called "El Fureides," the Paradise.[9] It is a perfect paradise for lovesick swains and damsels, and is resorted to in the latter part of every season, when times have grown dull at the Old White [Sulphur Springs] with a perfect *furore*. It is situated in a valley of real fertility (sulphur) around which are picturesque hills covered with trees and grasses of the most luxuriant growth. The grounds are laid off with considerable taste, and the buildings, which struck me as elegant and spacious, are said to be furnished with every convenience. There are the tables, chief attraction to a soldier, so often burthened with innumerable luxuries; the porches, delightful for promenades; and the great halls where nightly, in happier times, "the music arose with voluptuous swell, and all went merry as a marriage-bell." Now comparatively all is dull and almost tenantless. Such are the effects of War.

A mile to the east the Red Sweet is situated, and the line between Monroe

---

8. For every soldier killed in action during the Civil War, two died behind the lines from disease. The first contagious illness to strike a unit was usually rubella ("red measles").

9. Maria Susanna Cummins's 1860 novel *El Fureidis* tells the story of a Palestinian girl named Havilak, who embodied both purity and passion far beyond the constraints of Western civilization.

and Allegheny [Counties] is said to be between the two. The summit of the Alleghanies, the ridge that divides the waters of the James and the Ohio, we crossed a few miles beyond the Old Sweet, to the west. We are now in camp three miles north east of the Sweet Springs and two N.E. of the Red Sweet on the road to Covington. Mitchell's Map[10] locates both watering places in Alleghany.

A mile and a half N.W. of us, Capt. McDonald's Company of cavalry from Tazewell is quartered.[11] In the meadow below us are the tents of the 1st Regt., Col. Heath, and 2nd Regt., Col. Reynolds.[12] We belong to the 2nd Regt. but are under the immediate command of Major Thorburn,[13] who is one of the most glorious little fellows in the world, a gentleman in every sense of the term. Genial, gallant, gifted and experienced, under him our pathway to high honor and fame will be broad and straight.

He is exceedingly anxious that Rosecrantz's[14] battery of seven guns, formerly McClellan's, the only Yankee battery of any considerable strength now in Western Virginia, should be taken by his cavalry, and when he orders it we will certainly take it. It is probable that a separate Regt. of Cavalry will be formed and that he [Thorburn] will be promoted to a Colonelcy. Nothing could please us better. We expect to get sabers very soon, and with them in our hands we hope to be invincible.

From Camp Bartow, where my last letter to you was written, Genl. Floyd dispatched Sergeant [A. B.] Cook of the Dragoons on an expedition to Wise's Legion. He returned last night bringing Gen. Floyd with him. He reports that

10. John Mitchell was an Anglo-American cartographer who produced the first reliable maps of French and English settlements in North America.

11. Capt. John McDonald's Tazewell Troop became Company H of the 8th Virginia Cavalry.

12. Col. Henry Heth commanded the 45th Virginia Infantry. The 50th Virginia Infantry was under Col. Alexander W. Reynolds.

13. Charles Edmonston Thorburn had a unique Civil War career. The Norfolk native graduated from the U.S. Naval Academy and spent fourteen years in naval service prior to his 1861 appointment as major of the 50th Virginia. Thorburn subsequently commanded the regiment, served on Brig. Gen. William W. Loring's staff, failed to win reelection as an officer in the 50th Virginia, was a Confederate Navy purchase agent, and accompanied Pres. Jefferson Davis's party on the 1865 flight from Richmond. John D. Chapla, *50th Virginia Infantry* (Lynchburg, Va., 1997), 199.

14. Brig. Gen. William S. Rosecrans (whose name Sheffey consistently misspells in his manuscript letters as "Rosecrantz") succeeded George B. McClellan as commander of Union forces in northwestern Virginia.

Wise is very tyrannical, and that his men are much dissatisfied and regard him as out of his element & thoroughly incompetent as a military leader. He had many opportunities to cut the enemy to pieces but did not avail himself of them.[15] His headquarters now are near Lewisburg, about twenty five or six miles N.W. of us.

Wise & Floyd will operate under Genl. Lee, I presume, as he is reported to be coming towards us with 122,000 men. I rather think it is Gen. Loring who was sent after the death of Garnett to succeed him.[16] 12,000 North Carolinians are reported to be awaiting us at Jacksons River. We hope soon to be ready to meet the enemy. The people of the North West are much afraid of the Yankees, and we meet them constantly traveling southward or with their families and Negroes.

Please write to me and address "Covington, Alleghany Co., Va." & "care of Capt. Thompson of the Smyth Dragoons, Floyd Brigade." I must close now for I have not written home since I left Wytheville, and must do so this evening. I cannot tell you half the news, for something of interest is constantly occurring among us, but will write again very soon. We are entirely in the dark as to what is occurring in the East, however. I have not seen a paper since I left Wytheville. My duties are becoming innumerable, but I will try to [be] equal to every task. I wish I could strike up a correspondence between you and some of my sisters so that I could hear from them and they from me through you, but I believe you are not well acquainted with any of them but Maggie. I cannot write to you as often as I would wish, but suspect you would get very tired easily if I were to write oftener.

15. One of Henry Wise's few defenders has stated, "His lack of military training and experience, and his illness after the heated sessions of the convention approving the ordinance of secession, were sufficient reasons for his remaining in the quiet of his country home near Norfolk." Yet Wise always craved being in the center of action. E. Kidd Lockard, "The Unfortunate Military Career of Henry A. Wise in Western Virginia," *West Virginia History* 31 (1969–70): 40. Wise explained his first problems in western Virginia with typical bluntness: "We are treading on snakes while aiming at the enemy. The grass of the soil we are defending is full of copperhead traitors; they invite the enemy, feed him, and he arms and drills them. . . . A spy is on every hill top, at every cabin, and from Charleston to Point Pleasant they swarm." *Official Records*, 2:291.

16. Following the death of Brig. Gen. Robert S. Garnett at the July 13 engagement at Corrick's Ford, Lee placed General Loring in charge of Confederate forces in northwestern Virginia. The report of a reinforcing army coming from Virginia was groundless. On July 28 President Davis sent Lee to western Virginia with the hope that he would "strike a decisive blow at the enemy," or at least "organize and post our troops so as to check the enemy." *Official Records*, 5:767.

We are exceedingly anxious now to get our arms and to get into a fight. The work we have to do we want to do quickly. We will be here several days and are not certain what will be our direction when we leave. We may march immediately to meet the enemy, if we get our arms.

Love to all. Goodbye.

Headquarters Army of Kanawha[17]
Camp Tyree, AUG. 17TH, 1861

Miss Josie,

I write you at the request of Preston. He has been this evening sent with a portion of his Company to examine certain roads and localities near our present camp. He has been similarly occupied during the last few days and consequently unable to write you. His inability to do so has given him so much pain that at his suggestion I have taken the liberty to do so myself. He is perfectly well—in as poor spirits as could be expected *under all the circumstances.*

It would amuse you no little to see something of a soldier's life—particularly his quarters. For instance, I am at present writing flat on the ground under a bivouac of poles covered with leaves—in front of a large log fire—not ten feet from me is Genl. Floyd in the very graceful attitude (for a man of his stature) of sitting on the ground without hat or coat. All around me are blankets, &c.

The enemy are, according to best information, within ten or fifteen miles of us. The retreat of Genl. Wise from Charleston has surrendered the Kanawha Valley to the enemy.[18] We intend, however, that they shall not hold this beautiful portion of our state. I believe we can whip them—at any rate we intend to try them whenever they make a stand. But I must close.

Please present my compliments and kind remembrance to your mother and her family.

With high respect,
William E. Peters

17. The letter from Sheffey's brother-in-law and compatriot is included because it provides information on the lieutenant's activities as well as his environment.

18. Wise had occupied Charleston and won a fight at Scary Creek on July 17. His retreat began when larger Union forces moved toward the area. The general and his legion abandoned Charleston without firing a shot. Worse, they retreated seventy-five miles eastward to White Sulphur Springs.

Camp Sewell near top of Big Sewell Mountain
Fayette Co., Va., AUGUST 18TH, 1861

Dear Josie,

I intended to write to you from Lewisburg, but the scarcity of writing material and incessant engagements rendered it impossible for me to write during the few brief moments of my stay there. I wrote to my father, however, from there to post him more fully with regard to the condition of this part of Va.

I commenced a letter to you while at Camp Arbuckle, 4 miles west of Lewisburg, but in the midst of it, we were suddenly ordered to saddle up and started upon a forced march westward, leaving our tents and equipage all behind us. Since then we have been sleeping with our horses out in the fields and wildwoods with only the heavens or perchance the leaves of some friendly tree above us. I have been sent upon a scout down Meadow River and along Hominy Creek away into the heart of Nicholas [County] and just returned day before yesterday to this, the Sunday Road, as it is called by the people of the country.

Last night I went upon another scout and met with some little fun and frolic. It reminded me very much of the coon hunts and opossum hunts of my boyhood. For a part of the night Col. Lucius Davis[19] who, though very brave and perhaps able, is yet very excitable and imaginative, was with us. He commands the advanced guard of our army and is stationed about ten miles to the west, or rather a little to the north of west of us. He is at a place called Locust Lane, which was three or four days ago the camp of three or four hundred of the enemy. They retreated several miles west to Locust Mountain, where they are now reported to be about 1400 strong.

They were yesterday attempting to get behind us by marching around south of us on what is called the Chestnutburg Road. Today we have fallen back five miles to this point which is a strong position, and we will here await their coming, confident if they attack us here that we will rout them. If they do not attack us here in a few days, we will advance upon them again.

Last Thursday a body of our cavalry had a slight skirmish with several hundred of the enemy, near the place where we camped last night. None of our men were killed or wounded, but they report that nine of the enemy

19. Col. James Lucius Davis commanded the 46th Virginia Infantry, which was then called the 1st Regiment of the Wise Legion.

were slain. The first shot on our side was fired by Mr. Garlans T. Gerald of Tazewell,[20] who asserts that he killed his man, but as the Yankees retreated, bearing away their dead, and I was myself in the heart of Nicholas[21] at the time, I do not know what is the truth in the matter.

I requested Capt. Peters to write to you last night because I did not know, when I started upon the scout above mentioned, when I could find the opportunity, and I thought that as I had promised to write to you from Lewisburg, you might be uneasy. I have pressed pen, ink and paper today into service, and am glad that when all other enjoyments save that of thinking and dreaming constantly of the dear ones I have left behind me are taken away from me by the wild excitement of this kind of life, I can still steal away occasionally and write to you, the dearest of them all.

I must close now, for I have an infinite number of duties to perform and I do not know what moment I may be sent out upon another scouting expedition to reconnoitre the movements and position of the enemy. I do not know when I can write to you again. We are 34 miles from the nearest post office from which my letters could reach their destination, and as my trunk, paper, ink and pens are all 30 miles from here, it will be next to impossible to write frequently. Do not be uneasy about me. My fate is in the hands of the great God who has sided with us and I am content to abide the issue.

Twice during the last week, I have narrowly escaped death, once at night, when returning from a picket guard, my own men, excited to the highest pitch, came near shooting me for an enemy, and once when my faithful bay, by whose side I was sleeping, forgot that my head was not a stone, and came within a half-inch of mashing it into the same shape into which she transformed the hat that was upon it. I am beginning to think that I also am a creature of destiny, and that a mysterious Providence is watching over me who will preserve me for a happier fate.

Do not think that I ever forget you. Morning, noon & night, always and everywhere, I think and dream of you, and the happiness that awaits me when these troubles are over. I wish I could give you a detailed account of

20. Garlans T. Gerald was a member of the Tazewell Troop, later a company in the 8th Virginia Cavalry. The *Official Records* contain no reference to any fighting of note on August 15, 1861.

21. Nicholas was one of the principal characters in "The Miller's Tale," part of Chaucer's great 1385 work, *The Canterbury Tales*. Nicholas was a poor scholar whose life seemed so often in limbo and who boarded with a wealthy but miserly carpenter.

my experiences since I saw you, and I know they would be interesting to you, but I cannot now. Every night for a week I have slept under arms, coated, booted and generally with spurs on, also ready to move at a moments notice, and am beginning to think that the customs and habits of civilized life are very superfluous. Tents and houses are nuisances which, if they were abated out here, would cause most of us to suffer no inconvenience whatever. Great campfires, a merry greenwood and starry heavens are all the soldier needs aside from his blanket, arms, and flannels, to make him as luxurious as a monarch in the midst of marbled halls, surrounded by all the accompaniments of gorgeous majesty.

But, separated from you, I could never be happy anywhere, and I long for the time to arrive when this horrid war shall end and Peace shall once more reign supreme over the land. I would not have Peace, however, except upon our own terms, the terms the Southern government sought to make, which are that the Yankees shall forever give up every inch of slave territory, pay the expenses of this war, and let us alone forever.

We captured a Yankee mail a few days ago from which we gained some information, and found out the names of some of the sweethearts of the Yankees. We had a merry time reading the Yankees' love-letters, and if I could have found an opportunity, I would have sent you one of the richer productions. But I can write no more. Please write to me as soon as you receive this. Direct to "Lewisburg, Greenbrier Co., Va., Care of Capt. John H. Thompson of the Smyth Dragoons, Floyd's Brigade." The letter will be forwarded to me immediately. I am very anxious to hear from you.

I have written hastily and very badly, but you will look over that. Goodbye.

P.S. A scout has just come in who reports that the enemy is encamped 18 or 20 miles from here on the Chestnutburg Road. He could not ascertain what their intentions are but we will find out in a few days. If you see any of the folks from my home, tell them I am well & want to hear from them. Love to all.

Camp Gauley, North bank of Gauley [River]
Nicholas Co., Va., AUGUST 26TH, 1861

Dear Josie,

We have had a hot fight today and gained a glorious victory.[22] Have captured about fifty of the enemy, and killed a good many of them. I do not

22. The skirmish at Cross Lanes would occupy Sheffey's attention for two letters. At dawn on August 26, Confederates surprised the 7th Ohio Infantry as its members were cooking

know how many. Side by side with Capt. Corns of the Border Rangers,[23] I followed them in their flight for seven or eight miles. Three of our men were killed. I had only seven men of the Dragoons in the fight, the others being all on the south side of the river. None of the seven were hurt, nor was I.

Capt. Thompson of the Dragoons was entrapped yesterday at the Hawk's Nest with the balance of his company. Four of his men had horses shot under him, but only one man is missing. They will probably cross the river and join me herewith my forlorn seven. I have no time to rest now or to write. I wish I could hear from you. I suppose you have heard of the death by drowning of 3 of the Dragoons,[24] as I wrote to my mother and directed her to write to you. The boat went down with them and that circumstance was what separated me from the rest of my company. Please write to me. Direct to Lewisburg.

P.S. The troops defeated by us today were composed of the flower of the Yankee Army in the Northwest. Love to all.

Nicholas County, Va., Miller's House,
1½ Miles North of Camp Gauley, Aug. 28, 1861

Dear Josie,

Two days have now elapsed since "the Battle of the Cross Lanes," with regard to which I wrote you on Monday evening. I crossed the river at McVeys Ferry, called also Carnifex Ferry. Carnifex Ferry is at the mouth of Meadow River. Last Friday the 23rd, I was there, along with seven of the Dragoons, separated from the rest of my Company by the loss of the ferryboat, and the four men in it, three of whom, Hugh Scott, Jno. Jones, and Geo. Bear, were Smyth Dragoons. The river was much swollen, and, as the poor fellows went down the boiling stream, among the rocks, and into the furious rapids, the scene was sad and fearful beyond description.

For the first time in many years, I cried like a child. In the excitement of

---

breakfast. The Ohioans, unable to reach their weapons, were "overpowered by superior numbers and scattered." Floyd's claim that 45–50 Federals were killed or wounded is an exaggeration. Actual Union losses were 1 killed, 10 wounded, and 96 captured. Wise sarcastically referred to the affair as the "battle of the knives and forks." *Official Records,* 5:118–19, 809; "War-Time Reminiscences of James D. Sedinger, Company E, 8th Virginia Cavalry (Border Rangers)," *West Virginia History* 51 (1992): 59.

23. Capt. James M. Corns commanded Company E, 8th Virginia Cavalry.

24. George W. Bear, John L. Jones, and Hugh Scott were the three cavalrymen who drowned.

victory and pursuit, I have tried to forget the horror of that hour, but I can never cease to grieve over the untimely fate of the poor fellows to whom I had become so much attached. Had they been shot down in the fury of battle I should not have lamented them so much, for the price of Liberty is the blood of the brave.

The day after I crossed, I went with my own men on a scout to Peters Creek. Peters Creek runs West of us and its general direction is from NE to SW. The two main crossings of the creek are about eight miles from Camp Gauley, which is three or four hundred yards from the ferry above-mentioned, and are about 3 mis. apart. I went across the upper one and stationed 6 of my men a short distance beyond at a point where the road from here towards Sutton enters the turnpike from Gauley Bridge to Summersville. I scouted that road effectually for four or five miles and watched it until evening, expecting to capture the Yankee Mail, but they have not trusted their mail upon that road since the former capture, with regard to which I wrote to you, I believe, from Camp Sewell in Fayette.

Shortly before dusk, I recd. information from a long, lean, lank, lanthorn [lantern]-jawed specimen of humanity, who carried a rifle, longer, leaner, lanker and hungrier looking than himself, that the Yankees were advancing in force by way of the lower Crossing, to take possession of the Cross Lanes, at which point about one mile from where I am now writing, the nearest road to Summersville, the road to the Lower Crossing at Peters Creek, and the road to the upper crossing, about 6 mis. off. Concurrent, of course I was in a predicament. There was no other route for me—and no choice left except to double-quick the distance, and we did double-quick it, in double-quick time and order.

At the Cross Lanes we found a considerable body of cavalry, which was not there in the morning. It was dusk and I could not distinguish whether they were friends or foe. I advanced upon them with considerable confidence that they were friends for I knew the enemy had very few cavalry, but I determined, if the event proved otherwise, to dash thru and sell my life as dearly as possible. I was considerably relieved when I found they were Capt. Corns' men from Cabel [Cabell] and Wayne [Counties], who had also received information of the approach of the enemy and had been sent out to watch their coming.

By some Providence the Yankees had delayed their march and after passing the Lower Crossing of P. Creek had gone into camp 4 or 5 mis. distant from Cr. Lanes. The same thing I had intended to do, was done the next day by Lieut. [Alexander H.] Samuels and 8 of Capt. Corns' men, so I have heard. They dashed thro. the enemy at Cross Lanes and tho' volley after volley was fired after them, the hand of God was interposed and they escaped unhurt. I went on to camp with a heart full of thankfulness to Him who has thus far watched over me with more than a Father's care.

After reporting to the General, I returned to this house where I have been quartered since I crossed the Gauley, and have been treated with the utmost kindness by Mr. Miller and all his household. Tho' a mile and a half in advance of the camp & consequently full of peril it is a pleasant retreat, and I shall regret the necessity which must soon drag me away.

The next day, Sabbath, tho' it was, I went with 6 of the Dragoons, the other having unfortunately hurt his knee very badly. I went out upon the road to the Lower Crossing to Walker's within a mile and a half of the camp of the enemy. There I found Capt. Corns with 6 or 8 of his men. The name of his company is "The Border Rangers," and they were formerly commanded by Jenkins[25] who was Congressman for some time from the northwestern part of the state. Our object was to ascertain the position and numbers of the enemy as nearly as possible. I had been at Walker's but a short time, probably an hour and a half, when the scouts sent out by Capt. Corns to reconnoiter the camp of the Yankees came in and reported that three companies were advancing toward us.

I had picketed 2 of my men a quarter of a mile below Walker's to give notice of the approach in that direction. I brought them in immediately. We then retreated and took a position about ½ mile from Walker's stationing a line of pickets on the brush upon commanding points to watch them. We had scarcely stationed our pickets when the enemy reached Walker's. Unconscious of our proximity, they then fired 3 guns. Had they known we were near and advanced rapidly we would have had a rough time of it, for we had no idea they were as near as they were.

They remained at Walker's a short time, and having gained as much information as possible, we double-quicked to the Cross Lanes. The enemy, be-

25. Albert Gallatin Jenkins was a native of Cabell County in western Virginia. When he cast his lot with the Confederacy, a Wheeling newspaper branded him a "traitor son" whose property should be confiscated and himself hanged. Roy Watson Curry, "The Newspaper Press and the Civil War in West Virginia," *West Virginia History* 6 (1945): 255. Jenkins served in the Confederate Provisional Congress before taking command of the Border Rangers. For a period in 1862, he was a member of the Confederate Congress. Jenkins returned to military duty as a brigadier general and fell mortally wounded at the battle of Cloyds Mountain in May 1864.

tween seven and eleven hundred in number, reached Cross Lanes in the afternoon and went into camp apparently unconscious that we had crossed the river in any considerable force until that [Sunday] night. We supposed from their boldness that there were three or four thousand of them, and expected an attack that evening. Had they attacked us in our position we would have utterly annihilated them. They had orders from Genl. Cox[26] to retake the ferry, and the prisoners have since told us that it was their intention the next day to attack.

I rather think if we had delayed our attack a half hour the next morning they would have escaped us entirely. Their abandonment of the ferry has been a great error, for it is one of the great strategic points of approach to the country before us and our assumption of it was a military masterpiece. It brought us across the Gauley without the great loss of life we had anticipated and gave us a position where we think we can defy Abraham and all his kith, kin and kind.

We have utterly demoralized their brag Reg., the 7th Ohio, Col. Tyler,[27] and have killed, wounded, and captured more than a hundred of them. Since the battle, our men have been constantly in the woods and are constantly capturing the blue-coats and bringing them into camp. Eighty odd prisoners will be sent on toward Richmond this evening. One of the Yankees lived more than a day with his brains shot out, conclusive evidence that they can get along almost as well without them as with them.

The battle for a few minutes was hot and heavy. The Yankees upon their right wing fought like fiends. They had every advantage of position, and if they had shot a little better, would have given us some considerable cause for regret. Within twenty five minutes after our attack, they were flying in every direction through the woods. Had the country been open we would have captured all, but the most of it is a rugged wilderness. We did not find the true trail soon enough. Almost our whole army went down to the Lower

26. Union general Jacob D. Cox commanded the four infantry regiments that had driven the Wise Legion from the Kanawha Valley. Cox was an Ohio attorney and state senator who displayed solid military talents in the field. After the Civil War he was a governor, secretary of the interior, and a congressman.

27. Erastus B. Tyler won election as colonel of the 7th Ohio Infantry over James A. Garfield. For a Union account of this one-sided action, see George L. Wood, *The Seventh Regiment: A Record* (New York, n.d.), 43–59. A good Confederate summary is in Robert Leroy Hilldrup, ed., "The Romance of a Man in Gray, Including the Love Letters of James S. Peery, Forty-Fifth Virginia Infantry Regiment, C.S.A.," *West Virginia History* 22 (1960–61): 93–94.

Crossing after about a hundred and fifty, when the main body had taken across the hills and forest toward the sources of 20 Mile Creek. We did not find the true trail till late in the evening—or we would have captured them all as it was. Along the course of the main body, they seemed to have dragged their dead and wounded, and everywhere they scattered guns, canteens, haversacks, shoes, hats and coats, cartridge boxes & bayonets in tumultuous confusion. Col. Tyler was allegedly the first man to "make tracks." He brought his men into the difficulty and then deserted them.[28]

On our side, Major Hounshell[29] acted with conspicuous bravery, and it is a miracle that he was not killed. He seems to be perfectly reckless of his life. Twelve months ago, I would have been so too, but circumstances alter cases. I am willing to go into the front of the battle, but to expose myself unnecessarily as he does I am not willing. He and I have been much together. He delights in war. I sigh for peace. He is not a happy man, even in anticipation. If he were he would think as I do and if I were as he is, and as I have been, I would, as he says he is willing to do, sell my head for glory. Bah! How paltry it seems compared to my dreams of peace and happiness! But I can write no more. I have not heard from you since I left Wytheville. I suppose you have written. Please write as often as you can.

My company had been very much hurt in the fight at Hawk's Nest.[30] Five of the men were wounded, one is missing, and four horses were killed.[31] They were led into an ambuscade by Jenkins who, though a very brave man, has not three grains of discretion.[32] We will be all massacred if we follow unwittingly all the fools who are put over us to lead us. I will not go blindly into such a trap. Please write to me.

28. General Cox recalled that at Cross Lanes, Tyler "was new to responsibility, and seemed paralyzed into complete inefficiency." Jacob D. Cox, *Military Reminiscences of the Civil War*, 2 vols. (New York, 1900), 1:95–96.

29. A native of Wytheville and graduate of VMI, David Stuart Hounshell was at this time a major without a command. He later served with the 23d Virginia Infantry Battalion and the Virginia State Line.

30. On August 25 Captain Jenkins led some cavalry units into an ambush by the 11th Ohio Infantry concealed in a defile near Hawks Nest. The Confederates "retreated *pell mell*, strewing the road with guns, pistols, knives, and everything that would encumber their flight." Joshua H. Horton, *A History of the Eleventh Regiment (Ohio Volunteer Infantry)* (Dayton, Ohio, 1866), 41–42.

31. The missing soldier, John Easter of Marion, was captured and imprisoned at Camp Chase, Ohio. Jack L. Dickinson, *8th Virginia Cavalry* (Lynchburg, Va., 1986), 89.

32. Sheffey in time would markedly change his opinion of Jenkins.

Cavalry Camp at Cross Lanes, near Camp
Gauley, Nicholas Co., Va., SEPT. 6, 1861

Dear Josie,

Again out in the green wood, among the shadows of the somber old oaks, my thoughts revert, as is their constant habit, to her for whose love I am ever so grateful. Feeling assured that my letters, badly written as they necessarily are, are always welcome, I take advantage of every available opportunity to write to you. Time after time, as I turn from our Postmaster's tent, with the knowledge that among all the letters that come to me, the one most desired, most anxiously expected, has not come, I can scarcely conceal the bitter disappointment. Just a little line of love from you, an occasional message of affection, how it would strengthen me in the purpose which brought me into this uncongenial wilderness to fight, if need be to die, for our country and our right! However, strong may be his patriotism, his sense of duty and his trust in God, the poor soldier needs constant communion with the dear ones he has left behind him, to nerve and inspirit him, not so much in the wild tumult of battle as in the longer and sadder hours when he has nothing to do but to think of them. Without hearing frequently from you the long months that are before me will be sad indeed.

Mr. [J. J.] McMahan reached Camp Gauley last Tuesday the 3 inst. He is delighted with his appointment to the Chaplaincy of the 3rd Regt. I brought him out to my camp here which is, as I have written in a former letter, a mile and a half or two miles in advance of Camp Gauley, took him over the battle ground, explained to him the disposition of our forces and of the enemy and then sat him down to a sumptuous repast of corn bread, boiled corn and, I was going to add, corned beef but it happened to be older and tougher than any of that description. His teeth are good, however, and he seemed to enjoy the banquet considerably. His coming was as welcome as it was unexpected to me. He brought a delightful letter from my dear old mother who, God bless her, never forgets her absent darling. He returned to Lewisburg, which is about 60 or 70 miles S.E. of us on Wednesday for his baggage.

The 3rd Regt., Col. Wharton,³³ which after many delays has at last reached

---

33. Culpeper native Gabriel Colvin Wharton graduated second in his class at VMI and was a successful civil engineer in the West prior to the Civil War. He was colonel of the 45th Virginia for a month before taking command of the 51st Virginia. Wharton ultimately became a brigadier general in the western Virginia theater. After the war he was a prominent citizen of Radford.

us, is finely equipped, and the regularity and exactness of all its movements and arrangements are after the order of clockwork. Besides all military conveniences, it came accompanied by an excellent band. To our savage and unsophisticated ears, the dulcet strains seem, indeed, a delightful innovation.[34] Two other regiments will soon be with us.

Mr. McMahan and others who were with him as they came down the Sunday Road, which is the nearest road from the direction of Lewisburg to Carnifex's Ferry at the mouth of Meadow River, near which it intersects with the Saturday Road from the direction of Hawk's Nest, where Wise is with his Legion, heard heavy cannonading in the direction of Wise's forces.[35] That was upon the 3rd [of] Sept. It was evident that Wise was fighting. In the evening of the 3rd and morning of the 4th many rumors came to us as to the result, but all of them thoroughly unreliable. One report was to the effect that Wise had killed 300 of the Yankees, another 100, and another 80.

Still later, the report came that he had killed none of the Yankees but that by mistake, three of his own men had been badly wounded, among them Col. Crow,[36] a gentleman of fine character from one of the northwestern Counties, who was said to have had his chin shot off, and a very clever fellow named Williams who acted as my guide some time ago, in quite a tedious, and as I thought then perilous, scout upon the Sunday Road when the Yankees were there. Upon the 4th Genl. Floyd sent John D. Hutton[37] over to learn the truth of the matter. He returned, and I talked with him yesterday but he seems to know as little, almost, as the others.

The Hawk's Nest you are perhaps aware is a high, abrupt precipice, in Fayette, which overhangs New River or Kanawha about 9 miles S.E. of Gauley Bridge, which is near the mouth of Gauley. Below that precipice passes the turnpike road, a road which does not deserve the name, from Lewisburg *via* Meadow Bluff to Gauley Bridge. On either side of the Hawk's Nest for miles

34. The regiment may have looked impressive, especially with its own band, but a goodly number of its soldiers had not yet received any weapons. James A. Davis, *51st Virginia Infantry* (Lynchburg, Va., 1984), 4.

35. The skirmishing at Hawks Nest on September 4 was inconclusive, though Wise represented it as a Southern victory. He reported a loss of only 2 men slightly wounded. *Official Records,* 5:122–27.

36. Crow was a civilian. No active officer of that name is mentioned in any military communiqué of the time.

37. Capt. John D. Hutton was Wise's topographical engineer. See *Official Records,* 5:771, 849.

the country is wild, desolate and rugged in the extreme. It passes through defile after defile, where Nature herself has thrown up impregnable fortifications, where the laurel, the ivy and innumerable species of tangled undergrowth form thickets as impenetrable as any Mexican chaparral. About 4 or 5 miles E of the Hawk's Nest, the Saturday Road leaves the turnpike at a point called Piggott's Mill. Here was our camp the night before we came to Carnifex's Ferry. The Yankees had then retreated before us for thirty or forty miles.

That night the 21st ult., they were encamped two or three miles before us, near a point where a few days before they had ambuscaded two or three companies of our cavalry and infantry and had wounded four of our men one of whom, Stuart Painter,[38] from Wythe they succeeded in taking prisoner because our men supposing that he was shot through the heart had left him for dead on the ground. The Yankees confess a loss in that skirmish of four men killed and several wounded. In camp at Pickett's [Piggot's] Mill, the question came up whether we should attack the Yankees between it and the Hawk's Nest, or take the Saturday Road and drive them from the Ferry. The latter plan was wisely adopted. When we reached the Ferry, the Yankees had fled and we had no difficulty in crossing until the next day 23rd when the 4 men were drowned & the boat lost.

Wise was then ordered back on the Saturday Road to Dogwood Gap, a strong position, where he planted his cannon commanding the approaches beyond. His advance guard was thrown forward to the junction of the Saturday Road with the turnpike at Piggot's Mill, about a mile and a half or two miles beyond Piggot's upon the road to the Hawk's Nest to the house of a man name Tyree.[39] Near this point the Yankees were posted in force, where on Sunday, August the 25th, the Smyth Dragoons, from whom I had been separated by the loss of the boat at Carnifex's, the Tazewell Cavalry, Capt. McDonald, the Nelson Rangers, Capt. [Thomas P.] Fitzpatrick, the Lee Grays, Capt. [Daniel S.] Dickerson, and a company of Wise's Cavalry, Capt. Buck's,[40] led by Col. Jenkins, were ambuscaded and compelled to run a

---

38. Stewart Dabney Painter of the 45th Virginia was wounded in the left lung at Hawks Nest. He returned to duty and served with his regiment until captured in March 1865 at Waynesboro, Virginia. Scott, *45th Virginia Infantry*, 109.

39. Frank Tyree owned a stone tavern that still stands. Although arrested briefly by Union authorities, Tyree continued to keep Confederates informed of enemy movements. *Official Records*, 5:782; Tim McKinney, *The Civil War in Fayette County, West Virginia* (Charleston, W.Va., 1988), 40, 85, 191.

40. Sheffey here refers to Capt. John P. Brock, whose "Valley Rangers" company was part of Wise's 1st Cavalry Regiment. Lee A. Wallace Jr., *A Guide to Virginia Military Organizations, 1861–1865* (Lynchburg, Va., 1986), 52, 150.

gauntlet for more than a half mile of incessant and deadly fire from hundreds of the enemy concealed in the bushes on both sides of the road.

Our men escaped miraculously with a loss of but one killed, several wounded and two, Hester of the Dragoons and Duff of the Lee Grays,[41] taken prisoners. Several of the Yankees are said to have been killed. But the men most of them were thrown from their horses, and some of them lost guns, pistols, saddles, and clothing. Several of the horses were killed and others wounded. All that were not killed came out of their own accord. One horse, [William] Edwin Copenhaver's of the Dragoons, who was himself badly wounded, was shot through but bore his rider out of danger before he fell. The companies have all gone back to Camp Arbuckle, 16 miles W. of Lewisburg, except 10 or 15 from each Co. who are here. The others will be up in a few days—ought to be here now.

The next day, 26th, we fought our battle here at Cross Lanes—some of the particulars of which I gave you in my two last letters. Genl. Wise was then ordered by Genl. Floyd to advance upon the enemy at Hawk's Nest, which he did, and upon the 3rd inst. the day Mr. McMahan came over Sunday Road, he passed by Tyree's out to the Hawk's Nest, finding no enemy, they having retreated towards Gauley Bridge. Marching on two miles further, he found them posted in force on Broad Run or Big Creek as it is called indifferently. There the fight between the cannon occurred. According to Harman's report,[42] no harm was done on either side. Wise then fell back two miles beyond the Hawk's Nest in the direction of Tyree's.

Today (Sept. 6) Thompkins with his Regt.[43] was sent to him by Genl. Floyd. They will be able to drive the enemy through to Gauley Bridge, not withstanding the disadvantages they will labor under, for the retreating army in such a place as that has always infinite advantages over the one advancing. On the south side of the Kanawha, opposite the Hawk's Nest, at Cotton Hill between Fayette C.H. and the river, we have a large force under Gen. Chapman.[44] It is reported here that at that point a few days ago, a fight occurred

41. John Easter Hester remained a prisoner of war until exchanged in July 1862. He rejoined the 8th Virginia Cavalry and in August 1864 was captured and imprisoned again. Jerome H. Duff was an inmate at Camp Chase, Ohio, until his August 1862 release. He too returned to duty with Sheffey's regiment.

42. Edwin Houston Harman was captain of the Tazewell Rangers of the 45th Virginia.

43. Christopher Quarles Tompkins led the 22d Virginia, known then as the 1st Kanawha Regiment. In November 1861 he resigned from the army "because Confederate General Floyd fired on Tompkins's home during an engagement, despite Tompkins's protest." Robert K. Krick, Lee's Colonels (Dayton, Ohio, 1984), 323.

44. Augustus Alexandria Chapman led a brigade of fifteen hundred Virginia militia.

between the enemy, a detachment from forces led by Col. Jenkins, the same spoken of above, among which were Capt. Caskie[45] & his Company from Richmond. Without loss, they succeeded in killing some of the Yankees and in taking 25 prisoners. That, however, is only rumor.

We have a considerable force now at Summersville under Col. McCauslin [McCausland].[46] The Putnam Hornets (Cavalry) are there also.[47] Day before yesterday they pursued the Dutch Cavalry[48] who have been depredating on Birch Creek, 20 mis. north of Summersville, and captured their guide, a Union man named Fox. They ought to have hung him when they caught him. If we get hold of that cavalry, it will not be well for them, but "catching" is said to be "before hanging." They move too fast.

Now I have written you a long and, I fear, exceedingly uninteresting letter. Please write to me often. Here I am out of the world. I hear nothing that is going on anywhere except what's immediately around here. Will you not, for I fear I will become as ignorant of [events] in the world as a Rip Van Winkle after his years of slumbering among the peaks of the Catskills. I have not a letter from you since my company was in camp at Marion. I have not heard from you at all except through Mr. McMahan since I saw you at Wytheville. Any letter directed to me at "Lewisburg, Greenbrier Co., Va., Care of Capt. John Thompson, Smyth Dragoons, Floyd's Brigade" will reach me, for we had a regular post from there to the headquarters of the Brigade. I receive letters regularly from my mother and sisters, but though I love them with all the devotion of a true son and brother, I do no violence when I say that any time I would give up all from them, for one from you. They know it and love me none the less.

But you are tired [of] reading. [I hope] you can read this almost illegible scrawl. If anything of interest occurs out here, I will inform you of it. My kindest regards to all. Goodbye, and may God guard and keep as in the hollow of His hand my own darling.

45. Robert Alexander Caskie's small mounted company was then attached to the Wise Legion. The action mentioned by Sheffey was hearsay.

46. John McCausland graduated at the top of the VMI Class of 1857 and was teaching mathematics at his alma mater when the Civil War began. He was instrumental in the formation of a regiment mustered into service as the 36th Virginia Infantry.

47. Capt. Albert J. Beckett's mounted company from Putnam County was attached to the 36th Virginia Infantry during this period. Wallace, *Virginia Military Organizations,* 119.

48. Sheffey's reference is to a Union cavalry company with a significant number of German-speaking troopers, though the specific unit cannot be identified.

Marion, SEPTEMBER 13TH, 1861

Dear Miss Josie,

We received recently several letters from our brother, evincing intense anxiety at your continued silence and desiring us to give him information from you, rumors having reached him of the prevalence and fatality of the "Typhoid Fever" in Wytheville, which fill his mind with gloomy forebodings with regard to *your safety.* The desire to arouse his drooping spirits and also to allay our own anxiety—for our hearts echo the fears which pervade his— prompts me to write.

I truly hope that I may receive pleasant tidings to communicate to him or hear that he has been made the recipient of a bright little messenger which alone can lessen the cares and sweeten the hardships of his present life. A letter received from him this morning assures us of his perfect health and his enjoyment of the wild and exciting scenes to which his life as a ranger intro- duces him. He has for some time had command of a small portion of the "cavalry" as the others had been sent to Lewisburg with prisoners. Fearlessly they run over the country, capturing unionists; bringing in prisoners and I *suspect robbing* cornfields as they are said to live like princes, "faring sumptu- ously every day," which is not the case with those who have no *"fleet-footed* steed" to bear them away from the savory odor of *fried* meat.

The only things which dissatisfies him with his home in the "wild woods," is the thought that he cannot more frequently hear from the dear ones for whom he braves the dangers of a soldier's life. Altho' we write repeatedly, I fear that all our letters haven't reached him. This may probably be owing to the fact that he is constantly on the wing.

To ensure a prompt transmission, he desires us to direct his letters to Mr. Peters' care and to Lewisburg *as formerly.* I hear frequently from Mr. Peters, who writes most cheerfully—says that camp life agrees with him admirably, which is a great comfort to me, tho' I fear that he only lets me see the "bright- side." It takes such a long, long time for letters to reach me from that wild, out-of-the-world place. I cannot refrain from feeling anxious all the time yet I try to look forward hopefully to the time when "our glorious Flag" shall wave triumphantly over every inch of ground our brave soldiers now so nobly contest and they can return to peaceful homes to enjoy the fruits of their well earned victories.

I have written more than I intended; but I hope you will pay me back in the "same coin." I should be most happy to correspond with you. Be assured that your letters will ever receive a warm welcome and a cordial response. My mother and sisters write in love. I close with the hope that I may hear from you soon and *often*.

Affectionately yours,
Maggie S. Peters

Camp Sewell Big Sewell, Fayette Co.,
Va. SEPT. 15, 1861[49]

Dear Josie,

We fought General Rosecrans with 9000 men at Camp Gauley on Tuesday the 10th. We had but 1700 men at the breastworks, yet we whipped him and drove him back with great slaughter in every attempt he made to carry our breastworks. The great disparity of forces compelled us to fall back across the river during the night, and we have continued our retreat to the point where we will fight him again with increased forces. The battle of Gauley, considering the disparity of numbers, is as valiant as any that has been fought during the war. We did not lose a man, & from all the information we can get, the loss of the enemy was from 800 to 1000. They acknowledged a loss of only 25 killed and 80 or 90 wounded. But they were bringing in their dead for a day or two after the fight on the field around my old camp at Cross Lanes.[50]

I cannot give you a detailed account now, for I have much to do, and am wearied out with incessant labor. I am afraid, too, that this note will fall into the hands of the enemy, or I would write more fully. I am well & ready to go into another battle whenever the Yankees care to attempt it. Goodbye.

49. This and Sheffey's next letter describe the four-hour battle fought on September 10 at Carnifex Ferry. Floyd had moved his seventeen-hundred-man brigade into the Gauley River area in an attempt to sever communications between Rosecrans's Union forces to the north and Cox's Federals to the south. In dense woods and on high ground overlooking the river, Floyd constructed a mile-long system of defensive works in the shape of an inverted U. Rosecrans attacked in midafternoon. Rather than commit his superior numbers to combat, the Union general sent individual regiments forward one at a time through rough terrain. Confederate defenders easily beat back the five assaults before nightfall ended the contest. Floyd had to withdraw his small force overnight because the Federals had moved into a better position for new attacks. Union casualties at Carnifex Ferry were 17 killed and 141 wounded; Floyd's losses were 20 wounded. *Official Records,* 5:146–47; "War-Time Reminiscences of James D. Sedinger," 59–60; Isaac Noyes Smith, "A Virginian's Dilemma," *West Virginia History* 27 (1965–66): 177–80.

50. Darkness brought an end to the fighting. Union soldiers lying wounded near the Southern lines could not be collected until the following day. *Official Records,* 5:131.

P.S. I received a letter from you six or eight days ago and regret very much that my letters have not reached you. I have written very frequently.

Camp Arbuckle, Four Miles West of
Lewisburg, Greenbrier Co., Va.,[51]
WEDNESDAY, SEPTEMBER 16, 1861

Dear Josie,

I wrote you a short note day before yesterday from Camp Sewell on the top of Big Sewell Mountain in Fayette, twenty-six miles from here, to keep you from being anxious about me, by Madam Rumor. In it I spoke of the terrible battle of Gauley or Carnifex's Ferry, on the 10th inst. and of our movements in consequence. Knowing that a more detailed account will be interesting to you, I take advantage of the brief leisure afforded me by a temporary retirement to this point to write you more fully.

You have, I hope ere this, received another letter or two, written by me on the west side of Gauley. I have written you a series of letters, which, if you have received them, have given you a pretty full idea of our operations among the wildernesses of the North West. Yours of the 5th inst. stated that you had received but one from me. I have not written to you since the 7th inst. That letter, I presume, you have received ere this.

On the next day, Sunday September 8th, the report came to us that the enemy were approaching via Sutton and Summersville in large force. Col. McCausland had been in Summersville several days with his Regt. guarding our mills there and attending to the grinding of the grain of the country for the use of the army.[52] He had pushed forward his work so vigorously that 12,500 bushels of flour & meal, I believe, had been sent to our camp on the bluffs of Gauley. Capt. Corns with his company, the Border Rangers Cavalry, & the Putnam Hornets, Capt. [Albert J.] Beckett, were ordered to the vicinity of the enemy. They found them on Birch Creek (in Braxton) which empties into Elk, a few miles S.W. of Sutton. They had 250 or 300 tents and scattered their encampment over sixty or seventy acres of ground. That was

51. The encampment of Sheffey's regiment was at the James Arbuckle farm, one of the oldest and best-known estates in Greenbrier County. See Ruth Woods Dayton, *Greenbrier Pioneers and Their Homes* (Charleston, W.Va., 1942), 162–66.

52. For how successful McCausland and his 36th Virginia Infantry were in the quest for corn and wheat, see *Official Records*, 51, pt. 2:282, 285.

done to get plenty of wood and water, and probably to give an appearance of additional strength.

On the south of Birch Creek is a huge mountain called Powell's Mountain, over which the road passes. Up this mountain the enemy came in most elegant style.[53] Disposing his powerful advance guard, at times, into the shape of a V with his cavalry in the center of the acute angle, grandly, like a huge monster he drew his slow length along over bench and spur. Our scouts, deceived by the cavalry that were advancing upon them, and unconscious of the invisible wings that were encircling them, found themselves once or twice like the victims of Giant Grim,[54] enfolded in an embrace from which escape seemed utterly hopeless. But their own dauntless courage and the speed of their gallant steeds again and again bore them safely away.

Two or three of our foot scouts were so closely beset that the intervention of a friendly briar patch was all that saved them. Gunless, hatless, coatless, and almost breathless, they came to their friends, glad that they were not lifeless also, yet ready whenever called upon to run the same risks again. Twelve hours were consumed by the enemy in crossing Powell's Mountain. Our scouts were constantly firing upon them and killed several, among them a captain.

On Monday morning, Sept. 9th, I went on a scout upon the headwaters of 20 Mile Creek, which empties into the Gauley 5 miles about Gauley Bridge. At the mouth of this creek, as I have before written to you, the enemy has extensive fortifications. His forces were disposed up the Creek for four or five miles. On the Saturday before, 8 or 9 Yankees had gone up the Creek to the house of Anthony Bell, a secessionist who of course was not at home.[55] They abused his property shamefully, tearing to pieces everything of value. All the people are vile Unionists, and are in the ranks of the enemy. Two or three miles below is the house of a man named Osborne.[56] He was the guide of the

53. For more on the Powell Mountain skirmish, see Terry Lowry, *September Blood: The Battle of Carnifex Ferry* (Charleston, W.Va., 1985), 65–67.

54. In John Bunyan's *Pilgrim's Progress,* Grim is a huge giant who tries to stop pilgrims on their way to the Celestial City.

55. Confederate units such as Sheffey's would spend long periods of duty in what would become eastern West Virginia because the border counties were so decidedly pro-Southern in sentiment. Residents of such counties as Greenbrier, Mercer, Monroe, Pocahontas, and McDowell had voted 6–1 in favor of Virginia's secession from the Union. Hampshire County contributed more than thirteen companies to the Confederate armies, while only one Union company organized there. Curry, "Newspaper Press," 233.

56. This Greenbrier resident was likely William Osborne, who was in his early forties at the time of the Civil War. Larry G. Shuck, comp., *Greenbrier County Death Records, 1853–1901* (Athens, Ga., 1993), 215.

fellows who came to Anthony Bell's, and I was anxious to get hold of him. I sent footmen around the house to reconnoiter, but it was so enveloped in corn and trees and shadows that no discovery could be made, except that everything was as still as death. The Osborne's family had been there the day before and his horse was then in the field.

The appearance of things was exceedingly suspicious. I knew that some of the enemy were "there or thereabouts," and I had but ten men besides 3 or 4 secessionists who had gone with me from a house above. I have heard since that we had been already discovered, and if I had listened to the solicitations of several of the men & gone to the house, it is more than probable that several of us would have been killed without any chance for retaliation. I thought my judgment was best, and would not further imperil the lives of the party. We had reached the camp late that night having ridden 32 miles since the morning. I had been westward in the direction of General Cox. Summersville lay north, and to this point from the Flatwoods *via* Sutton & Birch Creek, General Rosecrans was advancing. Col. McCausland with his command came in on Monday evening, shortly before I reached the cavalry camp at Cross Lanes. His pickets had been driven in by the enemy.

The next morning, Tuesday, Sept. 10th, Capts. Corns & Beckett with their companies left Summersville, their pickets having been driven in. The enemy had camped 8 miles beyond Summersville & their march was a remarkable one. Within an hour after the arrival of the last men from Summersville, we were fighting with them at Cross Lanes, and compelled to leave some few of our tents. The tents left belonged to the Lee Grays.[57] I had had everything removed into camp which belonged to the men under my command. Two of my men, contrary to my wishes, had been sent on picket to Peters Creek at the Panther Mountain Road near the lower crossing. They were intercepted, as I anticipated, and only escaped by abandoning their horses and creeping through forests and gloomy laurel thickets to the fortifications.

The firing at the Cross Lanes commenced about 2½ o'clock. At three the firing began at the fortifications, and then for three hours and a half or four hours, raged the most terrific fight probably, considering the numbers engaged, which has been witnessed during the war. The roar of musketry, the shell reports of the Mississippi Rifles;[58] the deep booming of the cannon and

57. Recruited largely from Lee County, Capt. Alexander S. Vandeventer's Lee Grays became Company B of the 50th Virginia Infantry.

58. The Mississippi Rifle was a .54-caliber U.S. Model 1841 shoulder arm extremely popular with American troops during the Mexican War. It was the first percussion rifle adopted by the U.S. Army.

the bursting of the shrapnel; the shrill whistle of the grape and canister, and above all the wild screams, for it sounded so, of the rifle cannon ball, conspired to form an overture more grand and sublime than anything from the pens of Beethoven or Mozart or Haydn or Handel of any of those fellows.

Col. Heth commanded our right. Col. Reynolds and the artillery occupied the center, Cols. Wharton, C. Q. Tompkins & McCausland with Jackson's artillery[59] the left. About 2½ o'clock my two forlorn pickets, broken down by their long run through the brush, came up in front of the fortifications on the left. Instantly every man was on the alert, the cannoners stood ready to send the death-shot home to our own hearts, when a timely command from Major Hounshell prevented the catastrophe. Almost immediately afterwards, the firing began upon the right. The General was wounded in the arm during the action.[60] The fight upon the right was furious, but it was sometime before the enemy gave up their intention of forcing the right flank.

They then made a demonstration against the center. Col. William H. Lytle[61] at the head of a large body of men rode up to within 75 yards of our entrenchment. He was mounted upon a fine horse elegantly caparisoned. One of the Smyth Dragoons[62] under my command, who had gone to the breastworks by my permission, though contrary to the orders to the cavalry to "stand to their horses," fired at him with his double-barreled gun, loaded with musket cartridges and the gallant Col. fell to the ground. His horse came on up the road and was caught soon after within the entrenchments, but in the course of the evening breathed his last, having been shot by the same ball which had crippled his rider. Col. Lytle was a very brave man and it seemed almost a pity to shoot him.

59. Thomas E. Jackson was captain of the Kanawha Artillery, a battery that began its service as part of the 22d Virginia Infantry.

60. Floyd received a gunshot wound in the fleshy part of his arm, which seemed so trivial to him that he did not mention it in his official report of the battle. General Wise had been castigated earlier for his withdrawal from the Kanawha Valley. When Wise learned of Floyd's abandonment of the field at Carnifex Ferry, he shouted to his troops: "Men! Who is retreating now?" Henry Heth, *The Memoirs of Henry Heth* (Westport, Conn., 1974), 155.

61. The mounted Col. (later Gen.) William H. Lytle was at the head of his advancing 10th Ohio Infantry when a bullet passed through his leg and mortally wounded his horse. Lytle's gallantry in the engagement received widespread praise from Union officers. *Official Records,* 5:134, 138.

62. The historian of the 8th Virginia Cavalry states that a Private Minnifern of Sheffey's company was the man who shot Lytle, yet the regimental roster at the end of the book lists no such soldier. Dickinson, *8th Virginia Cavalry,* 24, 97.

The enemy had one Col. killed[63] and another, Col. Lytle, wounded. When Col. Lytle fell, his followers fell back and no attempt was made to carry our center. The enemy crowded a cane-patch pretty full about 3 or 400 yards in front of the center, but a few rounds of grape from our central battery slew them and the cane too. They then crowded [into] a house two or three hundred yards to the front of center, Patteson's house,[64] which we neglected to burn. It did not do them much good, however. They went up to the upper story in order to shoot our principal men, but a round shot from one of our guns aimed at the window made minced-meat of some of them, and made the rest bolt out of the doors and windows like frightened hornets. Another shot knocked down the chimney and sent the stones flying "permiscuously" among them.

In the evening they attempted to turn our left flank, and there just at dusk, the battle was fiercer than at any portion of the day. Col. Tompkins, under the impression that the enemy had succeeded in flanking us, had his men on the other side of the breastworks prepared to fight them from the outside, but the mistake was soon discovered and they got back to their own side of the fence speedily. The firing ceased a little after dusk. We had thus far gained a brilliant victory.[65] Not a man had been killed and but seven wounded. The loss of the enemy must have been terrible, though that, of course, will never be correctly ascertained. It was evident, however, that 1700 men, our number at the breastworks, could not maintain the position for another 24 hours against 8 or 9000, the well-ascertained force of the enemy. We therefore fell back across the river during the night, leaving a few cattle, a few horses, some tents and camp equipage and some stores of not much value. The retreat was in itself a brilliant affair, for the crossing of a river by a retreating army is always a most difficult feat to perform. We executed it without a single fatal accident. The next morning I was sent back to the river with Capt. A. J. Dick-

63. Col. John W. Lowe of the 12th Ohio Infantry led his men forward to attack the Confederate lines. He "had advanced but a few steps" when he was killed by a blast of canister. *Official Records*, 5:134, 138.

64. The Henry Patteson farm was the site of the actual fighting at Carnifex Ferry. But Sheffey's next sentence is puzzling, for the Patteson home was a one-story structure. Lowry, *September Blood*, 69, 72.

65. After the battle ended, Maj. Isaac Smith of the 22d Virginia Infantry took a message to the commanding general. He reached headquarters, Smith wrote in his diary, and "found Genl. Floyd's tent filled with officers. He was wounded slightly in the arm and had it bandaged and in a sling. Everything was stiller and more solemn than a funeral." Smith, "Virginian's Dilemma," 179.

enson[66] & 10 or 12 men and we brought away some of our sick men and one of the Yankee prisoners under the fire of the enemy. All day the cavalry packed sick men and tents over the Sunday Road to the turnpike 8 miles away, down the turnpike 1½ or 2 mis. to Dogwood Gap where Wise was encamped.

If he had done his duty & sent us the thousand men & artillery we asked for, we would have been at the top of Gauley Hill yet. Instead of that, he replied to Genl. Floyd, "I take the responsibility, sir, to refuse to obey your order."[67] No. He would rejoice over any reverse which might befall us. He is a candidate for the Presidency, I guess, and is beginning to envy old Gray Eagle's heavenward flight.

The next day, Thursday, Sept 12th, I was sent back with ten men towards the Ferry, but overhauled by a messenger from the General, who informed me that I had been sent on that perilous expedition contrary to his positive orders. He sent me, however, immediately towards the Hawks Nest down the turnpike, giving me at the same time the very pleasant information that the militia had run off the night before from Cotton Hill and that for aught he knew, I would find Genl. Cox or Genl. Rosecrans or both within two miles of him in that direction.

I had scarcely gone a half mile before I met Lieut Smith[68] of the artillery with still more pleasant information that from the top of Vaughan's Hill, he had himself seen a large body of troops advancing towards us. I threw out my pickets boldly, however, upon the high points, commanding the road, for a long distance, and advanced calling them in as I went, and doing the same thing at different points. In that way, I proceeded several miles beyond Tyree's, the point, you will recollect, where the cavalry under Col. Jenkins were compelled to "make tracks" so rapidly on the memorable Sunday the 25th of August.

66. In all likelihood this reference is to Lt. Andrew J. Dickinson of the 8th Virginia Cavalry's Kanawha Rangers.

67. Wise did not use these exact words, but he did repeatedly parry Floyd's calls for reinforcements with statements of his legion being under constant threat of attack. In Floyd's official report of Carnifex Ferry, he blamed Wise's failure to send troops as the primary reason why the Confederates had to abandon the field. *Official Records*, 5:147, 841–44. A prominent Lewisburg resident became so concerned at the sniping between the two generals that he wrote President Davis, "They are as inimical to each other as men can be, and from their course and actions I am fully satisfied that each of them should be highly gratified to see the other annihilated." Ibid., 864.

68. Lt. William H. Smith was second in command of the Kanawha Artillery.

I went to within a mile of the next and fully satisfied myself that there were no Yankees on that road east of the nest. I then came back a mile, turned to the right & scouted the Chestnutburg Road to a point opposite Piggot's Mill, which you will recollect from previous letters is at the junction of the Saturday Road with the turnpike that runs from Lewisburg to Gauley Bridge via the Hawks Nest. I further learned that it was an entire mistake about the Militia running from Cotton Hill. The body of men seen by Lieut. Smith was Militia going to Cotton Hill.

The next day the enemy came up the turnpike—Friday Sept 13th. We heard too that they were crossing at Carnifex's or McVeys Ferry & trying to get behind us by a march on the Sunday Road. So we fell back to Master's, two miles east of Locust Lane. The next day we received the further information that they were preparing to cross the Gauley at Hughes' Ferry, eight miles above Carnifex's Ferry—on Meadow River Road. As the united force of Genl. Cox and Genl. Rosecrans about the Gauley is now about fourteen or fifteen thousand men, we fell back to the top of Big Sewell, Wise and Floyd together. There we entrenched but the position was not tenable, and yesterday we fell back to Meadow Bluff this side of the junction of the Wilderness or Meadow River Road with the Turnpike. There we will fight them, notwithstanding the odds against us, looking to the God of our fathers, the God of battles, the God of the right to give us the victory.

But Wise will not obey Floyd and that circumstance will imperil the heart of our beloved Virginia. Plenty of troops are lying idle at Lynchburg and Richmond, but they will not send them to us. We will fight them ourselves. We cannot be defeated, for God will not allow it, but if we are, they must march up the steep rough hill, up the trembling stair way where victory awaits them, through their own blood and over their own dead. And when they reach the top, they will find some of the sentinels over the heart of our grand old Mother, faithful to their trust, stiff, stark, weltering in their gore, unwilling to witness the desecration of these dear old Mountains.

How grandly Old Virginia bared her bosom to the storm! She was the lightning rod of the Southern Confederacy. She received into her own bosom the bolt that was aimed at the hearts of her southern sisters. I could weep over the pollution of her soil—that which I have seen, if it were a time for tears. Already she is scathed and scarred by this infamous invasion, despoiled of her beauty, robbed of her happiness. Upon the banks of the Gauley, Desolation sits queen, and Famine and Woe are her handmaidens.

But I have wearied you with this long letter. I love to write to you and wish I could do so every week. Your letters—how delightful they are! To me they are full of beauty and grace, of heart & soul. Yet I have received but one.

Now, my darling, you are wise, discreet, prudent, and I have communicated much to you that would be of advantage to the enemy if they knew it. Our movements and strength must not be known to them. Our friends therefore must be careful about communicating any important information to any one who would reiterate in a letter to some Northern friend. We are much crippled by sickness and fatigue and our foes are strong.

Yet God will give us victory!

I look at your picture often, carry it near my heart. But it is not like you. It does you injustice. It has no life. I wish I could see you.

CHAPTER 3

Stalemate in Northwestern Virginia

After the battle of Carnifex Ferry, Sheffey's company lost its independent status. Nine cavalry companies attached to Floyd's infantry regiments were banded together by the Confederate War Department and designated the 8th Virginia Cavalry. Walter H. Jenifer, a former veteran trooper in the U.S. Army, became the regiment's first colonel.

The dominant theme in Sheffey's letters through the autumn of 1861 was the failure of John B. Floyd and Henry A. Wise to achieve anything positive—and the inability of Gen. Robert E. Lee to correct the situation. Dispatched by President Davis in late July to try and bring success in northwestern Virginia, Lee had suffered one setback after another in his first field command. Initially he had to work with a glory-seeking trouble-maker, William W. Loring, who regarded himself as Lee's superior. Lee sought to attack the Federals at Cheat Mountain, but twenty days of rain, plus green troops and inept officers, brought few good results from the dozen skirmishes waged over four days in mid-September. Lee's reputation had already suffered greatly when he joined Floyd's command at Meadow Bluff. Thereafter Sheffey would be a bystander to the Floyd-Wise-Lee squabble that crippled the high command.

So insightful an officer was Sheffey that his continuing admiration for the bumbling Floyd is surprising. By the last months of 1861, that general had demonstrated conclusively his unsuitability for field service. Even after the debacles at Carnifex Ferry, Cotton Hill, and elsewhere, Sheffey still regarded the "able" Floyd as the "Gray Eagle," who could and would accomplish military success.

The young cavalryman did see action in small clashes at Sewell Mountain, Armstrong Creek, Loup Creek, and Guyandotte. Weather and terrain seemed most of the time to be the principal obstacles to operations.

During this time period, Sheffey also had his first sight of the sickness and disease that plagued every field encampment of the 1860s.

SEPT. 24, 1861
Camp Arbuckle, 4 ms. west of Lewisburg

Dear Josie,

I wrote you from this place a few days ago a full account of our battle of Carnifex's Ferry. That letter I hope you have received ere this. I received your letter of the 18th day before yesterday. If I could receive such letters often, my life here notwithstanding the cloud and gloom would be a bright summer's day, and I as happy *almost* as a king.

I am about to send John Ross[1] home with my trunk etcetera & cannot allow any opportunity of writing to you escape me. We are henceforth permitted to carry no baggage, except upon our horses. Hence we are all parting with our trunks.

Gen. Lee is now with Gen. Floyd at Meadow Bluff, looking very much worn and weary.[2] Another battle with Rosecrans who is now at [the] top of Sewell, I think. I will write to you again as soon as I can. We are receiving some reinforcements. A splendid Mississippi Regt. came in yesterday and were ordered on last night at midnight.[3] They are very footsore to go into a battle. Cavalry have very little chance for distinction in this country, as there is scarcely level ground enough anywhere between this and Gauley for their maneuvre.

I have but a moment for writing. The stage is coming & I must close. Please write a line or two by John when he returns. He will stop in Wytheville. If victorious, we will march straight to Kanawha Valley where we will go into winter quarters. If alive and well, I will come home about the middle of December.

---

1. John Ross was a freedman employed by the Sheffey family as Pres Sheffey's manservant.

2. On September 22 Maj. Isaac Smith of the 22d Virginia Infantry was among a group of officers who called upon the newly arrived Lee to pay their respects. Smith found Lee "about 6 feet high, a most perfect figure, straight without stiffness, full chest, trim built in every respect, decidedly the handsomest figure I ever saw . . . and with the most remarkable faculty of keeping his own counsel I have ever known—perfectly circumspect in all he says, answering all questions civilly, but with good care that no one shall find out more than he intends them to know." Smith, "Virginian's Dilemma," 183–84.

3. The 20th Mississippi Infantry, under Col. Daniel R. Russell, and Col. William Phillips's legion of Georgia troops were both sent to buttress Floyd's command. *Official Records*, 5:848.

Camp Arbuckle, Four Miles West of
Lewisburg, Va., SEPT. 29TH, 1861

Dear Josie,

You will perceive from the date above that I am still at the same camp from which I wrote you with regard to our battle of Carnifex's Ferry. Amid the turmoil and confusion, rapid military movements and exciting preparations for battle around me, I have been condemned to a life of comparative monotone. Left by Major Davison,[4] commander of this post, I have many duties, but they compose a dull routine to which I cannot reconcile myself after the excitement of the few weeks past, and in view of the great events immediately impending. The greater portion of the cavalry companies here have been removed to the immediate scene of action, and I [am] left commander of the remainder, & of the post which is an important one. It was contrary to my earnest request, for I ardently desired to witness and to participate in the coming battle, the last, I trust, as I hope it will be, the most successful act in our part of the great tragedy. The majority of the Smyth Dragoons under Capt Thompson will, however, be there.

Our company and the Tazewell Troop now constitute Genl. Floyd's body guard. The greater portion, I believe, all of the rest of this cavalry have been disbanded or turned over to the command of the eccentric, I might say, insane, Col. St. Geo. Croghan.[5] Our commanders seem to be at a loss what to do with cavalry among these rugged mountains. It seems to me that it would be infinitely better if they were transferred to the plains of Manassas or the lowlands of Maryland where cavalry are appreciated and in demand and where horses can be fed. The Smyth Dragoons and the Tazewell Troop seem to be the favored companies, but even their horses starve necessarily.

We have now at Meadow Bluff about 11 ms. west of this point and near Big Sewell, 25 or 30 ms. west, between twelve and fifteen thousand men. Genls. Lee and Loring are with Genl. Floyd. Gen. Wise has gone to Richmond.[6] Gen. Lee is about the size of Gen. Floyd, has a huge iron grey mous-

4. Samuel Davison was a major in the Virginia militia.

5. St. George Croghan had been lieutenant colonel of the 1st Cavalry Regiment in the Wise Legion until late August, when he was placed in charge of all of Floyd's mounted troops. Croghan would be mortally wounded November 14, 1861, in a skirmish at McCoy's Mill. See Forrest Hull, "The Death of Colonel Croghan," *West Virginia History* 24 (1962): 20–21.

6. In the Floyd-Wise dispute, Wise always voiced his arguments to Lee while Floyd made his appeals to President Davis. The commander in chief had the last word. On September 25

tache and is the finest looking man in the army.[7] Gen. Loring is a little black-whiskered fellow with but one arm, but he is "a man for a' that."[8] Gen. Floyd, I fear, will also soon have but one arm if he is not more careful, for his wound received at the battle of Carnifex's Ferry has caused him a great deal of suffering, and he is very imprudent.

The enemy have about ten or twelve thousand men under the command of Rosecrans & Cox and are camped upon the top of Big Sewell. There has been constant skirmishing for a week past between the outposts of the rival armies, and it is contemplated that a general engagement will come off tomorrow, Monday. The enemy are strongly posted and we will have to be the attacking party. The attack will be attended with much loss of life, but if we succeed in dislodging them, their rout will amount to something like annihilation.

I have been anxiously expecting a call to the theatre of the conflict, and day before yesterday Cousin Sallie[9] promised that she would use her influence. In her solicitude for the General's welfare, she has probably forgotten it, or it may be that they think I can do more good taking care of the prisoners and property and men under my command here. I have been an active participant in one fight and present, only a nonparticipant, in a second because cavalry could do nothing. It is hard that I cannot have something to do with the third and most interesting of all.

The Gray Eagle, our General [Floyd], has made his mark and the Yankees fear him.[10] Had he been commander of 25,000 men, we would now be near

---

Wise received orders to turn his troops over to Floyd and return to Richmond. An officer in the 22d Virginia wrote of Wise's departure: "Nothing could be more humiliating—he despises Floyd, and now while all his ambitious hopes have been ruined, he goes back to Richmond in disgrace, and his old enemy takes his command." *Official Records*, 5:879; 51, pt. 2:313; Smith, "Virginian's Dilemma," 186.

7. This western Virginia campaign would turn Lee's hair from brown to gray.

8. William Wing Loring was a brusque and belligerent North Carolinian who had lost an arm during the Mexican War. The Confederacy's premier mapmaker said of him: "General Loring always struck me as lacking in nearly all the qualities necessary for a commander of an army. . . . He was always hesitating [in] what to do . . . and worse than all to my mind, he was always filling himself with brandy and thus incapacitating himself for his duties." Jedediah Hotchkiss to Fitzhugh Lee, Oct. 22, 1891, Jedediah Hotchkiss Papers, Library of Congress.

9. Sally Preston Floyd was the general's wife and Sheffey's cousin.

10. Here Sheffey let his admiration for Floyd obscure reality. The general was bold in advancing to a point of attack but indecisive thereafter. Union general Cox observed that Floyd's "inactivity puzzled me. . . . His courage had oozed out when he had carried his little army into an exposed position, and . . . at Carnifex Ferry he seemed to be waiting for his adversary to

the Ohio, camped perhaps upon the bank of the great river, and ready to repay the compliment of our Northern friends by a visit to their homes and hearth-stones. The time will come. The time will come when we will slay their household gods at their own altars as they have slain ours. *We* will not *forget,* and forgiveness is a virtue we have long forgotten.

We are strong now, but it is singular that a short time ago, when we were indeed weak and perhaps in peril, our friends here should have published such minute accounts, notifying the enemy fully of our condition. They are deceived by it, however, for they know little of our increased resources. I understand Gen. Rosecrans sent a flag of truce the other day to our commander with a dispatch that if he would go into winter quarters at the White Sulphur, he, Rosecrans would retire for the winter to Charleston.[11] I do not know, however, whether there is the slightest truth in the matter.

MONDAY, SEPT 30TH, 1861

The Confederate forces have this morning moved from Meadow Bluff to Big Sewell. It is expected that the battle will begin this evening. Lieut. Col. Spalding[12] of the Wise Legion is reported here to have been killed last night. He very imprudently advanced with 30 men to the enemy's camp and fired into it. Two volleys were fired at him and he fell a victim to his rashness. One of our scouts was killed yesterday by another of our own men—under the belief that he was one of the enemy.

Such occurrences are not rare. I was myself upon a scout while we were returning from Gauley—and was in imminent peril from the same cause. We were not informed that our pickets and scouts were upon the road, and were sent out upon a dark rainy night in the direction of the enemy without the countersign & under the belief that we would find nothing but Yankees. Capt [A. J.] Dickinson and I were together. We sent forward five men on foot as

---

take the initiative." Cox, *Military Reminiscences,* 1:97, 139. The best defense of Floyd is John M. Belohlavek, "John B. Floyd and the West Virginia Campaign of 1861," *West Virginia History* 29 (1967–68): 283–91.

11. This was wishful thinking on the part of the Confederates.

12. Lt. Col. James Willett Spalding, a native of Richmond, was commander of the 3d Regiment, Wise Legion (later the 60th Virginia Infantry). On September 29, having "been intoxicated for several days," Spalding took a company of soldiers and attacked the Union lines. He was killed immediately; his men dashed back to camp. Maj. Isaac Smith of the 22d Virginia noted disgustingly, "The whole thing was unauthorized and utterly foolish and of no use but very sad." Smith, "Virginian's Dilemma," 187.

skirmishers, and we had scarcely proceeded a mile and a half before they fired into our own pickets. The darkness of the night fortunately prevented a catastrophe. The pickets "made tracks" rapidly, some of them leaving guns & hats in the road. The folly of sending us uninformed upon such an expedition was inexcusable.

Having learned that we had fired into our own pickets, we advanced a mile or so farther and found about a hundred and fifty of our own men, on the alert for us. Had we come in contact with them first, we would have had a serious battle among ourselves. We were then informed that there were no more pickets below us, but we had been so deceived and vexed that we would go no further without a fuller assurance. The next day we learned that a number of pickets had been left beyond the point at which we stopped. Had we proceeded, they or we would have fallen victims to the singular ignorance of our own plans exhibited by our superiors.

Once below Locust Lane, I went with Col. Lucius Davis under cover of the night to surprise a house in which we were told a number of Yankees had taken lodging until morning. The house was surrounded by a dense forest—a perfect cottage in the wood, a "lodge" like that which Cowper wished for in a "vast wilderness."[13] We laid siege to it *a la militaire,* and carried the citadel *sans peur* like genuine chevalier Bayards,[14] but not *sans reproche,* for we disturbed the midnight slumbers and pastoral quietude of a harmless old man, woman, and helpless little one. The enemy had taken to themselves wings, or had crept into invisible coats like those I remember to have read of in the fairybooks of my boyhood. At any rate they were not to be seen. Thoroughly ashamed of ourselves, we again sought the "outer darkness." Suddenly the pawing of horses and a suppressed talking upon the hill above us attracted our attention. I asked Col. Davis if he had any pickets about there. "None, sir," said he, and he prudently remained at the house.

Slowly with arms ready, ear intent and eyes straining in the gloom, we felt our way up through the thick brush-wood. Every ten steps we paused to listen. The silence was audible and the darkness was *visible.* Up, up we went. "Halt" shouted a voice above us. We halted. "Who comes there?" asked the

13. William Cowper was an eighteenth-century English poet who suffered successively from religious mania, depression, and insanity. This quotation is from one of his better known works, *The Task.*

14. The original Bayard was a horse of incredible speed given by Charlemagne to the four sons of Aymon. The word came to denote any army commander known for alacrity; for example, Robert E. Lee has been called the "Bayard of the Confederate Army."

same strange voice. "Friend with the countersign," said we. "Advance one," said the voice.

We hesitated. Who knew whether they were friends or foes? Not we. Major [Col. Alexander W.] Reynolds and I were in front. I turned toward him and he toward me. It was fortunate that neither could see the expression of the other. It would have been ludicrous. He was my superior in rank, and I willingly accorded him the precedence. "Advance" thundered the voice. To hesitate was death. "Go ahead," said I. "Stand by me, boys," said he despairingly, and he went. The rest of us were ready and close behind him.

We could laugh about it afterwards, but it was peril then. We found a poor half starved picket of Col. Davis' of six or eight men, who had been out so long that he had forgotten them. The poor fellows would have been standing there yet, I suppose, but for that midnight adventure. Like the sentinels at the gates of the buried Herculaneum,[15] their skeletons *probably* would have stood there for years to come, the bleaching monuments of their unfaltering fidelity. All that will do to talk about. It is poetry, romance and fiddlesticks. It is not so pleasant to starve on post.

What a wild, strange life it is! Years ago, when I poured delighted over Horry's Life of Marion,[16] rapt in admiration of that strange romance of truth, I little thought I should ever witness anything like the scenes delineated upon those pictured pages. If I loved nothing, cared for nothing in the outer world, I could give myself up to it heart and soul, here at tattoo, when the tents stretched upon the hillsides grow taller and whiter in the darkness, reminding the southern[er] of the ghosts that figure so largely in negro mythology; and dark forms are gathered in groups about the fires or moving here and there through the lights and shadows. We see the originals of the pictures of Revolutionary camps and camp fires. Here are the spies and scouts, the half clad, sometimes half starved patriots, and the sleek and well fed tories. Here is the storehouse of materials from which Cooper and Gilmore Simms drew the "Spy" and "Katherine Walton."[17] Geo. Lippard[18] might have found plentiful

15. Herculaneum was an ancient city in southern Italy at the base of Mount Vesuvius. In AD 79 it and Pompeii were destroyed in a volcanic eruption.

16. Peter W. Horry and Mason L. Weems collaborated on *The Life of General Francis Marion* (Baltimore, 1815).

17. James Fenimore Cooper published *The Spy* in 1829. Twenty-two years later William Gilmore Simms completed *Katherine Walton.*

18. Despite a short life (1822–54), George Lippard became a successful American novelist and playwright. He wrote a number of historical novels but is most remembered for *The Monks of Monk Hall,* a tale of debaucheries among the socially elite.

employment beyond the Gauley. Before the winter is over, we will dream of Valley Forge, and it is probable that the next time we cross the Gauley, we will see something worse than the midnight passage of the Delaware through mush—ice and gloom.

But away from you and home and all that is near and dear to me. "I have no pleasure in them." *Here,* as it was with one of Shakespeare's best characters, "man delighteth me no nor woman either."[19] I prefer too the page and the picture, the prose and the poem about these things. The reality is too vivid to be pleasant. It is like the lightning, beautiful when it gilds the horizon, or plays upon the surface of the far off cloud. It glares too fiercely, and rends and scathes too ruthlessly when you are in the midst of the tempest.

But that is stuff and nonsense. Col. Spalding was killed yesterday about three o'clock. It was singular that he could have thrown away his life so unnecessarily. He was formerly Lieut. Spalding of the United States Navy, and was a man of considerable notoriety. He was between 30 & 35 years of age, it may be not so old, small of stature, probably 5 ft. 9 in. in height, 135 or 40 lbs. weight, a light, sandy colored moustache and goatee to match—a man of many bows and all the vivacity of a Frenchman. That is my idea of him, having seen him but once. He was a man of intellect, ambition and rash daring. His body has been taken to Lewisburg. He was shot through by two balls either of which would have produced instant death. Yet he clung with a singular death grip to his horse and was borne beyond the reach of the balls, otherwise his body—like that of Col. Washington[20] at Valley Mountain— would have fallen into the hands of the rascals who killed him.

Now I have written you a long prosy letter, are you not weary of it? I will write to you again, however, as soon as I hear from the battle of Sewell Mountain. I await anxiously the coming of every mail, hoping that it may bring as good news from you.

Your letter informing me that there was three cases of fever at your own home has rendered me very anxious. I hope you will not go about it. "The pestilence that walketh in darkness" is infinitely worse than "the arrow that flieth at noonday."[21] Just a line from you telling me that you are well is more

19. The correct phrase—"man delights not me; no, nor woman either"—is from *Hamlet.*

20. General Lee's assistant adjutant general, Col. John A. Washington, was killed in a September 13 skirmish along Elkwater Creek near Rich Mountain. Douglas Southall Freeman, *R. E. Lee: A Biography,* 4 vols. (New York, 1934–35), 1:568–70.

21. Sheffey slightly garbled this passage from Psalms 91: 5–6: "Thou shalt not be afraid for the terror by night; nor for the arrows that flieth by day; nor for the pestilence that walketh in darkness; nor for the destruction that wasteth at noonday."

prized by me than long letters from others, and if your letters just tell me about yourself alone, they are sufficiently interesting.

Forgive this soiled paper. It has traveled many a weary mile, and has a right to be soiled.

Camp Arbuckle, Four Miles West of
Lewisburg, Va., OCT. 12TH, 1861

Dear Josie,

I take advantage of the kindness of Mr. Joseph Williams of Smyth Co.,[22] who leaves here for home tomorrow morning, to send you a brief note. He will mail it at the first P. O. from which there will be a probability of it reaching you. The PMs in this country must be engaged in searching our letters for money & consequently destroying them, as they seem to utterly fail of destination in almost every instance. We are constantly writing to those we love, but our letters are not received.

John Ross reached home this evening with Squire Killinger[23] after a tedious trip of ten or twelve days. He brings letters from my house and yours and boxes from both filled with innumerable good things. The bright faces and happy hearts in this camp tonight testify our appreciation of the kindness of our friends. Our hearts are filled with gratitude above all men in the world. *Soldiers* can appreciate such kindness. Express my thanks, and those of my comrades, to your dear Mother and sisters. I doubt not all of you had a hand in that box. Capt. Peters, I fear, will not get a chance at its contents as he is at present in Richmond attending to business of importance, but he will appreciate the kindness nonetheless upon his return & he can take my word for it that they were incomparable, inexpressibly & immeasurably *good,* which will be of infinite satisfaction to him.

I wrote a letter to you since John left here. I suppose you did not receive it as letters which I mailed for home about the same time did not reach their destination.

Genl. Floyd has crossed New River at Bowyers Ferry with nine Regts. and

22. The 1860 census for Smyth County lists Joseph Williams as a fifty-seven-year-old farmer of above-average means living in the Seven Mile Ford area.

23. Many Killinger families resided in Smyth County at the time of the Civil War. Sheffey is likely referring to seventy-two-year-old Michael Killinger, shown on the census as a prosperous farmer in the Seven Mile Ford region.

a part of another.[24] He will attempt to make his way into the Kanawha Valley from the South.

Genl. Lee will remain at Big Sewell until Floyd has gained a position. It was scandalous that Genl. Lee did not attack the Yankees at Big Sewell.[25] Had Genl. Floyd been in command of the whole force, he would have killed or taken every one of them.

The sickness in the hospitals around here is horrid. Six dead men, I understand, were carried out of the Lewisburg hospitals today. It has pleased a kind Providence to preserve me [so] far. Since I have had some rest, my health has much improved. Capt. Peters also seems to have become much more vigorous & robust.

It is probable that our cavalry will be sent to Manassas. I hope they will. Our horses have starved here, and we can not here do ourselves justice.

We have gone through as many changes as a chameleon. First Thornburn was our commander, then Reynolds, then Davidson & others. Now we are formed into a regt. (8th Regt. Va. Cavalry) under Col. Jenifer, Lt. Col. Jenkins & Major Edmondson.[26] We are needed at Manassas—here nothing but infantry & artillery can operate to advantage.

24. Lee's new offensive plan called for Floyd to move south of the Kanawha River (formed by the Gauley and the New) and threaten the communications of Rosecrans's force encamped along the Gauley; Lee would then follow with his army. United, the Confederates would attack Rosecrans, drive the Federals from the Kanawha Valley, and gain control of the most fertile region of northwestern Virginia. Floyd began his march with four thousand troops but without the Wise Legion, which he "found to be in such a state of insubordination and so ill-disciplined as to be for the most part unfit for military purposes." *Official Records*, 5:901. In the ensuing advance, everything from weather to cooperation to secrecy of movement went awry for Lee. On October 20 he abandoned the campaign.

25. Lee had taken a strong defensive position atop Sewell Mountain in hopes that Rosecrans might attack. Heavy rains late in September swept away bridges, turned roads into mud, and cut off Lee from both supplies and Floyd's support. By the time reinforcements reached Lee, Rosecrans had determined to go on the defensive near the Gauley River. The lost opportunity at Sewell Mountain, on the heels of the failure at Cheat Mountain, brought a loud outcry against the Confederate commander, which he downplayed. "Genl. Floyd has the benefit of three [newspaper] editors on his staff," he wrote. Robert E. Lee, *The Wartime Papers of R. E. Lee* (Boston, 1961), 80. Col. Henry Heth termed Lee "the best-abused man of that day." Heth, *Memoirs*, 156.

26. All three officers had short tenures with the 8th Virginia Cavalry. Walter Hanson Jenifer attended West Point for two years and by 1861 was a captain of U.S. cavalry. He led the 8th Virginia Cavalry until May 1862, when he failed to win reappointment. Albert Gallatin Jenkins was not reelected in 1862 but quickly won a seat in the C.S. Congress. Patrick Muir Edmonston

I have not received a letter from you for a long time until John brought me your note today. Take good care of yourself. I am in constant apprehension that you will expose yourself to the terrible fever which seems to be raging in the South West, as much, almost, as in the army of the North West. Without you, there would be no future for me.

I wish you would consent to our marriage this winter. I could see you oftener then. But I may be killed before the expiration of my term, and leave you alone. You are better capable of deciding such matter than I.

Write to me as often as you can—and if you get sick much, it ought not to be concealed from me. This Brigade could not keep me away. But He to whom you have more right to look than I, will preserve and watch over you. Wild, wicked, destitute as I am, of that saving faith which led old Bunyan's Pilgrims safely up to the gates of the City of God, it is yet with an unfaltering trust that I confide you to His care. I do not look upon the dark side, and believing firmly in the Providence of God, I cast my eye beyond the wall of gloom to a season of brighter & happier days.

When my term has expired, I will leave it to you to determine whether I shall go again into the service, unless indeed the country imperatively demands the aid of all who can lend her a helping hand.

Again express my thanks to your mother. I hope the time will soon come when I will have a right to love her as I do my own. Kindness regards to all.

Excuse that corner up there. It just now very foolishly stuck itself into the candle.

The Smyth Dragoons were paid off this week up to the 1st of September. They are flush, happy & boisterously merry.

An exciting footrace came off here this morning in which some of them lost and others gained a good deal of extra change. As I am no sportsman, I know nothing of the pain of losing or pleasure of winning.

We are lying upon our oars here anxiously awaiting orders. We will be sent somewhere, I think, within the next few days.

Camp on Loup Creek
Fayette Co., Va., Oct 30th, 1861

Dear Josie,

I have been looking long and anxiously for a letter from you but as none will come, I again put pen to paper to write to you. I have not heard from

---

was a Floyd appointee. He became lieutenant colonel of the regiment, but there his service mysteriously ended. Dickinson, *8th Virginia Cavalry*, 82, 91.

you since John Ross came & that seems a weary age. We have been camped here on Loup Creek since last Friday or Saturday. We left Camp Arbuckle last Saturday week & came to Blue Sulphur.[27] Thence on Sunday to Green Sulphur, then on Monday to this side of New River at Richmond's Ferry. The River at that point is the line between Raleigh & Greenbrier [Counties]. Tuesday we left our wagons & hurried on with two or three days' provisions to Raleigh Ct. House.

The singular wildness of the country through which we passed was the subject of general remark.[28] Precipitous hills loftier than any I had ever seen, clad with ivy, laurel & vine, deep gorges down which the mountain streams ran foaming and boiling into gorges still gloomier and more cavernous, and a bridle-path that wound its serpentine track across, around and "through other," from base to top & from top to base, with a cascade here and there among the cliffs, conspired to form scenery of unusual picturesqueness, and occasionally of grandeur & sublimity. The road was enormously bad, and involuntarily we cast our eyes forward at every turn expecting to find on the next tree one of Jim Morris's[29] signboards with the significant inscription "No More Roads" engraved thereon.

Weary and worn, we reached Raleigh Ct. House late that night. The name of the place, I believe, is Beckley.[30] Little, scattering and insignificant as it was, nevertheless deemed worthy of a visit by the villainous Yankees or rather Hessians, for they were all imbruted Dutchmen. It was considerably damaged by them.[31] They fled from it in terror at the approach of our troops as they did soon after from Fayette. Leaving Raleigh at an early hour Wednesday, we came that night to Fayette Ct. House, near which place tentless, houseless,

27. The purpose of this cavalry foray was to disrupt the "first election for the counterfeit State of Kanawha"—the early attempt to organize a separate state government for the western Virginia counties. The raid was successful. Hila Appleton Richardson, "Raleigh County, West Virginia, in the Civil War," *West Virginia History* 10 (1948–49): 237.

28. See ibid., 214–17.

29. Sheffey was probably referring to Smyth County farrier James Morris, a member of the Smyth Dragoons.

30. The town was called Beckley until 1851, when the name was changed to Raleigh Court House. Later it became simply Raleigh and in 1896 became Beckley again. T. Harry Williams, *Hayes of the Twenty-Third* (New York, 1965), 100 n.

31. Lt. James Peery of the 45th Virginia Infantry wrote home from Raleigh at this time: "Everything is almost destroyed by the Yankees; they came to this place two or three weeks ago; remained here about 10 hours, plundering people's houses and doing everything that was mean; most all the citizens have moved to adjoining Counties, except a few families." Hilldrup, "Romance of a Man in Gray," 98.

homeless and hungered, we bivouacked until Friday or Saturday.[32] On Thursday morning I visited Capt. Peters and the General at Headqrs., about six miles below town near the base of Cotton Hill. They were all very well but the Captain was so busy that I could get little opportunity to talk to him.

Friday or Saturday we were ordered over to this creek and are now encamped within two miles of the Kanawha line. Nine miles from us, opposite the mouth of this creek, is a steam boat landing up to which the stern-wheels and occasionally larger boats such as the Mose McClellan, into which Col. Clarkson fired not long ago, come every day.[33] But we have fired into them so often that they are getting shy, and no longer come up with shout & merry whistle as of yore. To defend this landing, two six pounders are stationed on the opposite side and they vent their impotent malice in smoke, bluster and harmless balls every day or two at our (Col. Jenkins!) pickets & scouts.

Two or three days ago, our scouts fired with good Enfields into a skiff that was coming to this side filled with men, & reported that they had killed two. We have heard since that both were officers. Day before yesterday some scouts we sent over on Armstrong Creek, captured a Dutch Yankee who had strayed from his fellows & was hunting "papaws" up the creek. Armstrong is the next creek below us and is the Kanawha line. The next is Paint, which empties into Armstrong & the next Cabin Creek. Then I believe come the waters of Coal River, which heads near Raleigh Ct. House, flows in a great arc to the south & west of us around the sources of the creeks I have mentioned, and empties into the Great Kanawha below them. Fourteen miles from here at the mouth of Armstrong is a body of Hessians numbering from 800 to a thousand.[34] They are all as Dutch as "sauerkraut" (I believe that is the Dutch orthography). Their commanders alone are white men. At this point we are about 6 or 7 ms. from Headqrs.

Genl. Floyd has all the ferries guarded, Bowyer's, Miller's, Hamilton's,

32. For three days, the 8th Virginia Cavalry's James Sedinger reported, the men "lived on baked pumpkin and parched corn—all that we could find to eat." "War-Time Reminiscences of James D. Sedinger," 60.

33. In mid-September Col. John N. Clarkson took command of Floyd's cavalry. He was an Albemarle County native who moved in 1834 to Kanawha County. His wife, Anna, was the sister of Confederate general Jubal A. Early. Union authorities at the time of Sheffey's letter were labeling Clarkson a "guerrilla chief." *Confederate Veteran* 15 (1907): 40; *Official Records*, 5:288, 411, 675. For details on Clarkson's raid, see *Official Records*, 5:377–78, 924.

34. The Second Brigade in Rosecrans's army was known as the Bully Dutch Brigade because so many of its members were of German descent. In the brigade were the 9th, 28th, and 47th Ohio Infantry. Lowry, *September Blood*, 53–57.

Montgomery's and Dempsy's, and is now prepared to throw shot & shell into Gauley Bridge. Occasional quarrels with many growlings have already been heard between the cannon, but the conflict is expected to commence in genuine earnestness tomorrow. Our wagons came up two or three days ago, and we are once more happy nomads, dwelling in tents. Just a little while ago, a scout came in and reported that forty Dutchmen are at the mouth of this Creek. The scamps will not come away from the protecting range of the batteries on the opposite side. If they do, we will try & make mince-meat of them.

Thompson Stewart of the Smyth Dragoons died last Monday week, near Camp Arbuckle.[35] We have about 25 sick men. Capt Thompson and I are the only commissioned officers of the Co. here. The other two Lieutenants are sick.[36] We have now a line of expressmen to Newbern who run through in 18 hours. You will therefore direct to "Newbern, Pulaski Co., Va., Care J. H. Thompson, Smyth Dragoons, Floyds Brigade."

I have not the pleasure of an acquaintance with any of the belles of this aboriginal valley, this Happy Valley, where Jenkins is Rasselas and Fitzhugh is Imlac,[37] but they are numerous and daily impelled by a feeling of curiosity, or a womanly love of admiration. They come to our headqrs. with their tiny feet daintily encased in elegant five-toed slippers "A no. 12," and their sylph-like forms arrayed like "queans" not "queens" of Sheba.[38]

The quarters of our gallant Col. [Jenifer] & handsome Adjt. [Richard B. Kennan] are in an oak-hewn palace with Gothic chimney of primeval sandstone tapestried walls and tassellated floors, denominated a Northern Methodist Church. Upon the quaint old wall, in huge chalk characters that resemble not only the sanscrit but syriac and Hebraic also is graven everywhere the name of the reigning belle of the valley, Miss Johnson, in-dweller between two of the ruggedest hills in a' this goodly land. No kith of General Joe's[39] is she, yet a merry, rosy, bonnie lassie, like Burns' Highland

35. Thompson M. Stewart was a late addition to the Smyth Dragoons. He enlisted in July 1861.

36. The other two lieutenants were William C. Copenhaver and Hezekiah Hannan.

37. Another reference to the two travelers of Johnson's *Rasselas;* the characters lived in Happy Valley, home of the Prince of Abyssinia.

38. According to 1 Kings, Queen Sheba visited Solomon and in vain sought to disprove his great wisdom. In this version of the story, Sheba was so impressed by Solomon that she married him and gave birth to a son who founded the Assyrian dynasty.

39. Gen. Joseph E. Johnston then commanded the principal forces defending northern Virginia.

Mary.[40] Like Canaan this is a land of milk and honey—and buckwheat cakes and grapes, not grapes indeed of Eshcol, but of a more deliciously flavored species, known in the elegant phraseology of the country as "Possum Grapes." The ladies I have spoken of are all *"Union men,"* and though they smile at our gay cavaliers, yet each could "smile and smile & be a villain still"[41] and would lead us into an ambuscade with the utmost *sang-froid.*

But I have written enough of nonsense. Please write to me as soon as you can. Kindest regards to all.

Cavalry Camp, one Mile SE of Fayetteville
Fayette Co. Va., Nov. 3RD, 1861

Dear Josie,

As I expect to start down the Kanawha tomorrow,[42] to be gone "out of hearing" of the civilized world for a long time, I take advantage of the leisure afforded by this gloomy day to write to you again. I have as you perceive no pen and ink with which to make legible the scrawl I shall inflict upon you. Your letter of the 22nd ult. reached me at the camp on Loup Creek several days ago. I wrote to you from that camp the day before I received it.

Since then I have had some of the experiences of the soldiers of the 1st Revolution. On the 1st inst. Friday, about 12 o'clock N, our pickets near the mouth of the creek came in and reported that they had been fired upon by a large body of the enemy who were advancing toward us. The position was one of peculiar peril as there were roads from Armstrong Creek upon our left & up Laurel Creek upon our right by which a force might be thrown behind us, and effectually prevent our egress. The tents were struck therefore & wagons packed as speedily as possible. The guards were detailed & the train started with instructions to make their way out beyond the junction of

40. Highland Mary was the beloved of Robert Burns and the subject of several of his poems.

41. The quotation is from *Hamlet.*

42. On November 5 (coincidentally the day Lee departed northwestern Virginia for Richmond), the Wise Legion, under Colonel Clarkson, and Lieutenant Colonel Jenkins's 8th Virginia Cavalry set out to attack the Union recruitment camp at Guyandotte along the Ohio River. The Confederates reached their objective five days later. Cavalry charged into the town and captured 110 Federals. The arrival the following day of Union reinforcements caused the Southerners to withdraw. *Official Records,* 5:411–12; Dickinson, *8th Virginia Cavalry,* 26–27.

any of those roads. The rest of us, perhaps 250 in number started immediately down the creek to attack the foe.[43]

After going about 3 ms., we dismounted and sent our horses back under command of Capt. Thompson, detailing one man out of every four to lead. That left us about 200 men. I took command of the remainder of the Dragoons. Having walked very little for years, the march for the first mile was very fatiguing to me. I improved, however, as we advanced, and before we had gone 3 ms., I could have left the majority far behind. We soon discovered that the enemy were not coming up the creek, but had gone up the left fork of the creek, apparently with the intention of cutting off our train of wagons by a quick march up the Laurel Creek road. Whatever may have been their intention with regard to us, they abandoned it.

Leaving the main fork of the creek to our left, we made our way across to the left fork over steep hills & deep hollows where it seemed that never man had trod before. Getting up their trail we followed it rapidly for several miles. They fooled us by leaving the road and going across to the river in the direction of Montgomery's Ferry. There were only about 200 of them, and if we had received notice in time to set a little earlier start, we would have paid them up for some of their misdeeds. That day they entered the house near which our pickets had been stationed and took the covering from the beds. The poor woman who lived there had a sick child, and with merciless cruelty they unrolled the blankets from around it and carried them away, leaving it to shiver in the cold. The day of retribution will come yet.

When we were following that band, the reports of the cannon from Cotton Hill were reverberating through the mountains;[44] and as we were there not more than 3 or 4 ms. from that scene of operations, we could hear almost every report distinctly. Late in the evening we gave up the chase. We were then seven or eight miles from our camp of the night before & the rain was pouring down in torrents. Ceaseless, pitiless, came down the rain, and the creeks were ever in our way. We must have crossed the left & the main

43. Sheffey's regiment was part of a new Confederate offensive. Late in October Floyd embarked on a campaign to occupy Cotton Hill, the high ground overlooking the junction of the Gauley and New Rivers. See McKinney, *Fayette County*, 101–13.

44. Shortly after Floyd began fortifying Cotton Hill, a heavy concentration of Union forces and atrocious weather convinced him to fall back to Monroe County. Five days after the general began his retreat, orders arrived from unknowing authorities in Richmond for him to hold Cotton Hill as long as possible. *Official Records*, 5:254–57, 286–88, 955; Cox, *Military Reminiscences*, 1:137–44.

branches of Loup Creek almost a hundred times. But it was as comfortable in the water as out of it, for the mud was horrible. Soon the shadows deepened around us and the night grew black as ink.

Reaching the camp of the night before, we determined to tarry until morning. Enormous fires we built with Union rails, but they did not stop the rain, nevertheless we were merry as crickets. I had sent away blankets & over coat with my horses & most of us were in the same condition. We found a large piece of beef that had been left upon a log by the wagoners. Most of us had had nothing to eat since the night before, and were savage. With forked sticks & knives we broiled the beef & ate voraciously *minus* salt.

Then a determined squad went forth, true votaries of Mercury, the god of thieves, and pressed two Union bee gums. The gums came in laden with stores of honey & the honey comb rich as ever grew in Hybla or on Hymetus.[45] (Heaven save the classics!) A few poor luckless wights were stung. What mattered it? One Border Ranger,[46] a rara avis on all occasions, eat bees and all. One stung him on the lip & to have revenge he bit the bee & was stung in the mouth & then, enraged, he "bolted" him head, honey, sting and all. A Border Ranger can't be killed, but they are such wanderers, that occasionally one of them is taken prisoner. On the 30th ult. one of them was captured on Morris Creek, by a picket guard of the Yankees. His name is Bramblett,[47] & he was a fine, brave fellow. He will find 3 others of his troop in the pens at Camp Chase.[48] Two of those were captured when Rosecrans came to Summersville & were only taken after a chase of seven miles.

Yesterday morning we again took up our weary march on foot. After walking six miles, we met our horses. As we could not forage longer on Loup Creek, we came across to this point & it is anticipated that we will start down to Coal River tomorrow.

Genl. Floyd, I understand, is preparing to go into winter quarters at Cot-

45. Mount Hyble in Sicily and Mount Hymetus in Greece were both famous for their honey.

46. Deserved or not, the Border Rangers had a reputation as the most undisciplined company in the 8th Virginia Cavalry.

47. Sheffey is in error on the identification of the captured Border Ranger. William H. Bramblett was captain of the Grayson Cavalry (Company C) in the regiment. The soldier taken prisoner was likely Pvt. George W. Russell, who went blind while a prisoner at Camp Chase, Ohio. Dickinson, *8th Virginia Cavalry*, 104.

48. Most of the Confederates captured in northwestern Virginia were sent to this prisoner-of-war camp near Columbus, Ohio.

ton Hill. The suffering here is terrible. How infinitely better it would be to fight the Yankees through. We had rather be killed, than frozen & starved. But our shoulders are to the wheel, and the God of our people will help us in His own good time.

The skirmishing at Cotton Hill is constant, but there is as yet no beneficial result. The rain continues and the cold increases. God only knows what is to become of the poor soldiers. Blessed are the careless and the light-hearted amongst us who laugh at the horrors, and fear not the Grim Monster who reigns around us.

Genl. Floyd is an able general. His great mistake is in overestimating the powers of endurance of his men. A wonderful man himself, in his young days capable of bearing any amount of fatigue, he imagines that every man ought to be able to stand what he could have stood at his age. He thinks his men are giants with frames of iron, & sinews of whalebone. The medical department is terribly mismanaged. The physicians themselves drink up the brandy and whiskey that is sent here by the government for the sick—so I hear.[49] If true verily they will have their reward.

I am writing in comfortable quarters, actually slept last night in a feather bed. I had almost forgotten there were such things in this cheerless universe. I dreamed last night of the old saying of Sancho Panza,[50] "Blessed be the man who invented sleep," and I thought he would have spoken more forcibly had he added "in feather-beds."

But I have written an amount of abominable nonsense & must close lest I weary you. Write to me very often. If I could get a letter from you every week or two, I could endure anything. I shall have to endure a great deal. In a few more days, I shall be able to appreciate the sublime poetry of those glorious old rhymes.

> And first it blew
> And then it snew
> And then it sin to friz.

You see I have not quite forgotten all the poetry I used to know.

49. Army surgeons of the Civil War had to cope with a host of problems, ranging from lack of knowledge and overcrowding to supply shortages and ignorance among the soldiers of basic hygiene. See Robertson, *Soldiers Blue and Gray,* 145–69.

50. Sancho Panza was the squire of Don Quixote in Cervantes' novel. A short, potbellied rustic, Panza had much common sense but little "spirituality."

Marion, Smyth Co., Va.[51]
DECEMBER 1ST, 1861

Dear Josie,

I left the company at Russell Ct. House,[52] day before yesterday to see Col. Clarkson, then about six miles from my camp. When I reached the point at which I expected to find him, he had set out for Abingdon. I followed him rapidly, expecting to come up with him at the ford of the N. Fork of [the] Holston, knowing that the river was past fording. He had, however, swum his horse across and I followed suit and came up with him at Abingdon. Came with him on the cars as far as Marion, intending to return to Russell [County] in the morning to bring the men under my command to Smyth [County]. But I was considerably used up by the trip and sent a trusty servant back instead with written orders to them. They will be here tomorrow and I shall keep them here for some time, unless we are needed in some active service. I will be in Wytheville as soon as I can have them comfortably quartered, which may take me several days. I have a good many already in the county, most of whom are sick. Fevered and emaciated, the poor fellows are scattered from here to Lewisburg. I must gather them around me here, that the atmosphere of home may revive them, and the kind hands of loving do something to alleviate their sufferings.

I have now innumerable cares upon me, but I shall find time to be constantly with my own darling. I am free now to go and come when and where I choose, but I must see first to the comfort of those who look to me for everything. I am Captain, 1st Lieut., 2nd Lieut., Commissary, Q. Master, &c.

Col. Clarkson has treated me with marked kindness and my original opinions of him are naturally rapidly changing.[53] Without any application from me, he has given me leave of absence *ad libitum* for as long as I choose, and then when I requested it, he has allowed me to bring my company home and

51. Late in November, following the Guyandotte raid, the 8th Virginia Cavalry went into winter quarters at "the old meeting ground" in Russell County. Dickinson, *8th Virginia Cavalry*, 27. The day after Sheffey wrote this letter, Floyd received orders to return with his command to Dublin [in Pulaski County, Virginia]. The Confederate efforts in northwestern Virginia were over for the season. *Official Records*, 5:975.

52. Lebanon is now the name of the seat of Russell County.

53. A 1906 obituary of Clarkson stated that "his noted bravery, his readiness to fight wherever the occasion required it, gave him the reputation of a daring and fearless man." *Confederate Veteran* 15 (1907): 40.

quarter them here until such time as he may see fit to order me elsewhere. This will give me time to gather them together, clothe them, and recruit them and their horses. The wound of our beloved Captain will disable him from military service for the rest of the year,[54] and as I shall have to fill his place, I desire to enter the Spring Campaign with as good a company as I can possibly make out of the worn remnant of our gallant band.

Capt. Thompson, I understand, is worse than he has been. He will probably lose his leg, perhaps his life. I shall go to Tazewell Ct. House in a day or two. I will come to Wytheville this week if possible.

54. During the Guyandotte raid, Capt. John H. Thompson received a wound that ended his military service. By 1863 he was a Smyth County delegate in the Virginia General Assembly. *Official Records,* 29, pt. 2:768.

CHAPTER 4

DISAPPOINTMENTS DAMPEN PATRIOTISM

Frustrations continued for Sheffey through the first half of 1862.

In the larger picture the Civil War was not going well for the South. Nor did the 8th Virginia Cavalry have any chance to enhance the opportunities for victory. The regiment spent a protracted period of guard duty near Princeton, Virginia. Its principal responsibility was blocking one of the logical Union approaches to the Virginia and Tennessee Railroad.

Sheffey's regiment was now part of the fifteen-hundred-man "Army of New River," under Brig. Gen. Henry Heth, an officer for whom Sheffey had little respect. There were the expected skirmishes between small groups of opposing cavalry; but when full-scale action developed at Giles Court House, Princeton, and especially Lewisburg, the Confederates seemed to snatch defeat from the jaws of victory.

Conditions inside the 8th Virginia Cavalry were unpleasant. The unit was at half-strength. Sheffey's letters show little allegiance to the regiment, which was the army organization that soldiers generally called home. The Marion native was soon appointed captain of the Smyth Dragoons, but his relations with his colonel and lieutenant colonel were anything but cordial.

Meanwhile, by mid-May 1862 Sheffey's loneliness for Josie had turned to near anger over her unwillingness to marry. He suggested that the two either wed or cease the interminable waiting. That apparently brought an invitation for him to visit her in Wytheville to discuss their relationship. Sheffey did so, but little seems to have been settled. Indeed, his first letter after the couple's meeting emphasizes the attractive and interesting young ladies the officer was meeting in the town where his regiment was encamped.

Princeton, Mercer Co., Va.
JANUARY 28TH, 1862

My dear Josie,

Long separated from any convenient post office, I have had no opportunity to write to her whom I love better than my own life. Here in Col. Jenkins' room at a late hour of the night, I snatch a moment to devote to you. I came up this morning from my camp at Round Bottom opposite Pennington's Ferry on New River, seven miles N.W. of Peterstown on business with different officers. It was a long ride through almost unfathomable mud. I return early tomorrow and then in a day or two we all start for a more active scene of operations in Raleigh, where we will wipe out in some slight degree, I trust, the stain cast upon our swords and shields in Sommerset.[1]

You will hear from me again soon. I hope when I can be more at leisure, but do not wait for me to write *please*. You are very *naughty* not to let me know what you are thinking about these long winter days. Heigh-ho! which everybody writes and nobody says. Time passes like the fleet eagle, yet the days are so long. They must be very pleasant and very brief where you are. I could write you some news but the Col. is waiting for me to come to bed. He leaves us tomorrow for the Confederate Congress.[2] I had rather anyone else would leave.

I directed the Proprietors of the South. Lit. Messenger to send it to you.[3] I presume you have received the January No.

Camp at Round Bottom
On New River, Mercer Co., Va.
FEBY. 13TH, 1862

Dear Josie,

I wrote you a brief note some time ago from Princeton, which I hope you received. I have waited anxiously for an opportunity to write you a long letter, but the time will not come. I returned yesterday from a fatiguing trip

1. In mid-November 1861, Confederate forces had moved into eastern Kentucky and encamped at Mill Springs near the southern bank of the Cumberland River. Soon a Union detachment occupied Somerset on the opposite bank of the river. Inexperienced troops fought inconsequential skirmishes from December 1 through 13. But the Confederates were unable to cross the Cumberland. See *Official Records*, 7:7–12. Meanwhile, Jenifer and the 8th Virginia Cavalry were on the alert in Mercer and Raleigh Counties, Virginia, for Federal raiding parties that were arresting pro-Confederate citizens. Ibid., 51, pt. 2:452–53.

2. Colonel Jenkins had only recently returned from a skirmish in eastern Kentucky with Federals under the command of Brig. Gen. James A. Garfield (later president). Jack L. Dickinson, *Jenkins of Greenbottom: A Civil War Saga* (Charleston, W.Va., 1988), 49.

3. The *Southern Literary Messenger* was one of the most respected literary journals in the nation. George William Bagby was then editor of the Richmond-based monthly. An early contributor to the periodical was Edgar Allan Poe.

occasioned by a false alarm, and am ordered tonight to move out with all possible dispatch to a point forty miles away in a difficult direction—to the Flat Top Mountain at the line of Mercer & Raleigh [Counties].[4] Col. Peters with the 45th [Virginia Infantry] is down the river somewhere near the mouth of Bluestone. I have not seen him.[5]

Please write & let me know what is going on in the delectable city of Wytheville, and in the world outside of this in which we move. The news— the rumors of disaster and defeat which reach our ears—are deplorable if true.[6] Our people must keep their heads up. We will "trust in God and keep our powder dry."

It is becoming very difficult to get food for horses & I wish on that account I were in the infantry service but it matters not. The enemy took six horses & two men of our Regt. prisoners last week.[7] We will take as many as an offset, if they will give us anything like a fair chance. A few more defeats will make our people desperate, and I care not how soon they become so.

Please write to me. I will write again as soon as possible.

Direct to "Lieut. JP Sheffey, Comdg. Smyth Dragoons, Care Col. WH Jenifer, 8th Regt. Va. Cavalry, Dublin, Pulaski Co., Va." & your letters will all reach me. I have not heard from you since I left Wytheville, and know not whether you are still among the living or in the land of spirits.

> *Camp Flat Top, Mercer Co., Va.*
> FEBRUARY 24TH, 1862

Dear Josie,

The days lengthen into weeks, the long weeks into months, and still you will not write. Letter after letter overflowing with the dear love of mother and sisters and the friendship of friends come to me yet I lay them aside, disappointed, because they are not from you. Yet I do not despair, but meet each courier, each dispatch-bearer, who comes to us from the great city of

---

4. For a description of Flat Top Mountain, see Richardson, "Raleigh County," 264.

5. Colonel Peters describes his trepidations at Pack's Ferry in *Official Records*, 51, pt. 2:463–64.

6. In the preceding six weeks, Confederate forces had suffered defeat at Mill Springs, Kentucky; Fort Henry, Tennessee; and Roanoke Island and Elizabeth City, North Carolina.

7. Compiled service records for the 8th Virginia Cavalry show only Edward S. Guthrie of the Border Rangers being captured at the February 9 skirmish at Jumping Branch. See "War-Time Reminiscences of James D. Sedinger," 61–62.

Princeton, with the full and certain assurance that this one at least brings a missive from you. What is the news in the gay world outside of these mountains? Will you not tell me? They shut me in from light and love, from joy and happiness, and from News like the walls of a dungeon. I am as miserable as any "prisoner of Chillon" or of the Bastile, or of Camp Chase in Ohio, and will surrender myself to the Yankees or incurable blues within a fortnight if you don't write.[8]

For me, there is no world, where you are not, and if I cannot hear from you, I will write to the P. M. General to abate the postal arrangements between Wytheville and Princeton as a nuisance and an unnecessary expense. Yet that might be selfish. We have tried to build up a little world of our own out here, but the universe we thought to fashion has proved as chimerical and visionary as Utopia itself.[9] We live here like Greenlanders and Esquimaux Indians,[10] warming our frozen bodies with fats and oils, and shivering like Switzerlanders in the midst of glaciers and peaks covered with ice and snow. Hourly, the old god of the winds lets loose his furies, and we sit cowed and trembling as he knocks off our hats and rends our tents. At the dead hour of the night, when all Nature, except our pickets, is wrapped in the arms of— (I've forgotten his name)—Jack the Frost rallies his forces, and assails us so successfully that we will soon be minus toes and noses. Our tents—some of them—are torn into fragments and we have been compelled to borrow from Capt. French,[11] who was so fortunate as to get into houses with his troops. Some of us have built wigwams after the order of Apache or Comanche, and as we become more advanced in civilization, we will go to burrowing in the earth, *a la* groundhog and prairie-dog.

We have parts of three companies here, much reduced by sickness and other causes and our duties are burthensome. We are seven miles in advance of any other force in N.W. Va. and have to picket four or five roads which form a junction near us. The Yankees are pretty strongly posted at Raleigh Ct. House, eighteen or nineteen miles from us, and they can easily visit us

8. In Lord Byron's 1816 poem, *The Prisoner of Chillon,* three brothers who are victims of religious persecution die in the same prison cell in the Swiss town of Chillon. The Bastile was an infamous state prison in Paris during the French Revolution.

9. Sir Thomas More, in his fifteenth-century romance, gave the name "Utopia" to an imaginary island where everything was perfect.

10. "Esquimaux" is an archaic spelling of "Eskimos."

11. Capt. William Henderson French led a Mercer County unit, Company D, 8th Virginia Cavalry.

whenever they see fit.[12] We sent out yesterday a scouting party on foot, to go within four or five miles of Raleigh Ct. House. They have not yet returned and I am rather uneasy about them. Ten of the Dragoons are with the party, and if they were lost, our troop would not easily recover from the blow. But they can only be taken by treachery, and I hourly expect their return.

The Yankee force at Raleigh is estimated at from 250 to 1000. The difficulty here is that the people are so untrue and so faithless that we can rely upon nothing they tell us. We cannot know whom to trust. We have some brave men here, and some who are infinitely cowardly. Some of them (not mine) keep their horses saddled from morning to night and from night till morning ready for a run. Some few of my own men I fear have caught the contagion but they are very few.

The position we occupy here is not defensible against a superior force, but we are compelled to occupy it on account of forage. There is a position two miles in front of us and another two or three miles to our rear where we could defend ourselves much more successfully than at this point.

March 4th. Since writing the above, our foot scouts came in bringing a number of cattle, horses, sheep and two prisoners. Their hunt was quite successful. They went under the guidance of the Wood Rangers[13] or as we call them here, Bush-Whackers, of whom there is quite a number constantly with us dressed in bark-dyed apparel with their long rifles and deer-skin pouches. Well may the Yankees fear them for they rarely draw a bead and pull a trigger without bringing a pigeon.

To-day is the anniversary of the inauguration of Abraham Lincoln. How eventful has been the twelve months passed! What sufferings we have endured! Pandora has let loose the furies,[14] and were it not for Hope, rising,

12. The 23d Ohio Infantry, under Col. Rutherford B. Hayes, was then at Raleigh Court House. The town stood where the road from Lewisburg to Kentucky crossed the turnpike from Great Falls to Wytheville. Union control of the county seat therefore hampered Confederate communications. Moreover, stated one Federal officer, the 23d Ohio was "untiring in making reconnaissances, sending out scouts, and swearing Union men" into Federal service. *Official Records,* 5:696. For Jenifer's view of the latter policy, see ibid, 5:1052.

13. No unit with the name "Wood Rangers" was then officially part of the Confederate forces. An Indiana soldier described the bushwhackers as "a lot of thieving, bloodthirsty, moccasin-wearing cut throats" who, "too cowardly to fight in the open, would, when outnumbering our pickets three to one, murder our camp guards." Charles H. Ross, "Scouting for Bushwhackers in West Virginia in 1861," *War Papers—Military Order of the Loyal Legion of the United States: Wisconsin Commandery* 3 (1903): 399–412.

14. In Greek mythology Pandora was the first woman. Jealous gods each gave her some power to cause the ruin of man. Those powers were placed in a box that Pandora was to entrust

white-robed and beautiful, high above them all, our hearts would be sad indeed. The blow by which our Kentucky Army has been smitten to the earth has dispirited all,[15] except those who like myself are ever hopeful. But from the graves of those who fell at Ft. Donelson, as from the dragon's teeth in the ancient myth,[16] a new host of armed men will spring to vindicate our lost honor, to restore our late prestige, and to avenge the murder of the heroes who have fallen.

The South is awakening at last to the peril that threatens us, and accursed will be the sluggard who still cries "Yet a little more sleep."[17] They must and will be up and doing. If out of her million and a half of fighting men, the South can speedily bring six hundred thousand into the field, the victory will still be ours. That only can avert a long and cruel war. To me, at least, it is some cause for joy, that the gallant "old Floyd" has again arisen above the detractions of the enemies crowned with well-won laurels. He and Price and Beauregard are our trump cards.[18] When they are caught, we may well tremble for the result. *Vae victus*—woe to the conquered, is already the war cry of our foes, but every Southern rill and river will yet run red with Northern and Southern gore before they can carry out their infamous policy.

One of our dispatch bearers, a Border Ranger, was shot a few nights ago by some scoundrel in the bush. He was not killed, however, and is now at Princeton doing well. Capt. Bowen was fired at in a similar manner.[19] He

---

to her husband, Epimetheus, who unknowingly opened it. All of the evils of the flesh sprang forth and have ever since afflicted the world.

15. On February 16 Brig. Gen. U. S. Grant forced the surrender of Fort Donelson, Tennessee, and its twelve thousand defenders along the Cumberland River. With the vital Cumberland and Tennessee Rivers now under Union control, Kentucky was lost as a potential Confederate state and all of Tennessee lay open to invasion.

16. According to Greek legend, Cadmus slew a dragon and sowed its teeth. A number of armed men then sprang forth from the ground and moved to kill him. Cadmus threw a precious stone among the men, who in their fervor to claim it, then killed one another—save for five who became allies to Cadmus.

17. This is a partial quotation of Proverbs 6:10.

18. Sheffey was building on weak hopes here. Floyd, the senior officer at Fort Donelson, ungallantly fled to safety prior to the garrison's surrender. This act ended his service as a field commander. Maj. Gen. Sterling Price led Confederate forces in the Trans-Mississippi Department and had done little since a limited success at Lexington, Missouri, the previous September. Gen. P. G. T. Beauregard, after 1861 victories at Fort Sumter and First Manassas, ran afoul of Pres. Jefferson Davis. In late January 1862 Davis banished him to the West as second in command to Gen. Albert Sidney Johnston.

19. Capt. Henry Bowen commanded the Tazewell Troop (Company H) of the 8th Virginia Cavalry.

returned the fire with his six-shooter, and from the manner in which the fellow yelled and fled, he thinks he has given him his *quietus*. A few nights ago, an old man named Moomaw (I am not sure of the orthography) had a horse stolen from him by a Yankee or Union man we have not yet ascertained which. Moomaw and his son succeeded in getting ahead of him, and as came along, they fired three shots at him with their double-barrels. The fellow dropped from his horse and escaped through the bush leaving his hat and revolver. The hat had a shot hole through it and the horse was shot in two places, so that we have every reason to believe and hope that he also has gone to that "undiscovered country from whose bourne no *horse thief* e'er returns."[20]

But I am wearying you and will close. Present my kindest regards to all, and do not forget how anxiously I look for letters from you.

> *Camp Round Bottom, Mercer Co., Va.*
> MARCH 20TH, 1862

My dear Sisters,

Some time has elapsed since I returned with the "Smyth Dragoons" from the chilling upper air of Flat Top Mountain to the more genial climate of New River and the bonnier "banks and braes" "here or hereabout." We are to leeward of a huge knob that throws a protecting wing over our torn tents and Esquimaux hovels. The effects of the exposure on Flat Top still make themselves manifest by the occasional breaking down of some one of our number. One of our bravest men, Haynes Thomas died recently at his home in Burke's Garden whither I had sent him. I allowed his two brothers to go to his bedside but they did not get there in time.[21] We will miss him very much, for though a very dissipated and wicked man, he knew no fear.

The enemy are now reported to be advancing towards Lewisburg and towards Princeton.[22] The militia of Monroe and Greenbrier [Counties] have

20. This quotation is from *Hamlet,* with one deviation: Sheffey substitutes "horse thief" for "traveler."

21. Haynes M. Thomas of the Smyth Dragoons died March 7, 1862, of disease. His brothers were A. M. and John L. Thomas.

22. Federal general William S. Rosecrans spent much of the winter planning and gaining approval for a spring offensive. His target was the Virginia and Tennessee Railroad in southwestern Virginia, the only link connecting Richmond and the western theater. The strategy called for two Union columns to advance simultaneously on Abingdon. One would march direct from Gauley Bridge; the other would move via Raleigh Court House and Princeton. The

been ordered out en masse. This country has been eaten out, and is almost as barren as if the army worm or the locusts of Egypt had swept over it. It is a barren desert—a wilderness *minus* those great necessaries of Dragoon life, corn and hay. The Cavalry will soon be removed westward, and infantry will take their places. Our troops are said to be fortifying at Brushy Ridge, seven miles west of Lewisburg, and are expected to fortify somewhere near Cross Roads in this County south of this point.

The clouds are darkening above us, and God only knows what we shall see when the veil is rent. Perhaps the Goddess of Peace will spread her white wings over the land and the glorious sun again look down upon us all brightly and beautifully. Perhaps the Furies will preside in the midst of the storm. For myself, I laugh at the horrors and defy the tempest. We will send many a Yankee soul howling to its long home, before we yield even to overwhelming odds. But our foes are a brave and determined race, and too many of our people are infinitely cowardly. The more worthless men's lives are, the more highly they seem to prize them. Some of them might learn lessons even from our foes, for they occasionally exhibit a degree of heroism which is very commendable.

Not long ago, sixteen of the 45th and eighteen of the Border Rangers surrounded eight of the Pennsylvania Dragoons near Jumping Branch in this county, killed three of them at the first fire and wounded a fourth.[23] The horse of a fifth was killed and fell upon him, fastening him so that he could not extricate himself. The wounded man and the three who were unhurt stood their ground against the odds until their pistol shots were all expended, then escaped. The man entangled by his horse refused to surrender but was taken by force. Such bravery, though it be that of our enemies, is worthier of all honor.

We must have a spirit in the South akin to that which animated the Greeks at Thermopylae and Marathon,[24] before we can succeed in achieving our in-

---

Union army was on the verge of getting underway when Rosecrans was removed from command in favor of Maj. Gen. John C. Frémont. Cox, *Military Reminiscences,* 1:192–96. For Confederate dispositions at this time, see *Official Records,* 5:1077–78.

23. A company of Pennsylvanians served in the 1st West Virginia Cavalry. Darl L. Stephenson, *Headquarters in the Brush: Blazer's Independent Union Scouts* (Athens, Ohio, 2001), 12. James Sedinger of the 8th Virginia Cavalry mentioned this skirmish in "War-Time Reminiscences of James D. Sedinger," 61.

24. During their wars with the Persians (540s–330s BC), the Greeks won a stunning victory at Marathon (490 BC) and later suffered a heroic defeat at Thermopylae (480 BC). After the former, an athlete named Pheidippides ran twenty-six miles to convey news of the battle to the Athenians, a feat that later inspired the modern marathon race.

dependence. We must be as willing to accept the crown of Martyrdom as the Waldenses,[25] or as the venerable sage in the strange tale of Tom Moore's, the Epicurean,[26] or as John Rogers with his wife and eleven small children besides LC. But how many cravens there are among us who will kiss the road and bless the hand that smites them—who will bow the rod and bless the hand that smites them—who will bow the knee to Baal,[27] and swear fidelity to the vile despot who has usurped the throne of Washington! But our people are at last alive to the impending peril, and the next few months will exhibit a series of battles as desperate as any on record. If they do not, I know nothing of the signs of the times.

Our troops ought never to have surrendered at Donelson. That has done us an injury which is almost irretrievable, and whoever was to blame for it ought to be accursed in the eyes of the South forever.[28] Well, well—Hope on, is my motto but I wish I were in the infantry where I could have better chance to do something. Our men do not evince much disposition to re-enlist. If they would enlist in the infantry service and elect me their Captain, I would be in a glorious element. Capt. Thompson has been appointed Major of this Regiment.[29] If another man were elected Captain over me in this company, I would not longer remain with it, for I have done and suffered far more for it than anyone else. I do not apprehend opposition, however, in case of an election. I have been necessarily rigid at times and have made some enemies. They may perhaps attempt to defeat me, but they will not succeed. These remarks are, of course, entre nous. Fitzhugh, our former Major, is now our Lieut. Col.[30]

Josie was in Richmond at the Inauguration,[31] or rather the day thereafter, and seems to have enjoyed herself. I am glad she went. Uncle Hugh [W. Sheffey] paid Mrs. [E. N.] Brown a good deal of attention during the winter, and Josie speaks highly of him.

25. The Waldensians, founded by Peter Waldo, were a religious sect declared heretical by the pope in 1215. The persecutions that followed drove many members underground.

26. Thomas Moore was the national poet of Ireland during the romantic period of literature. His most popular novel was an 1827 work, *The Epicurean.*

27. Originally a Syrian name for all gods, Baal has come to be the title of any false god.

28. Unknowingly, Sheffey was censuring his kinsman Brig. Gen. John B. Floyd.

29. Capt. John H. Thompson's wound prohibited him from accepting promotion.

30. On March 22 Colonel Jenifer named Henry Fitzhugh as lieutenant colonel of the 8th Virginia Cavalry.

31. Jefferson Davis was formally inaugurated as president of the Confederate States of America at ceremonies on Capitol Square in Richmond on February 22, 1862.

I am not surprised at his paying attention to Elle Brown for I know she was the belle of the city. I understand Guy Sanders,[32] and Miss Nat Sanders, Rob Crockett[33] and Miss Jinnie are married. At last I am almost left alone. I too will be married this summer or be free forever from all entangling alliances with women. More anon. Love to all.

> *Camp at Round Bottom*
> *Mercer Co., Va.,* MARCH 23RD, 1862

Dear Josie,[34]

Your letter of the 14th inst. was gratefully received. It was the first I had received from you since I was in Wytheville. No one but myself can appreciate the pleasure it gave me.

Some time has elapsed since I returned with the "Smyth Dragoons" from the chilling upper air of Flat Top Mountain to the more genial climate of New River and the bonnier "banks and braes" around Round Bottom. We are to leeward of a huge knob that throws a protecting wing over our torn tents and Esquimaux. hovels. The effects of the exposure on Flat Top still make themselves manifest by the occasional breaking-down of some one of our number. One of our bravest men, Haynes Thomas, died recently at his home in Burke's Garden wither I had sent him. I allowed his two brothers to go to his bedside, but they did not get there in time. I shall miss him very much for though a dissipated and wicked man, he knew no fear.

The enemy are now *reported* to be slowly advancing toward Lewisburg and towards Princeton. The Militia of Monroe and Greenbrier [Counties] have been ordered out *en masse.* They will constitute quite a formidable force. Monroe alone ought to furnish quite a thousand men.

This county, Mercer, has supported the cavalry well, but at last it is eaten out. It is almost as barren as if the army worm or the locusts of Egypt had swept over it.[35] It is a desert—a wilderness *minus* those great necessaries of Dragoon life, corn and oats and hay.

---

32. Samuel Guy Sanders, a Wytheville clerk, was then a sergeant in the 4th Virginia Infantry. James I. Robertson Jr., *4th Virginia Infantry* (Lynchburg, Va., 1982), 71.

33. Sheffey was probably referring to Robert Crockett Jr., a Wythe County attorney and soon-to-be lieutenant in the 4th Virginia. Ibid., 46.

34. Sheffey obviously made a copy of his March 20 letter to his sisters. Much of this letter to Josie is a verbatim account.

35. Chesterfield County native Henry Heth was in command of both the 45th Virginia Infantry and the region where Sheffey was stationed. Heth's soldiers came quickly to dislike his discipline and arrogance. The general commanded an inadequate force in northwestern Vir-

The Cavalry will soon be removed westward and infantry will take their places. Our troops are said to be fortifying at Brushy Ridge, seven miles west of Lewisburg, and are expected to entrench themselves also somewhere near Cross Roads south of this point.

The clouds are darkening above us, and God only knows what we shall see when the veil is rent. There are some of us who will laugh at the horrors and defy the tempest, who, like stormy petrels, will feel themselves in their element when the thunderpeals are loudest and the billows ride mountain-high. I prefer peace for the sake of those I love, but for myself I care little. We will send many a Yankee soul howling to its long home before we yield even to overwhelming odds. But many of our foes have evinced that they belong to a brave and determined race, and some of our own people are infinitely, shamefully cowardly. The more worthless men's lives are, the more highly they seem to prize them. Some of them might learn lessons of heroism even from our foes, for they occasionally exhibit a degree of bravery which is very commendable.

Not long ago sixteen of the 45th and eighteen of the Border Rangers surrounded eight of the Pennsylvania Dragoons near Jumping Branch in this county, killed three of them at the first fire and wounded a fourth. The horse of a fifth was killed and fell upon him, fastening him so that he could not extricate himself. The wounded man and the three who were unhurt stood their ground against the odds, until their pistol shots were all expended, then escaped. The man entangled by his horse refused to surrender but was taken by force. Such bravery, though it be that of our enemies, is worthy of all honor.

We must have a similar spirit throughout the whole South, a spirit akin to that which animated the Greeks at Thermopylae and Marathon, before we can be successful in achieving our independence. We must be as willing to accept the crown of martyrdom as the victims of St. Bartholomew[36] or as the venerable sage in that strange tale of Tom Moore's, the "Epicurean" or as the Waldenses and Albiginses,[37] or any other people who have been called upon

---

ginia, so to retard Union movements, he adopted a "scorched-earth" policy, even convincing Mercer County farmers to destroy their livestock and crops at any approach of enemy forces. Hilldrup, "Romance of a Man in Gray," 91; *Official Records,* 12, pt. 3:836, 839.

36. Sheffey here refers to the victims of the St. Bartholomew's Day massacre (August 24, 1572), in which French Catholics slaughtered Huguenot Protestants in Paris. The killing later spread throughout France.

37. The Albigenses were a religious sect in the south of France. They flourished from 1020 to 1250 before being exterminated for heresy.

to suffer and die for a principle. But the messenger who is to carry out our mail is waiting and I will close.

Capt. Thompson has been appointed Major of this Regt. I do not know whether he has accepted. Fitzhugh, our former Major, is now our Lt. Col.

I am glad you were in Richmond and regret you were not there in time to hear the President's Inaugural. My beloved Uncle deserves no credit for paying so much attention to Mrs. Brown, for I doubt not she was the belle of the city during the winter. Nonetheless I am gratified that she has formed a good opinion of him, for he is one of my favorites, a genial companion, a true and warmhearted friend.

I learn that Rob. Crockett and Miss Jennie are married at last, as are also Guy Sanders and Miss Nat. There must be a perfect mania for Hymen[38] in *la belle monde*. These mountains are not a part of it, yet we occasionally hear of such things out here.

More anon. Kindest regards to all. Write soon.

Camp at Crumps[39] on New River
Mercer Co., Va., APRIL 14TH, 1862

Dear Josie,

I received your letter of date this morning. Your letters, as well as my own, are like angel's visits in their rarity, but unlike mine, they resemble the visits of the angels, in the happiness, the gladness, the gloom-dispelling sunshine they bring with them. I would not mind the tedium, the living burial of this life in the wilderness, if I could hear from you regularly. My own letters are, I doubt, not very interesting, for aside from the fact that I have little time to write well, if I were able to do so, and less opportunity to write to you as I could wish, on account of many constantly around me, this military life here on account of the inactivity of our Yankee friends affords very little interest to write about.

We have been some time at this camp and in advance of all the Confederate forces in North Western Va. But our enemies do not evince much disposition to pounce upon us. If they were to attack us in our present position, I think some of them would be hurt, but they will not attempt it. The roads behind us are impassable, on account of the immense masses of trees, earth

38. Hyman was the Greek god of marriage.
39. The 1860 Mercer County census lists William Crump as a sixty-six-year-old farmer with a wife, son, and five grandchildren living on an estate valued at more than $124,000.

and rock which the vernal thaws and rains have precipitated into them.[40] We have constituted ourselves a band of roadworkers to no avail. The falling earth and crumbling cliffs crash our fabrics before we begin them, and the river and clouds send their floods to wash away our banks faster than pick and spade can fashion them. So we are thinking of abandoning the task as a bad one, and trusting to the roads upon the opposite side of the river for the outgoings and incomings of our transportation. That is but a broken reed and we and our horses must suffer very much in the next few days. The boats have been all destroyed upon the river by order of Genl. Heth except the one left for our use at this point, and this is but a frail and leaky bark.

There are two companies at this point, the Grayson Cavalry, Capt. [William H.] Bramblett, Co. C, and the Smyth Dragoons, Co. A. The Grayson Cavalry is a large company made up of brave and able-bodied men, but like this troop, they are indifferently armed and have suffered much from exposure and sickness.

From orders received from Headquarters this morning, we learn that Major Henry Fitzhugh, as whole-souled a fellow as I know of, has been assigned to duty in this Regt. and will take command of the post at Princeton and all the cavalry in the vicinity. What Col. Jenifer proposes doing, I know not. I think he has never loved his Regiment or these mountains, and these mountains and this Regiment have as little affection for him. He exceedingly desires that this Regiment should reenlist, but I do not know a single company in it which has any such present intention. All will probably reenlist but not in the 8th Regt. Va. Cavalry.[41]

We have been too much maltreated and mistreated, too much deceived and humbugged, too little cared for. We have changed our commanders as the chamelion its hues. We have begged for arms, and they have been promised time and again. Yet many of us still have no arms at all, and others nothing but the old cast-barreled shot-guns not good for a pheasant even at twenty steps. We have time and again seen our horses, once noble and vigorous, die of starvation and fatigue. As for me, I am riding my fifth horse—a coal-black steed is he, as symmetrical and brave, and proud and beautiful as a horse can be—but before our remaining six weeks have passed away, per-

40. It had been raining incessantly for the week preceding Sheffey's letter. Rutherford B. Hayes, *Diary and Letters of Rutherford Birchard Hayes,* 5 vols. (Columbus, Ohio, 1922–26), 2:222–28.

41. At that time the 8th Virginia Cavalry did not have three hundred men present for duty. This number was less than a third of the prescribed strength for a regiment. *Official Records,* 12, pt. 3:98.

haps I shall drag him also by the neck to some equine Golgotha,[42] and consign his spirit to that "undiscovered country from whose bosom no horse returns." It is not strange that we should weary of a Regt. which for twelve months has been vertically buried—buried beyond the reach of all but sickness and suffering, exposure and fatigue—buried where neither Fame nor the opportunity of Glory, nor Love, nor Hope nor Happiness could find us.

In a different field, with the company under my command, I could have won golden opinions, and a name. So could we all. Week after week, as we have sent our sick comrades away where they could be cared for, or as we have stood by the deathbed and the grave, we have trembled in the presence of the Angel of Death. Not so would it be with us, if he could come to us in the gorgeous raiment of a Spirit of Light, pointing us from a field like that of Manassas or Shiloh[43] to a heaven of Glory—an endless immortality of Fame.

To share in the glory of such victories would reward a man for being a soldier. It would be something to live for, which he could, jubilant and exulting, throw something for himself into the jaws of the frowning Azrael. But to be "cabined" in a hovel, "cribbed" in a corn-crib, and "confined" by sickness in a camp compared with which a colier's camp is a comfortable residence, or to die and be put away "unknelled, uncoffined and unknown" fifty miles from civilization, is horrible in the extreme.

I do not know what I shall do in the next few months. To me, the future is as misty and uncertain as the present is irksome. My own conduct will depend to a large extent upon your wishes. I shall not commit myself to any course without consulting you, unless such an opportunity of advancement offers—that it will be necessary to seize upon immediately. I do not intend to go into the service with any less rank than that I have held. I had rather be free and untrammeled, ready for the opportunities that I know will offer themselves. And I know I am more capable of filling a higher position than many who from mere favoritism have been placed above me. I would have very little self-love if I did not think so.

I heard with pleasure that Rob Crockett was married, and regret it is not so. I would be gratified to hear of anything that would contribute to his happiness. If he desired it, and Miss Jennie really loved him, she ought to have married him. The time may come when he will weary of delay and despair

42. Located on an elevation in northwest Jerusalem, Golgotha was the place of Jesus' crucifixion.

43. Two of the first major battles of the Civil War occurred July 21, 1861, at Manassas, Virginia, and April 6–7, 1862, at Shiloh, Tennessee. Manassas was a Confederate victory; Shiloh was not.

forever of the consummation for which he has waited so anxiously and so long. I have nothing to do with his affairs, but it is passing strange that the cowards who stay at home can marry, while the soldier who has more need of some one to care for & to love him, and who goes forth to battle for right and justice and the honor of woman, must wait. It is the soldier who needs the shield of love to save him from perils more imminent, more fearful than those of the blood-washed field, to guard him from the pollutions and contaminations of camp, from the sirens that sing to him in the tent of the reveler and the debauchee, from the vices that walk unbridled forth to tempt and lure him to his ruin.

Oh, God! How many are the victims! How strangely comes the profane jest, the maudlin song from lips that twelve months ago were pure as the pure heart of a woman! Only those will escape unscathed, around whom the shield of an all-absorbing love is thrown to rescue and to save. Next to the love of God, a species of love almost ignored among soldiers, the love of a soldier for his wife is purest, noblest, most exalted, best.

The love of lovers is vague, ideal, intangible, variable. Hence, in nine cases out of ten, long engagements end in disappointment, in the estrangement of both, or the alienation of one and the despair of the other. Lovers know nothing about the philosophy of "Bear and Forbear." But the love of Man and Wife, that alone of all the species of earthly affection is supposed to be through life until death, self-sacrificing, devoted, pure, perfect, sublime. But I wander and weary you; I have been rather communing with some of my own strange ideas than writing interestingly to you.

Our political skies are now rapidly brightening, but without a miracle, long, long years must pass before Peace will smile upon our distracted land. It was my opinion from the first, and I hope I may yet be mistaken. We have the work of years before us, and then the labours, the toils, the sufferings of the present will have their reward. But in the long period that is to elapse, our "individual cares," our individual happiness, cannot, ought not, to be totally absorbed by the concerns of the nation. The war should be left to those engaged in it, and our people not engaged in it should go to their accustomed avocations zealously as before. I admire patriotism and I love the new-born country which, already like the infant Hercules, had overcome the enemies that would have strangled it in its cradle.[44] But we have too little of

44. Hercules was the mythological Greek hero of incredible strength. When the jealous goddess Hera sought to kill him and his twin brother, Iphicles, by having two poisonous snakes placed in their crib, the infant Hercules strangled both serpents.

that patriotism which teaches every one his true duty and strengthens him to perform it. We cannot all be soldiers, yet almost all have forsaken their proper avocations and, if not soldiers, are idlers. They are not tilling their fields, they are not putting in their crops. Unless the negroes do the work, we shall in another year want meat and bread, the vital sinews of war.

I have very considerable patriotism, patriotism enough to induce me to risk my life anywhere to aid in bringing about the blessings which we all know will accrue to us if we succeed. But there is one love above my love of country, above my love of everything else on this earth, and that is love for you, my darling. Our government may be upturned, our country may be swept from the face of the earth, and we be left to mourn among the ruins. But if your love for me through all remains changeless, unchangeable, my own will grow stronger through the lapse of years and we will be brighter, for you are linked with all my dreams of that which is to come.

On this one subject alone, am I an enthusiast. For you I would peril everything except that which to the true man is dearest, his honor. But how coldly you do write. You write as if you were merely "interested" in me, merely my friend. I believe that in your heart there is boundless, illimitable treasure of love. It cannot be otherwise, and sometime I will find it. But you keep watch over it now as Argos did over the love of the mythic maiden,[45] or as the angels did over the garden of Eden. (That is a prettier simile than if I had said "as the Dragons over the treasures of the Hesperian gardens" though they were faithful too.)[46] And now you are either mad or merry. I don't know which, and I must quit. I have written you a long prosy, uninteresting, nonsensical epistle, and have wearied you unpardonably, but you must forgive me, and love me, even as I love you, dearest.

Camp 8th Va. Cavalry, Union, Va.
MAY 25TH, 1862

Dear Josie,

A long time has elapsed since I have found an opportunity of writing to you, and I doubt not you are anxious to know what is occurring in this por-

45. According to Greek fable, Argus was a huge creature with one hundred eyes. A jealous Hera assigned Argus to watch his wife, Io. When Argus failed to do so, Hera changed him into a peacock, with his eyes in the tail feathers.

46. The Hesperides were three sisters who, with the dragon Ladon, guarded the golden apples that Hera had received as a wedding gift in the "garden of the Hesperides." Hercules slew the dragon and carried away some of the apples.

tion of the belligerent world. Of the occurrence at the camp at Shannon's,[47] at Giles Ct. House and at Camp Success near the Narrows of New River,[48] you have doubtless heard in detail. I will not trouble you with a further account of them.

My life since I left Wytheville has been an exceedingly stirring and eventful one, but checkered with far more of shadow than of sunshine.

As soon as we reached Camp Success, our Regt. with the exception of two companies, the Border Rangers and the Kanawha Rangers, was again dismounted and our horses sent back to be pastured near Dublin Depot.

On the 13th inst. Cos. of the Regiment were reorganized. I was elected Captain of the Smyth Dragoons. On the 14th was held the election of field officers, resulting in the choice of Col. Corns, Lt. Col. A. F. Cook, and Major Thomas P. Bowen. The legality of the latter election was disputed by Col. Jenifer, who used every means to secure the election of Lt. Col. Fitzhugh, but to his chagrin was decided to be valid by Genl. Heth.[49]

The Regt. has at last something to depend upon, something to hope for. General Marshall[50] had driven the enemy from Princeton but later in the

47. Sheffey was referring to a May 1 skirmish at Clark's Hollow. Four companies of the 8th Virginia Cavalry had a brief but spirited fight with Federals before retiring back to Princeton. Williams, *Hayes*, 108–10; Dickinson, *8th Virginia Cavalry*, 29.

48. On May 10, Colonels Jenifer and McCausland with over one thousand men attacked the Union garrison at Giles Court House. The Federals fell back to a second position, were driven from there, and retired to the Narrows, only to be forced to withdraw again. The Confederates had regained that valuable approach to the Virginia and Tennessee Railroad. Casualties in the Giles fighting were 4 wounded on the Confederate side, 2 killed and 5 wounded on the Union side. *Official Records*, 12, pt. 1:491–95; 12, pt. 3:145, 176–77; Hayes, *Diary and Letters*, 1:262–63. Unaware of the small casualties, a member of the Grayson Cavalry in Sheffey's regiment wrote a friend, "We completely routed the enemy after half an hour [of] sharp firing." Fielding R. Cornett to Rosamond Hale, June 2, 1862, Fielding Raphne Cornett Papers, University of Virginia, Charlottesville.

49. Sheffey's complaints of Jenifer and Fitzhugh must have been personal. Fitzhugh was then receiving praise from Heth for every action in which he participated. *Official Records*, 12, pt. 1:450, 493.

50. Kentuckian Humphrey Marshall was a West Point graduate, colonel of cavalry during the Mexican War, congressman, and ambassador. In October 1861 he was appointed a Confederate brigadier general. A Kentucky staff officer wrote in mid-1863, "The want of Gen'l Marshall's brains is most evident in the management of the command, even to the perception of the soldiers." Edward G. Guerrant, *The Headquarters Diary of Edward O. Guerrant* (Baton Rouge, 1999), 311. In his retreat through Princeton, Marshall ordered the town burned. Only a few homes were saved. Richardson, "Raleigh County," 260.

day had been compelled to fall back two miles. Wharton was advancing from Cross Roads to sustain him. We thus had the enemy completely between three fires.[51] At this juncture, if any reasonable degree of strategy had been exhibited by General Heth, we would have captured the whole Yankee force. The men, footsore and weary as they were, were eager for the fray. We lay down in an open field near Johnson's, where the 45th had its former unfortunate fracas with the enemy, expecting to be ordered to the attack in the morning. But about twelve o'clock that night, we received orders to march in the reverse direction.[52]

It was as inexcusable and unaccountable a movement as any that has been made during the war, the dicta of more military pens than this to the contrary not withstanding. All that night we retreated and reached the camp at the Narrows late the next day, having accomplished nothing but the utter exhaustion and demoralization of our troops. Such a retreat from victory has been rarely known in the history of any war. Then, to relieve his own chagrin and vent his spleen, the singular General who has command over us sentenced some men who had fired their guns upon the march, contrary to the Regulations of the Army, to be ironed down in jail for the term of their enlistment. Their conduct should have been punished, but the punishment was so greatly disproportioned to the offence that it could only have been dictated by the utmost malignity of a malignant heart.

Two of my best men are among the victims of this cruel order.[53] I interceded for them in vain. He turned upon me at first with all the venom of a viper, and I was about to retire when he proposed to release the forty or fifty men under arrest, if all the captains and colonels would sign a paper making themselves responsible for the conduct of their men in this respect. That

51. According to Marshall's official report, he suggested to Heth the idea of a "lateral movement" whereby Marshall, assisted by Wharton's and Heth's commands, would trap the Federals around Princeton in a three-pronged vise. Three factors crippled the plan: Marshall's hope for secrecy never materialized; Wharton was tardy in arriving; and Heth failed to fulfill his part of the assignment. Marshall seized Princeton but had to retire when heavy Union forces approached. *Official Records*, 12, pt. 1:513–17; Cox, *Military Reminiscences*, 1:210–16.

52. The order to withdraw came from Marshall, not Heth. The latter got to within 4–5 miles of Princeton. Then, Marshall reported, "hearing in the country from somebody that I had been repulsed and was retreating, he fell back in the night to the mouth of East River." *Official Records*, 12, pt. 3:516.

53. The compiled service records for the 8th Virginia Cavalry do not show any Smyth Dragoons being arrested by Confederate authorities for a protracted period of time. Heth's statement was likely a threat.

would have put all the officers not only in his power but in the power of their men, and no sensible man would have acceded to it.

The same day we were again ordered to march, and with 2300 men crossed to the opposite bank of New River. The men were completely exhausted and in no fix for the march before them.[54] I informed Col. Jenifer of the condition of the dismounted cavalry, and he suggested that the officers should procure *knee-pads* for the men who couldn't walk. Fortunately we are at last rid of him.

On the 20th we marched from the bank of New River opposite the south of Wolf Creek to camp at Hugh Tiffany's. On the 21st we reached the Salt Sulphur, on the 22nd we marched from Salt Sulphur to Greenbrier Bridge, where the picket of the enemy was stationed. We lay upon our arms in a gorge near the Bridge. These excessively long marches were enough to have broken down fresh men. Our men were broken down before. After about three hours sleep upon our arms, were aroused and at 3½ o'clock AM advanced to attack the enemy at Lewisburg three miles off.[55]

The pickets at the Bridge were easily driven in, some of them killed and some captured by the mounted companies of our cavalry under command of Col. Corns. Lt. [George W.] Holderby was wounded and Lt. [Alexander H.] Samuels of the Border Rangers had his horse shot there. The whole force was double-quicked to the hill overlooking Lewisburg. The men advanced with the utmost enthusiasm, and the enemy was said to be in full retreat. Genl. Heth evidently thought that the victory would be exceedingly easy. The dismounted cavalry under command of Lt. Col. Cook had been ordered to act as a reserve, and to keep about 300 yards in the rear of the main body. Co. A was the advance of this reserve.

After cannonading awhile from the hill, the whole force, 45th, 22nd, W. W. Finney's Battalion[56] and artillery, were allowed to dash down into the town, helterskelter, pell-mell, without wings, without line of battle, without skirmishers, without any proper arrangement. The houses were filled with the

54. Heth drove the "new and undisciplined" men so hard toward Lewisburg that the columns were "much run down" when they reached the town. Dozens of sick and weary stragglers were left in the wake of the march. Otis K. Rice, *A History of Greenbrier County* (Parsons, W.Va., 1986), 268–69.

55. Seven actions took place in and around Lewisburg. This contest on May 23, 1862, was the largest.

56. Lt. Col. William Wood Finney commanded the undersized 189th Regiment of Virginia Militia from Craig County.

enemy. So was the street at the farther end of the town, and the force upon the enemy's right and left must alone have been superior to ours. A reserve was drawn up beyond all these. Our reserve was then ordered to follow close upon the heels of the main body and halted in the town at a point where the fire from both wings of the enemy concentrated. Here many of our men would have been killed had not Lt. Col. [Cook] allowed them to kneel upon their knees while we were awaiting further orders. The men were as cool and determined as any set of men I ever saw.

Then the battle began in earnest. Suddenly the popping shots were condensed into one terrific crash, and the Belgian rifles of the enemy, carrying each a ball weighing an ounce and a half—many of the balls explosive— roared with ceaseless fury upon the right and left. The General was near us when that peal of thunder broke upon us. It was something he had not anticipated. Our men were effectually ambuscaded, and for *that* General Heth alone was to blame.[57]

The reaction was almost immediate. The oldest regulars would have faltered under such a surprise. The 22nd had deployed to the right. The 45th and Finney's Battalion were in the centre and upon the left. Major Edgar was shot down.[58] Many other officers were killed, wounded or taken. Detachments of batteries had been indiscreetly rushed down into the street and upon the left and the horses were shot down. Four of our best pieces of cannon were captured. Finney's Battalion, after fighting bravely, mistook an order of their commander and began to retreat. The 45th saw this and followed the example, many of them flying in the wildest confusion.

Genl. Heth ordered the reserve which was as yet unbroken to form a line in the field upon the left and stop that flight. Under the fire of the enemy, our men obeyed every order to the letter, but we might as well have tried to

57. Heth with a superior force had blocked a Federal lunge at the Virginia Central Railroad near Covington. The Union commander, Col. George Crook, fell back to Lewisburg. Heth launched a dawn attack on May 23 and initially had the upper hand over the Union garrison. Suddenly the 2d West Virginia Infantry made a charge of its own and broke the center of Heth's line. The Confederate retreat quickly became a rout as men threw away arms and equipment as they fled the field. Union losses were 13 killed, 60 wounded, and 6 missing. Heth's casualties were a stunning 80 killed, 100 wounded, and 157 missing, plus the loss of four cannon, twenty-five horses, and three hundred stands of small arms. Boyd B. Stutler, *West Virginia in the Civil War* (Charleston, W.Va., 1963), 179–83; J. J. Sutton, *History of the Second Regiment, West Virginia Cavalry Volunteers, in the War of the Rebellion* (Portsmouth, Ohio, 1892), 53–54.

58. Maj. George M. Edgar, as well as Colonel Finney, were captured in the battle. *Official Records*, 12, pt. 1:807.

stop the wind as to check that disgraceful rout. Up to this time, we had not been allowed to fire a gun. It is useless to give the further details of this disgraceful affair. It was disgraceful in the extreme whether the fault be upon the shoulders of the general or the men.[59]

My own men, I know, behaved with perfect coolness and did nothing they were not ordered to do, and everything they were ordered to do. So did the whole reserve. The 22nd Regt. fought with the utmost bravery and held the enemy's left completely in check. The panic in Finney's Battalion and the 45th was occasioned by the surprise. The whole fight did not last over 30 minutes. In that time our loss was 186—40 killed, 40 wounded and 106 taken prisoners. The affair is the most disgraceful of the war and can only be wiped out with blood.

But Genl. Heth is pursuing a very mean and dastardly course in endeavoring to shirk the responsibility and throw it upon his men. But in that he will signally fail. He is responsible for the surprise and the consequent reaction. If he had used the proper precautions, his men would have continued the fight with the utmost enthusiasm and bravery. The victory would have been won notwithstanding the odds which I believe—and if I can trust the evidence of my own senses—know to have been against us.

But I have written enough. I hope soon to be led back to the attack of Lewisburg. If we are taken back, we will wipe out whatever of disgrace may attach to all who were engaged in this affair. Please write soon to me.

Camp at Union, Monroe Co., Va.
MAY 30, 1862

Dear Josie,

But a few days have elapsed since I wrote to you, giving you an indifferent account of our disastrous affair at Lewisburg. We are (I mean our Regt.) still encamped at the beautiful little town of Union. It is a pity it bears such a

59. In his official report Heth was candid in shifting responsibility for the defeat. "One of those causeless panics for which there is no accounting seized upon my command. The only excuse that can be offered for the disgraceful behavior of three regiments and batteries is that they are filled with conscripts and newly officered men under the election system." Ibid., 813. See also ibid., 12, pt. 3:242, 255. The 8th Virginia Cavalry's Fielding Cornett declared: "We lost this victory by nothing in the world but bad generalship. I do not think that I ever saw hail fall thicker and faster in my life than the bullets fell around us that day." Cornett to Hale, June 2, 1862, Cornett Letters.

name. I have frequently passed through it, but was never before impressed with its exceeding loveliness. In the winter it looked as bleak and dreary as some inhospitable village of Patagonia or Greenland.[60] In the summer the fields are robed in riches verdure, stretched away drearily in the scorching sun, as dry almost as the wastes of Sahara. But again I revisit it, and the fairy wand of May has transformed it strangely. How happy I could be if you were here! The society here is fine, and the people have treated me and others of our number with marked kindness. But a less favored spot nearer to the dear old town of Wytheville would be infinitely more delectable.

Since I wrote to you, the enemy have evacuated Lewisburg and fallen back towards Meadow Bluff. What the cause of the movement and what their designs are, we cannot yet ascertain. Perhaps the successes of Stonewall Jackson have had something to do with their backward march.[61] Perhaps they intend to come in upon our rear via Pack's Ferry. A few days will develop their plans. A few of our scouts were in Lewisburg today. They were followed by a body of Yankee Cavalry as far as Greenbrier River. Further than that, those fastidious gentlemen do not seem inclined to come. They came nearer one day last week, but two mounted companies of our Regt. pursued them and they went back much more rapidly than they came. The enemy treated the people of Lewisburg very shamefully, and they also shamefully neglected our wounded men there. One of our surgeons will, I think, go over tomorrow to attend to the latter.

We are still without our tents and without our baggage. We are a forlorn, destitute set of fellows but as merry as crickets for a' that. We have learned to take everything easy, and have become real hardened stoics. From our frequent perambulations about the country, in the way of forced marches and the like, we might also be classed among the philosophers of the Peripatetic school.[62] We have been drilling every day, and the Regt. will soon be thoroughly disciplined.

60. Patagonia is an arid, grassy region east of the Andes Mountains in Chile and Argentina.

61. Maj. Gen. Thomas J. "Stonewall" Jackson was then amid his spectacular 1862 Shenandoah Valley campaign. By this date, Jackson had won victories at McDowell (May 8), Front Royal (May 23), and Winchester (May 25). Union general John C. Frémont, who had succeeded Rosecrans as commander of the Mountain Department, was moving with a large force to try and intercept Jackson's army near Winchester. The Union elements operating against Heth were left much on their own. *Official Records,* 12, pt. 3:264.

62. Peripatetics were a school of philosophy founded by Aristotle and so named because they walked down the streets as the Greek philosopher taught his disciples.

I have not heard from you for a long, long time. Please write to me very soon. I do not know whether you are still in Wytheville or whether you have sought refuge in the old North State [North Carolina] or further south. Please keep me informed of your movements if you do take it into your head to run away.

I would get a leave of absence and come home for a short time, if I thought you cared to see me, but I don't believe you do. If you would consent to a consummation of our engagement, I would come and stay until you would get very tired of me. You are very cruel thus to put me off. There is no reason for it. Everyone knows that this war cannot end for years. Long ago I had set my heart upon a consummation of this engagement, and I was led to expect that whatever might be the condition of the country, I would not be deferred longer than a twelvemonth at furthest. The twelvemonth has passed away. So as reasonably will another and another and another with like result. And I am still to pursue blindly the receding hope like one who follows an *ignis fatuus* [foolish infatuation], "Hope deferred maketh the heart sick."[63] I cannot believe that you really intend to defer our marriage another twelve-month. If so, our engagement is indeed becoming exceedingly "indefinite." I have thus far performed every duty of a soldier with the most scrupulous fidelity. I have stood to my post faithfully and well, and am now entitled to some rest. If you will consent to our marriage, I will ask it; otherwise I shall not. My lot in the long years of war before me will be one of hardship and suffering, privation, danger, and toil, but there are goals yet above me to be reached, honors to be attained, prizes to be won. With your help, I can attain them. Thus far I have not receded nor, God willing, shall I. Whatever may be my lot, whether of suffering or pleasure, if you love me, you ought to be willing to share it. If you are not willing to share it, you do not love me. If you decide upon nothing, if you determine nothing except to remain in *status quo,* our engagement will be a mockery, meaning nothing.

Let us consummate it. You will not regret it. You will certainly not be less happy or less free, and you will make infinitely happy one who loves you with a love amounting to adoration. Write as soon as possible.

63. This famous line is from Proverbs 13:12.

Camp at Union, Monroe Co.
JUNE 20, 1862

Dear Josie,

Since my return from Wythe, I have been encamped at Union.[64] Nothing in the belligerent line has transpired of interest. I went upon a scout in the early part of the week in which we were quite successful but had no engagement. Major Bowen was in command and we numbered about 250 men. After proceeding about twelve miles towards Anderson's Ferry on the Greenbrier, we discovered a squad of men about 300 yards in advance of us in a wood, who seemed to be watching us and acting very singularly. Dividing the command into three divisions, we charged immediately in real John Gilpin, Jehu style,[65] but the apparitions had disappeared as suddenly as Macbeth's vision.[66] Though we followed the road for miles at full gallop, we could discover nothing of them. Since then, buildings have been burned at Rocky Point near that place. I presume it was done by those fellows, but whence they came or whither they went is more than I can imagine.

After our *distinque* charge, we crossed Greenbrier River and were soon upon the trail of bodies of the enemy who had been there earlier in the day. We were about two hours too late. Lying down upon a hillside covered with heavy grass, we slept and froze till midnight. Then starting out in a new direction, after burning a large wheat-rick containing three or four hundred bushels, we recrossed the Greenbrier at Poppaw Ford with about two hundred fine cattle, which the enemy would have taken away the next day. So that our expedition was not without its result.

The country through which we passed is one of remarkable fertility. Tablelands covered with cornfields, wheatfields and meadows, level bottoms matted with the most luxuriant grass, hills both gentle and rugged but overgrown everywhere with the finest blue-grass, constitute a majority of the landscapes.

64. It is somewhat strange that after journeying to Wytheville to discuss the future with Josie, Sheffey made no mention in his letter of their decisions. Perhaps his praise of several young ladies he met in Union was an approach of jealousy to get Josie to accept a quick wedding date. If so, the strategy did not work.

65. John Gilpin was a William Cowper character who had great difficulty staying on a horse. In 2 Kings, Jehu of Israel raced furiously around his kingdom on a chariot to slay his several rivals.

66. *Macbeth* begins with three mysterious witches who appear before the victorious Macbeth and tell him of other successes he will accomplish.

Most of us will regret the order that removes us and our horses from this land of grass. The people, with the exception of some few of the penurious nabobs, Oliver Beime for example, are very kind and hospitable.

Our camp here is in a beautiful sugar grove and is the most pleasant we have ever had since we left Wytheville.

The ladies are accomplished and some of them beautiful. When I first came here, I boarded at the house of Mr. [George W.] Hutchinson, the Clerk of the County.[67] His wife [Georgia], he being away, received me with great kindness and I lived like a prince. Miss Ann Hutchinson is a young girl of 14 or 15, not pretty, not particularly interesting, but good hearted, and her kindness added not a little to the pleasure of my sojourn there. Both her mother and herself are very fond of flowers, and from the number of bouquets I have received from that quarter, they must think, and rightly too, that I have the same failing.

A few days after I had gone to Mrs. Hutchinson's becoming "ennuiyes," I concluded I would get acquainted with a young lady opposite, the chief ornament of the neat residence of E[dwin] M. Brown, Esq. I went and was introduced. Mrs. [Caroline] Brown is a little woman, once very beautiful, still intellectual, and exceedingly talkative. She is a Heiskel from Staunton and is an old graduate of Kalorama, the school of my grand aunt in Staunton.[68] I was received with the utmost cordiality and felt more at home than I had done anywhere in this region.

Miss Emma Brown is a young lady of about 18 summers, dark hair, dark eyes, medium height, quite graceful, with cheeks as rosy as "the vale of cashmere" and complexion which at night seems fair as the most polished Parisian. She is at times very beautiful, sings, plays, talks tolerably, and is moderately interesting, but she has a melancholy cast and is not particularly intellectual. Besides there is a skeleton in the house, a something the mere sojourner cannot fathom. The ladies of Union, with perhaps one or two exceptions, do not seem to visit there, though Miss Brown visits them, and she has a sister living in the town, a single girl who is not allowed to go to her father's, but Brown is a man of wealth and his daughter has many admirers.

After a few days at Mrs. Hutchinson's, I went to Dr. [J. Alexander] Wad-

67. All of the individuals identified in this letter were Monroe County citizens, information coming from the 1860 census and Oren F. Morton, *A History of Monroe County, West Virginia* (Staunton, Va., 1916).

68. In 1831 Maria Sheffey established in Augusta County the Kalorama Seminary for the education of young women. Augusta County Historical Society, *Augusta Historical Bulletin* 12 (spring 1987): 8–9.

dell's. He is a Staunton man and has been living in Union for two years. Mrs. Waddell is one of the most excellent women I know of and treated me with great kindness. Young ladies frequently came to his house and we had very pleasant evening parties, musical "soirees" &c. There I became acquainted with Miss Bettie Caperton, daughter of Mrs. Gaston [Harriet] Caperton, and with Mrs. [Elizabeth] Akers and Miss Virginia Keenan, old graduates of Kalorama, and the latter an acquaintance of my boyhood & an old schoolmate of Mag's [Margaret Sheffey Peters].

Miss Bettie Caperton is a *petite* young lady of 16 or 18 years, dark hair, dark eyes, features very small but well-defined, graceful in face, beautiful. She is too petite, too *spirituelle* & too inanimate. Here is the beauty of statuary, yet she is sensible, high toned, agreeable, and in short a clever girl. Miss Alice Caperton is more en bon point—I believe that is the word. She, like Miss Bettie, plays exceedingly well but does not sing. About the same age and height, she is dumpier and not pretty at all, though her face is a pleasant one and she also is a sensible clever girl. The family is a very good one and is among the aristocrats of the burg.

Miss Keenan is now, I presume, over 25 and has changed a little but not sufficiently to prevent me from recognizing her after a lapse of years. She is not pretty but agreeable and plays well upon the guitar but does not sing. Mrs. Akers is a young widow and a very pleasant woman. She is a sister of Miss Kate & Miss Cynthia Byrnside, old schoolmates of Mag's and acquaintances of my own. She sings & plays well upon the piano. These widows are charming institutions, and I am compelled to quote frequently from old "Weller to save the hearts of some of my soldier friends."

Miss Harriet Krebs is a young lady who lives in a small house upon one of the cross streets. She was the prettiest frequently at McDonald's. She is the prettiest woman in the place, tall, fair, with raven hair, eyes dark, lustrous, glorious, and a mouth as bewitching as everything ever dreamed of in the days of witchcraft. She is intelligent, agreeable and, in short, a woman that a man might accidentally fall in love with. I speak, of course, as an outsider, a mere observer, student of character. Indeed, I regard a susceptible man as one species of a fool, and feel certain that I was never one of them. I have loved but once truly—that was the love of my boyhood & youth & earlier manhood. I hope it will be the love also of my whole future life.

But the belle of the place is Mrs. [Susan M.] Tiffany,[69] the widow of Capt.

69. Susan McDaniel Tiffany was the widow of the 27th Virginia Infantry's Capt. Hugh S. Tiffany, who was killed at First Manassas. Morton, *Monroe County*, 410; Lowell Reidenbaugh, *27th Virginia Infantry* (Lynchburg, Va., 1993), 180.

Hugh Tiffany who was killed at Manassas. She is emphatically the talking woman with her rich, dark hair brushed back from her brow, her words falling like the pattering of a hailstorm, & while exhilarating her listeners like a "hailstorm" of another kind, while her eyes flash & sparkle like the lightning in the midst of the tempest. Her widow's weeds contrasting with her blonde complexion, she is a dangerous specimen of that exterior species of woman kind known as young widows. She was a McDonald & relative of the Alexanders at Newbern. Miss Krebs seems to be her intimate friend and almost constant companion, but in her presence the conversation of Miss Krebs is like the gentle ripple of the streamlet compared with the thunder & clatter & flash of the hailstorm aforesaid. Indeed, Mrs. Tiffany is a most nervously intellectual woman. By "nervousness" applied to her, I mean not weakness but strength, nervousness like that of the flying steed, the soaring eagle, the inspired orator in his flights of eloquence.

And now I have written a real womanly gossiping epistle for which I hope you will forgive me, as I have nothing else at present to write about. Please write to me very soon and do not altogether forget.

CHAPTER 5

JENKINS'S RAID

Throughout the late summer and early autumn of 1862, Sheffey continued to write Josephine Spiller of the numerous young and attractive women he was meeting during his army travels. He still hoped that jealousy might cause his fiancée to yield to the point of setting a wedding date. When that did not succeed, Sheffey in November bluntly asked Josie to make a decision one way or the other relative to their marriage.

Meanwhile, the captain experienced the most exciting action of his Civil War career. It involved a five-hundred-mile ride through the Union-held counties of northwestern Virginia.

The idea for the raid came from Gen. Robert E. Lee. Union troops were departing western Virginia in a steady stream to reinforce Maj. Gen. George B. McClellan's Army of the Potomac. Lee suggested to Maj. Gen. W. W. Loring, commanding forces in the mountainous region, that he take advantage of the lightly defended area by raiding Federal posts and regaining the vital Kanawha Valley.

Brig. Gen. Albert Jenkins was selected to lead the raid. With five hundred mounted troops (most of them from Sheffey's 8th Virginia Cavalry), Jenkins made a circular sweep that took him first as far north as Weston, near the birthplace of Thomas J. "Stonewall" Jackson. Then his horsemen galloped west, crossed the Ohio River, and became the first Confederate force to enter Ohio. Jenkins completed the circuit by riding east toward Charleston.

One Union officer sought to downgrade the exploit, stating, "Little real mischief was done by this raid, but it added to the confusion, and helped to disturb the self-possession of the commanding officer" in western Virginia. The man in charge was Col. Andrew J. Lightburn, a childhood friend of Stonewall Jackson. In truth the Jenkins raid was a positive event just before the twin Confederate disasters of Antietam in the East and Perryville in the West.

Camp Ellis, Monroe [County], Va.
JULY 20TH, 1862

Dear Josie,

Since I wrote to you last, our life has been one of little interest though full of toil & hardships. These, however, are to such an extent the characteristics of our every day life that we have become accustomed to them, and most of us have learned to bear everything that befalls us with stoical fortitude and endurance.

Shortly after the date of my last letter, I was ordered upon an expedition to the northward of Lewisburg. We travelled rapidly all night for three successive nights, keeping close in the day to prevent the enemy from ascertaining our whereabouts and purposes. But they found us out nevertheless, though it did them more harm than good, for we are told that they laid an ambuscade for us through which Capt. Everett[1] and I with our companies passed unscathed. They did not fire upon us, thinking that we were their own cavalry whom they had sent around to intercept us.

Shortly after we passed through, we are told by Mrs. Hanna,[2] who lately came through their lines, their own cavalry came into the ambuscade, supposing in the darkness that these were we. The infantry fired into them immediately. The cavalry, thinking on the other hand that we had ambuscaded them, returned the fire, and thus they battled it out among themselves. Eleven wagonloads of dead and wounded men were hauled to Meadow Bluff, if we can credit Mrs. Hanna's report.[3] She is a very reliable woman and strongly southern.

After four days absence we returned to Union. The expedition was virtually a failure, though we went to the northward of Meadow Bluff and our scouts were within a mile and a half of the Yankee camp at that place. We

1. Capt. Henry Clay Everett was then in command of the Border Rangers of the 8th Virginia Cavalry.

2. The Hanna family was large in number in Greenbrier County. No way exists to pinpoint the identity of this particular lady. For example, see Shuck, *Greenbrier County Death Records,* 107–10.

3. This report was pure fabrication. No major action occurred in West Virginia during the June 20–July 20 period. The only mounted force in the area was the 2d West Virginia Cavalry. Its historian wrote, "The country around Meadow Bluff was well suited to grass, the inhabitants seemed to be quite well to do, and taking it all in all, this was the most pleasant season we experienced during the war." Sutton, *Second Regiment, West Virginia Cavalry,* 55.

Head Quarters,

DEPARTMENT OF SOUTH-WESTERN VIRGINIA,
SALT SULPHUR SPRINGS, August   1862.

GENERAL ORDERS, No.

By direction of the General Commanding is hereto appended a list of those absent without leave from the 2nd Brigade of this Command. All such absentees are ordered to report to their respective Regiments, Battalions or Companies within ten days from the publication of this order. Those so reporting within this period will be assigned to duty without further trial. Those failing to report within the prescribed limit of time will be proceeded against as deserters. The absentees from Maj. Jackson's Battalion of Cavalry will be allowed fifteen days to report.

By Order of   Maj. Gen. W. W. LORING.
August 20th, 1862.   W. B. MYERS, A. Adjt. General.

A List of Men absent from the 8th Va. Cavalry.

B. F. Aiken,	R. B. Diggs,	Andrew Greer,	William Lacy,
John P. Aiken,	Kinser,	Henry Davis,	Sampson Simmons,
J. W. Anderson,	Smith,	Stephen F. Jones,	J. B. Beckwith,
W. Anderson,	Spencer,	D. A. Taylor,	Simonton,
J. Anderson,	Coleman,	C. Wesley,	W. W. Hamilton,
D. W. Bean,	Kidd,	J. Cossett,	J. Ralsin,
J. H. Copenhaver,	Peerry,	Wm. M. Boone,	T. R. C. Blankinship,
S. M. Copenhaver,	Thornhill,	J. W. Bowyer,	W. H. Russel,
Wm. E. Copenhaver,	Fitzpatrick,	Wm. R. Thornton,	A. Hornbert,
W. W. Thompson,	Ferguson,	A. J. Woodall,	Edwin Lambert,
J. Park,	Stewart,	H. Davidson,	Paul C. Smith,
Thomas Copenhaver,	Jones,	Fletcher,	J. W. Harman,
A. B. Cook,	Staples,	Muse,	Wm. C. Sogner,
A. P. Cole,	Ballon,	A. B. Nash,	J. E. Maurice,
John J. Hester,	Spencer,	J. D. Morton,	M. B. Ranbirne,
S. T. Morrison,	Joseph Faber,	J. B. Perdue,	William Stevens,
L. G. Maupin,	H. A. Bourn,	S. W. Sinclair,	J. Strader,
J. M. Saunders,	J. D. Pickett,	Ely,	J. J. Stafford,
J. L. Thomas,	J. Austin,	Thompson,	A. T. Snyder,
James R. Evans,	William Austin,	A. P. Handley,	P. R. Snyder,
James Nuckles,	Martin Nelson,	P. M. Russel,	W. G. Panley,
Thomas Smith,	Henry Nelson,	J. V. Ralson,	J. P. Lambert,
John C. Hite,	M. Honk,	J. E. Shelton,	T. P. Hereford,
James W. Mathews,	E. W. Greer,	A. Page,	William A. Smith.

J. M. CORNS,   A. C. BAILEY,
Col. 8th Va. Cavalry.   Adjt. 8th Regt. Va. Cavalry.

D. A. ST. CLAIR'S POWER PRESS, WYTHEVILLE, VA.

A broadside listing absentees from the 8th Virginia Cavalry in August 1862. It was printed in Wytheville. *Courtesy of the Virginia Historical Society*

brought back with us several of the vilest Union men of that region and sent several others "to that bourne from which no traveller returns."[4] When we reached Union, we found our tents all gone and the army on the "qui vive" for a combat, as the Yankees had crossed at Alderson's Ferry and were advancing upon Union. We passed on immediately in the direction of Alder-

4. This quotation is from Hamlet's famous soliloquy.

son's Ferry. The Yankees, deeming "discretion the better part of valor,"[5] prudently and hastily retreated.

So they would have done before when they went to Union if Heth had shown fight. It is easy to perceive that he is no longer in command.[6] Our men succeeded in killing one and wounding three or four others, but they had killed the day before one of the Bland Rangers and wounded severely three others.[7] So that we have made nothing after driving the enemy across the river at Alderson's Ferry. We came back five miles to Wolf Creek Church, where we remained in bivouac till day before yesterday.

We are now a mile nearer the Ferry. We have not seen our tents or baggage since we started on the trip north of Lewisburg. Within the last few days, we have had two communications with the enemy by flags of truce. I had the pleasure of listening a few evenings since to the conversation of the notorious Capt. Bill Powell of Canton, Ohio.[8] He has more than once been accessory to the murder of our men after they had been taken prisoners, and if he ere falls into our hands, woe be unto him. His flag of truce this time protected him.

It is reported here that Murfreesboro has fallen into our hands.[9] The news everywhere is cheering, but the war, though already virtually decided, is to be a protracted one unless the European powers interfere, of which there is as yet little hope.

I am tired of it as all are, but as I have staked my life, hopes, happiness all upon the prize, I can bear it through swimmingly to the end. I hope soon to hear from you. Almost everybody seems to have forgotten me. Letters even from home are like Angel's visits.

You will excuse this scribbling. I have nothing to write upon but the blue

5. In Shakespeare's *King Henry IV* appears the statement, "The better part of valor is discretion."

6. In the third week of June, Heth received orders to report to Chattanooga for duty in the western theater. *Official Records,* 12, pt. 2:707.

7. The Bland Rangers was Company F of the 8th Virginia Cavalry.

8. Sheffey may have been undeservedly derogatory about William Henry Powell. The highly respected Powell was a Wheeling iron and cut-nail manufacturer when the war began. He then led a company in the 2d West Virginia Cavalry and ultimately would rise to the rank of brigadier general.

9. On July 13 Confederate general Nathan Bedford Forrest and fourteen hundred hard-riding cavalrymen surprised a larger Union force occupying Murfreesboro, Tennessee. With a loss of only twenty-five men, Forrest captured the town, twelve hundred Federals, four cannon, and a half million dollars' worth of military supplies.

grass sod and nothing to write with but a pen as bad as the pen of him or her who first wrote the famous couplet in which there is more truth than poetry

My pen is bad. My ink pale
My love for you will never fail.

Camp Caperton,[10] *Monroe Co., Va.*
AUGUST 15TH, 1862

Dear Josie,

I received your letter of inst. a few days ago, and take advantage of the first opportunity for reply that offers itself. When your letter was handed to me, we were engaged in a general review of all our troops. Maj. Genl. Loring[11] & Brig. Genls. Williams[12] and Jenkins[13] were present, and the two latter addressed the troops and the large concourse of citizens. For their speeches I cannot say much, though they both have the reputation of accomplished orators. Genl. Williams, formerly Col. under Genl. Marshall, is now Brig. Genl. in command of this (formerly Heth's) Brigade of Infantry. Genl. Jenkins, formerly Lt. Col. of the 8th Va. Cavalry, is in command of this Brigade of Cavalry. It consists as yet, however, only of a Regt. and Battalion. We are expecting Col. Lucius Davis's Regt. also.[14]

Since I wrote to you last, the flight of Time has been as swift as sometimes is the flight of Love. We have been so constantly employed that we have taken little note of the passing days. Upon a recent expedition of over 200 miles, we again foiled the enemy, though he laid every trap to catch us. We succeeded in bringing out 400 cattle.

10. The encampment was named for Allen Taylor Caperton, a resident of Union and member of the Confederate Congress.

11. Loring had commanded the Army of the Northwest until the January 1862 Romney campaign, when he made the mistake of challenging Maj. Gen. "Stonewall" Jackson's authority. Although promoted to major general, Loring was transferred to command the obscure Department of Southwest Virginia.

12. John Stuart Williams had been a Kentucky attorney who won fame leading infantry during the Mexican War. In April 1862 he received promotion to brigadier general. The majority of his Civil War service would be in the southwestern Virginia–Kentucky region.

13. On August 5, 1862, Jenkins accepted promotion to brigadier general. He left his seat in the Confederate Congress and returned to field duty.

14. Sheffey was referring to the 10th Virginia Cavalry, under Col. James Lucius Davis. The unit remained with Lee's Army of Northern Virginia.

While we were encamped at Wolf Creek Church, we were engaged in constant scouting, and skirmishes with our pickets on the river and scouting parties of the enemy were not infrequent. Our next camp was at Cross Roads, where the road from Rollingsburg and the road form Alderson's Ferry form a junction. While the Regt. was encamped there, I was with my company on picket 8 miles distant at the river. The people there are as patriotic and enthusiastic as I have known anywhere. The ladies constantly supplied our pickets with food, and more than once brought it to them from a distance of a mile or two. Some of them are beautiful, sensible and accomplished, and I have formed some pleasant acquaintances and some firm friends among them. They constantly kept us informed of the movements of the enemy, and the Yankees in consequence hated them with the most malignant hatred.

While there, I went upon a scout with 20 men in the direction of Meadow Bluff. When I had proceeded 5 or 6 miles, I met a squad of Yankees with a Flag of Truce. Lt. C. E. Hamilton from Ironton, Ohio, was in command.[15] I conducted him to Dr. Clays[16] at Alderson's Ferry, where I remained with him and his men until the next evening, when communications were received from Genl. Loring. Lt. Hamilton expressed himself highly gratified with the treatment he had received. He was a very gentlemanly and intelligent man. I had several arguments with him in which I flatter myself he was worsted. Still he professed to stick pertinaciously to his opinions.

Several things occurred while we were there to deepen my own hatred of them. Families which had been driven from the little town of Palestine opposite, by the inhuman order of the Yankee Col. Comd.,[17] were moving. Among them were Mr. & Mrs. Dyer and their two daughters, one of whom is beautiful and both interesting. Enthusiastically southern as they were, it was with pain that I saw them driven from their homes. The old man had, of course, to keep out of the way through fear of the enemy.

The women had packed all their little household wealth in an ox-wagon which a little boy was driving. Just as the team entered the ford, the wagon was overturned into the water. Almost everything was ruined. The Yankees

15. Lt. Charles E. Hambleton, a former neighbor of William H. Powell in Ironton, Ohio, was in Company B of the 2d West Virginia Cavalry.

16. Thomas G. Clay is listed in the 1860 Monroe County census as a forty-six-year-old dentist.

17. This reference is probably to Col. Eliakim P. Scammon, who was in charge of Union troops in that area. Col. Rutherford B. Hayes observed of Scammon, "The colonel is too nervous and fussy to be a good commander." Hayes, *Diary and Letters,* 2:319.

sat upon the bank and gazed upon the scene with stolid indifference. Lieut. W[illiam C.] Copenhaver (whom I had kept with me, having sent the remainder of the co. under command of Lieut. [Andrew] St. John to camp,) and I entered the stream, and by dint of hard labor succeeded in saving everything that could be saved. But bonnets and beds, silks and soft soap, laces, and dyestuffs, china-ware and hard-ware were mingled together in weeping, dripping, inseparable confusion. The whole scene was as picturesque as could well be imagined, and would have afforded a study for the artist who used to paint the back of Fisher's Comic Alamanac.[18]

The goods and chattels were at last hung upon the fences and spread upon the grass to dry. The curling, wreathing vapors were rising gallantly in the hot sunshine, and all Nature and the rest of us were rejoicing over what we regarded as a signal success; when suddenly a dark cloud came wrathfully over the hills; the windows of heaven were opened, the rains fell, and the goods were again much increased in value provided they could have been sold by weight. In sadness and despair I left the scene to ruminate over the miseries of this sublunary existence. The same evening my Yankee guests bade me farewell and I returned to camp.

The next morning at 6 o'clock we set out upon the expedition mentioned in the first portion of this epistle, crossed the river at Edgars Ferry, passed through Lewisburg and Frankford, passed on to the edge of Pocahontas, recrossed the river at Burn Ford, next morning drew up for the night on top of a mountain in Alleghany, back to White Sulphur, across to the Old Sweet next night, then to camp at Union.

A few of our cavalry had a slight skirmish with 30 of the enemy's cavalry yesterday. Nobody hurt. The enemy recently attempted another visit to Union—but failed signally. McMahan shook his fist in their faces at Packs Ferry and they "skedaddled" there. Two thousand of them crossed at Alderson's Ferry, came a short distance this side and, becoming alarmed, retreated rapidly at that point. They know that Heth is no longer in command here and that they will get a fight whenever they dare to come within striking distance of us.

Occasionally in our experience, there are occurrences, romantic as the incidents immortalized by the pens of old-time novelists and poets. Among these is the following. Six or eight weeks ago, several of the cavalry were

---

18. *Fisher's Comic Almanac,* published annually in Philadelphia, was a popular periodical of the day.

wounded in a skirmish at Johnston's on the Greenbrier River. One of them was found in a meadow with three balls through him by Miss Virginia Alderson, a noble-hearted girl of Greenbrier.[19] She had never seen or heard of him before, but he was a Southern soldier. She had him taken to a house, dressed his wounds, each of which was supposed to be mortal. Deserting her own home, she took up her abode at his bedside.

Day after day, night after night, week after week, she watched as a ministering angel there, and contrary to the expectation of all, he began to recover. He is now well, a man of handsome face, of noble form, of good head and gallant heart. And when the shrill fife and the beat of the enlivening drum, the rattle of musketry, the roar of cannon, and all the horrid notes of discordant war are heard no more in the land, Miss Alderson will become Mrs. Robinson,[20] and I intend to dance at their wedding. She has promised that I should be there, if I am in the land of the living—which, however, is doubtful.

But I weary you. Don't forget to write. Excuse this paper. I can do no better at present.

Camp Tompkins,[21] Twelve miles below Charleston Ka[nawha],
SEPTEMBER 21–22, 1862

Dear Josie,

Your letter of 6th inst. reached me here yesterday and I hasten to reply. After a circuit of more than seven hundred miles, we have reached this point conscious of having accomplished an expedition, equal if not superior in daring, endurance, and in splendid results to any that has been made during the war. I look back over it as I would over a strange dream or the memory of some wild romance with some thing of pleasure and much more of pain.

On the 24th [of August], Genl. Jenkins set out from Union in Monroe with a command consisting of about six hundred men, namely five companies of the 8th Va. Cavalry, 1st Co. A (Smyth Dragoons), Co. C (Grayson Cavalry, Capt. Richmond G. Bourn), Co. E (Border Rangers, Capt. Henry

19. The 1860 census for Greenbrier County does not list anyone named Virginia Alderson, although several families of that surname lived in the county.
20. The soldier in question was likely William Robinson of the Grayson Cavalry of Sheffey's regiment. Dickinson, *8th Virginia Cavalry,* 104.
21. Named in honor of Christopher Q. Tompkins, first colonel of the 22d Virginia Infantry.

Clay Everett), Co. H (Capt. George William Shotts [Spotts], Tazewell Troop-
ers), Co. I [Kanawha Rangers, Capt. Charles Irvine Lewis] and Co. K (Big
Sandy Rangers, Capt. Joseph Martin Ferguson); and five companies of [Wil-
liam Lowther] Jackson's (Cavalry) Battalion under command of Capt. Walter
[Waller Reed] Preston, with a detachment of artillery under command of
Lieut. Allan Fowler.

Passing through Lewisburg, the command encamped on the night of the
24th in the beautiful country between Lewisburg and Frankford. Dr. Baker[22]
and I went down to Mr. Robinson Stuart's,[23] where we were entertained as
became the whole-souled people of that portion of Virginia. Mr. Stuart has
two daughters, Miss Virginia and Miss Gussie, who vied with each other in
endeavoring to make our time pass as pleasantly as possible.

Miss Virginia is very beautiful. Her hair is of the richest, glossiest brown
and her eyes of that large, dark, lustrous, Castilian cast of which Byron
dreamed when he wrote, "I love a dark eye in woman." Her mouth is large
but finely formed, and her teeth white as any pearls that ever glistened upon
the neck of the fabled Gulnare or Nourmahal.[24] It is a treasure of gems in a
casket of carol, and in her complexion the purity of the lily is blended in
delightful harmony with the blushing freshness of the delicate rose. Then her
voice is rich and glorious, sweet, deep, musical, beyond anything I had expected to find in one so young. She is about sixteen or seventeen. There is
little enthusiasm in this description. I like the other the best. Though not
beautiful, Miss Gussie is a fine talker and a pleasant companion. We spent
two evenings there and also visited others in the neighborhood who had
treated us and our friends kindly in darker hours one year ago.

Leaving Capt. Bouldin's Co.[25] of Jackson's Battalion at that point, we set

22. Claiborne Henry Baker was surgeon of the 8th Virginia Cavalry. In May 1861 he had
enlisted at Marion as a private.

23. William Robinson Stuart had extensive land holdings in Greenbrier County. He was
also the father of six children. According to the 1850 census, the fourth sibling was Hanna
Augusta, obviously the Gussie mentioned by Sheffey. Virginia R. Stuart, the youngest of the
children, was not listed in the 1860 census because she was attending one of the private schools
in Wytheville. When Sheffey met the two sisters in the autumn of 1862, Gussie was nineteen
and Jennie fourteen years of age. See also Sheffey's letter of March 7, 1863.

24. In Lord Byron's narrative poem *Corsair,* Gulnare was queen of the harem and the most
beautiful of all the slaves in the kingdom of Seyd. Nourmahal, an Arab word meaning "The
Light of the Harem," was one of the women in the seraglio of the Caliph Harun al Raschid.
Thomas Moore highlighted Nourmahal in his poem *Lalla Rookh.*

25. Edwin Edmunds Bouldin led a company raised in Brunswick County. It later became
part of the 14th Virginia Cavalry.

out on the morning of the 26th ult. for Pocahontas. Passing Frankford, white with waving handkerchiefs and bright with the smiles of rejoicing beauty, we left the valley and the meadow, the stately homestead and the farms abounding in evidences of wealth and luxury, and found ourselves among the shadows of mountains, among glens and defiles—tangled with the wild vine and dense with the undergrowth of the wilderness. Now the journey became wearisome, and for miles no signs of life varied the deep solitude of the mountain wild. But the fertility of those mountains is remarkable, and wherever the timber and undergrowth had by any chance been cleared away, the grass grew in spontaneous luxuriance.

Camp at Sterrett's,[26] *1½ Miles below Buffalo*
Putnam Co., Va., SEPT. 22ND, 1862

We, you perceive, are incessantly upon the wing, and have very little opportunity to write. We are again thrown in advance of the infantry and will be expected to guard them as we were upon the wild banks of old Greenbrier. I shall try to give you a detailed account of our expedition through the North West, but under the circumstances will, I am afraid, fail to make it interesting.

Passing into Pocahontas, late in the evening [of August 26], in making a long descent, we came upon a scene of surprising loveliness. Attended by a cohort of clouds "all gleaming in purple and gold," the sun was going to his rest behind as sweet a valley as ever burst upon the vision of weary cavaliers in the wilderness. Its name is "The Levels," but it ought to be called *"El Fureidis"* so much is it like the beautiful valley in the novel of that name.

In the heart of "The Levels" nestles a little village, neat white and peaceful as the village in "El Fureidis," and upon a hill-side surrounded by towering poplars, and moss-grown oaks, smooth beeches—and the sweet shadows of the maple, stands a white church with yellow blinds, that reminds one of the church overlooking the village in that same strange delightful tale. Here too were pretty women glad to welcome us, and, by the roadside beyond the village in the midst of a group of girls, stood a dark eyed, dark-skinned, gypsy-looking maiden, with hair black and glossy as the raven's wing, beautiful

26. According to the 1860 Putnam County census, B. H. Sterrett was a well-to-do sixty-six-year-old farmer. On September 21 Sheffey returned to Buffalo from Charleston and resumed his recollections of the Jenkins raid on the same sheet of paper where his previous letter ended.

enough to have been the original of Rebecca, the Jewish heroine of Ivanhoe.[27] This valley is several miles in length.

Passing Hillsboro, we selected our bivouac at the western end of the valley on the banks of Mill Creek. Here we were joined by a new company which had been made up in Harrison Co. and was commanded by Capt. Annesy.[28] We had brought Enfield rifles[29] along for them, and they were soon thoroughly armed. We bade adieu to "The Levels" on the morning of the 27th and with increased members resumed our journey northward.

Now we came within the theater of the last Marlin's Bottom, a little valley stretching to the right beyond Greenbrier River & Greenbrier Bridge. We found Loring's deserted huts and broken camp-kettles, with the remains of the fortifications of Major Jackson and Genl. Edward Johnston [Johnson].[30] The position of our men at Greenbrier Bridge was a very strong one, and any amount of Yankees could have been quieted there. Now mountain after mountain exhibited evidences of old preparations for battle. At one place the timber had been cut away by Lee for two miles down a deep mountain-gorge, but he might have known that Rosecrans never would fight him there.

That night we bivouacked by the Big Springs of Elk in a valley covered with the heaviest Blue Grass. Along this valley for miles all the fencing is destroyed, but there are few cattle there, and the grass even in the woods exceeds anything I have ever seen. That night [August 27] a Lieutenant [William B. Bannister] of the Kanawha Rangers, who had that day come from Col. Imboden[31] whose command of 300 partisan rangers was near Huntersville, was sent back to him with a dispatch from Genl. Jenkins. He was fired upon by a picket of the enemy and returned to us, having made a very narrow escape. The next morning we fired off our guns, reloaded, and set out

27. In Sir Walter Scott's novel *Ivanhoe* (1819), Rebecca is the daughter of Isaac the Jew. She loves Ivanhoe, who has shown great kindness to her and her father. When Ivanhoe marries Rowena, Rebecca and her father leave England for a distant country.

28. Capt. Thomas D. Armesy's unit ultimately became Company B of the 14th Virginia Cavalry.

29. Many of Jenkins's troopers were then armed only with shotguns. *Official Records*, 12, pt. 3:951. Although the Springfield rifle was the most popular shoulder weapon in the Civil War, both sides imported large numbers of English-made .57-caliber Enfield rifles. The Enfield and Springfield were so similar in construction that their parts were interchangeable.

30. Sheffey's reference was to the November 1861 campaign where the charismatic Edward Johnson acquired the nickname "Allegheny."

31. Augusta County native John Daniel Imboden led the 1st Regiment, Virginia Partisan Rangers. It subsequently became the nucleus for the 62d Virginia Infantry.

prepared for battle. We had left Huntersville seven or eight miles to the right. Everywhere along this road stood the chimneys of burnt houses, silent witnesses of the cruelty with which the enemy had conducted their portions of the last year's campaigns.[32]

I have written enough to weary you and will close. I will write again in a day or two though I doubt that any of my letters will reach you from this point. Our skies are brightening, but our losses [elsewhere] are terrible. I regret to hear of so many casualties among the [Smyth] Grays. The Smyth Blues also suffered terribly. Capt. Gibson, I understand, was killed.[33] His family are left very desolate.

Please write as soon as you can. We are very anxious to hear now from our armies in the East. We get no papers here but Yankee papers and they are so one-sided.

> *The Jenkins Raid:* AUGUST 24–SEPTEMBER 21, 1862
> *Camp at Sterrett's 1½ Miles below Buffalo—Putnam Co., Va.,*
> *Kanawha Valley*
> SEPT. 25, 1862

Dear Josie,

I wrote to you a day or two ago, giving you an account of our expedition up to the 28th ult. I will now continue the detail, but will doubtless be interrupted before I proceed far.

Put upon our guard by the report of Lieut. Bannister of the Kanawha Rangers, we left the Big Springs of Elk on the morning of the 28th ult. prepared for battle. We now came to the waters of the beautiful Valley River and began to wind through and around the long, level meadows of Tiger's [Tygart] Valley. Ascending the Valley, a sudden turn brought us into full view of the immense fortifications behind which Rosecrans long defied the menace of Lee. This is the point from which Rosecrans made his swift but unfortunate expedition against Genl. Floyd whom he found at Carnifex's Ferry.

32. For the campaign at Huntersville and the Union destruction of property that ensued, see Stutler, *West Virginia in the Civil War*, 147–51.

33. Unfounded rumors then abounded of battle casualties. The Smyth Grays of the 50th Virginia Infantry had not been actively engaged since May. The Smyth Blues of the 4th Virginia Infantry fought in the August 28–30 battle of Second Manassas. Regimental losses were 21 men, including Capt. Andrew E. Gibson, who was killed. He is buried in Marion. Robertson, *4th Virginia Infantry*, 19, 52.

The mountains that bound this valley are rugged and precipitous. The valley, generally about a mile in width, is narrowed at the point fortified to about four hundred yards by spurs that run down from either mountain. To the tops of these spurs the timber is almost entirely cut away. Across the valley from foot to foot of the spurs extends a ditch about eight or nine feet wide and ten or twelve feet deep. A few feet behind this impassable ditch, along the top of a swell that here occurs in the bottom, a massive earthwork is thrown up extending also from mountain to mountain. Upon the top of the mountain on our right, Rosecrans had placed a number of mountain-howitzers which were afterwards captured by Lee when Rosecrans went off on his wild-goose chase after Floyd.

At the foot of the mountain on the enemy's left stood barbette batteries erected of stone and earth and wood commanding the whole valley. Upon his right, also in rear of the earthwork on a bench of this mountain fifty or sixty feet above the valley, batteries commanding every approach had been stationed, some defended by heavy earthworks, others by parapet breast-works consisting of heavy logs arranged one above the other, strengthened by braces and by large masses of earth filled in against them. Upon this side at the very extremity of the earth work stands a square, neat little white house, probably the headquarters of Genl. Rosecrans.

Passing the breastworks we found ourselves among the deserted dirty huts once occupied by the scum of Yankeedom. Moving rapidly up the valley now gradually widening, we were welcomed by the waving handkerchiefs of three ladies dressed in deep mourning upon the south side of the valley. Immediately the greeting was responded to by a loud cheer which was repeated again and again. This shouting was unfortunate, as we were now very close to the enemy. Within a few minutes our advance-guard was engaged with the picket of the enemy. The picket was routed immediately but not until they had wounded Charley Tompkins,[34] one of the General's aides, and shot the horse of Lieut. [John E.] Thompson of the Border Rangers.

The chase now became exciting, but the pickets seemed to live a charmed life. One of them was killed, one wounded and two taken prisoners. The remainder escaped.

The man killed was named Gibson.[35] After running more than a mile

34. Charles Tompkins, a civilian volunteer aide to Jenkins, was wounded in the arm. *Official Records*, 12, pt. 2:757.

35. According to Jenkins, Gibson was one of two brothers "notorious through all that section for the persecution of their loyal neighbors, guiding the Yankees through the country and exciting them to deeds of violence." Ibid.

across the valley, he stopped & fought his pursuers with the utmost despera-
tion to the last. He was in the act of shooting Genl. Jenkins when he received
his death-wound. A little girl at the picket post whose "bould soger lad" was
in danger of being taken, wrung her hands and cried in an agony and despair
but, I believe, love lent wings to her chosen one and he made good his retreat.

Our advance-guard hurried rapidly on to Huttonsville, about five miles
off. This little town had been burnt by the Yankees the week before for its
secession proclivities, and its site was now guarded by a picket of 35 or 40
men. One of these our advance guard shot in an orchard near that place &
returned with him to us. This attack upon the pickets was merely intended
as a feint to distract the attention of the enemy who, under command of
Cols. Kelley & Crook, was stationed 3000 or 4000 strong at Beverly, 15 miles
distant.[36] Therefore, Genl. Jenkins at a distance of three miles from Huttonsville reversed his column and left the squad of men at Huttonsville to rest in
peace. That night (28th) we bivouacked outside of the fortifications of Rosecrans, and if the works had only been faced the other way, we would have
awaited Kelly and his whole force behind them. It was proposed that night
but it was found impracticable to defend the works as they were against so
overwhelming a force.

Accordingly before daylight (29th) we "got out of the tall grass" of Tygart
Valley and, sending back to camp our artillery and broken down horses, we
struck across toward Upshur through the wilderness of Rich Mountain. For
hour after hour, we followed that rude bridle path. The science of the road-
makers had never been heard of in that wild region. At length an opening
appeared, and the skeleton of a cabin was to be seen among the trees, but
roofless and silent was that dwelling of the *quondam* woodsman. The inhabitants thereof belonged to the traditions of long ago. At last we came to the
castle of one who claimed to belong to the *genus homo,* but the question was
at least debatable. He told us that we had yet sixteen miles to travel before
we came to the haunts of civilized humanity.

Now down steep declivities and up precipitous ascents, among huge,
mosscovered boulders that had been hurled from the peaks by the convul-
sions of some primeval period, we wound our weary way. In His plans of
irrigation, Providence seems to have altogether overlooked this delectable
corner of this vineyard; and soon to the cooling hollows rushed man and

36. Brig. Gen. Benjamin Franklin Kelley had some fifteen hundred men posted at Beverly.
Brig. Gen. George Crook had left the region for duty with the Army of the Potomac.

horse in agony, and sought in vain for water to cool their parched tongues. Upon the beeches along the path the initials of adventurers and long past dates were carved. He who had made his way through that Godforsaken wilderness was worthy of record. Towards night we reached a cool mountain stream, one of the tributaries of the Little Kanawha. The men threw themselves upon the bank and the horses plunged their nostrils beneath the waters, and both drank like the wanderers of the desert at the springs of the oases.

Night came on—dark night in the wilderness. Losing the path, rider and horse went plunging over logs and brush, rocks & cliffs, while curses not loud but deep added to the gloomy horrors. Some built fires in the woods and rested till morning. But the most of us, finding our way to the path again & taking the tail of the horse in front with one hand & the bridle of the next horse with the other, made our way at length out of the mountains of Randolph into the fields of Upshur. In those mountains, the command lost thirteen men, but we understand that after many adventures, they have all at length made their way back to the counties of Greenbrier & Monroe.

All bright and beautiful dawned the morning of the 30th [of] August upon our simple bivouac. We had with small force invaded the lands of the enemy, and we were soon to pay the penalty or receive our reward. The latter we began to get immediately. The fields and stables we passed were now filled with splendid horses which we took without hesitation and kept without remorse. Arriving at Centreville, where a Union company was to have been organized that day, we captured twenty or thirty prisoners whom we immediately paroled. Our coming was a complete surprise and everywhere prisoners fell into our hands. Passing Centreville at a John Gilpin gait,[37] we came across a squad of Union men who opened fire upon us. Capt. [Joseph Martin] Ferguson was shot through the knee and crippled for life, but dearly did we avenge him.[38]

No one else of our men was hurt until we reached "Buckhannon," (or Buchanan), though the firing was frequent. Within a mile of Buckhannon, the 8th Va. & one or two companies of the squadron were dismounted to fight on foot. The remainder of the squadron was left on horseback. The

37. This is a reference to William Cowper's humorous ballad, *The Diverting History of John Gilpin, Showing How He Went Further Than Intended and Came Home Safe Again*. Gilpin was a poor horseman. In attempting to get to a family party some distance away, he endured a wild ride both to and from his destination.

38. Joseph Martin Ferguson was captain of Company E (the Fairview Rifle Guards) when wounded. The injury was not entirely crippling. Later in the war he returned briefly to duty before being elected to the Virginia House of Delegates. Dickinson, *8th Virginia Cavalry*, 83.

enemy, about 150 strong, had made good preparations to receive us. But we soon flanked them, and after about fifteen minutes of tolerably hot skirmishing (for them), they were in full flight. Eight or nine were killed, 36 surrendered, and the remainder escaped.[39] Lt. Col. Cook of our Regt. was badly wounded and we were compelled to leave him & Capt. Ferguson at Buckhannon.[40] One of my men was wounded, but I succeeded in bringing him through, and he is now almost well or was when I started him home. One other man was wounded slightly and that comprised our loss. Col. Cook's horse was shot, and he himself was shot as soon as he got off the horse.

The remainder of the day was employed in destroying stores & arms which, to the value of more than a million of dollars, had fallen into our hands. We destroyed 5,500 stand of Enfield Rifles, 1,000,000 rounds [of] Enfield Cartridges (i.e., 1,000 boxes), and more than 100 fine wagons & ambulances. We took a splendid brass six pounder. The amount of clothing appropriated or destroyed may be imagined when I tell you that besides numerous stores in the town, the immense Court-house of four stories was packed, jammed & crammed from basement to belfry with everything a soldier's heart could wish. We poured out of the commissary depots, coffee, sugar, rice, hominy, molasses, etc., until the mixed mass was almost knee-deep in the street for a considerable distance, and we allowed the people to carry off whatever they needed in the commissary line.[41]

I can write no more at present. Please write to me as soon as possible.

Camp at Ruffners,[42] One Mile Below Red House, Putnam Co., Va.
OCT. 5TH, 1862

I will take advantage of a few leisure moments this morning to write to you again; as I have but a few drops of ink, you will excuse scribbling, blots, etc.

39. In the action at Buckhannon against what Jenkins called "the Lincolnite bushwhackers, or Home Guard," the Confederates inflicted casualties of 12–15 killed or wounded plus 20 captured (including the captain in charge of the post). *Official Records,* 12, pt. 2:758–59.

40. Colonel Cook was shot in the thigh. The wound was severe but not mortal.

41. Jenkins reported, "On taking possession of the town we commenced the work of destruction, at which the whole command labored assiduously until midnight." *Official Records,* 12, pt. 2:759.

42. The 1860 census lists fifty-year-old G. Ruffner as one of the most prosperous farmers in the county.

We are encamped at Sterrett's one and a half miles below Buffalo,[43] from which camp I wrote to you last, from Sept. 21st to Oct. 1st. On the 20th, ult., our picket at the mouth of Eighteen, about five miles below camp, was surprised. One was killed, one wounded and one taken prisoner.[44]

Last Saturday morning, Sept. 28th about day-break, I was standing at Sterrett's gate listening to distant firing in the direction of our lower picket. After awhile, a fellow appeared down the road jogging along at a snail's pace. In course of time he came to where I was standing. He was about to pass me when as sudden notion struck him and checking up his *rosinate*[45] he said with slow, measured tones, "Yer would better be siftin. The pickets is gone up, all but me, and the Yankees is comin."

There was fortunately a heavy fog. The Yankees opened fire almost immediately upon [Maj. George] Jackson's squadron, now the 14th Cavalry. They came in on one side of the field in which we were encamped as we went out upon the other. I was thrown in the rear, and we then, as we had only about 300 men, retreated slowly 2½ miles up the valley to a point one mile above Buffalo. I was then sent back with my company and a piece of artillery under command of Major [James W.] Sweeny to check the advance. We went back through Buffalo and crossing a bridge over a creek found ourselves within 75 yards of their advance. We could not then see further than that on account of the fog.

We immediately opened upon them with the howitzer, and they upon us with their rifles. A couple of shell[s] thrown amongst them, however, made them as silent as the grave. But they were busily engaged in flanking, and we fell back about 50 yards to this side of the bridge. From this point we shelled them again. Throwing out our scouts into the fog to give us notice of their flank movements, we fell back slowly to the upper end of the town, about 300 yards from the bridge.

43. Buffalo is alongside the Kanawha River, midway between Charleston and the Ohio state line at Point Pleasant.

44. Sheffey omitted any reference to the September 26–27 action in which the 91st Ohio Infantry drove a portion of Jenkins's cavalry "panic stricken" across the Kanawha River near Buffalo. If the Ohio regiment had received expected support, Col. John A. Turley later stated, the expedition "would doubtless have accomplished all that [was] desired, even to the capturing of Brigadier-General Jenkins and his entire force, as he slept in a private residence in Buffalo on the night previous." *Official Records*, 19, pt. 2:6–7.

45. Rocinante was the bony mount of Don Quixote, the famous hero of the novel by Cervantes.

Here I was standing upon the bank of the river when a skiff with two rangers in it shot out from the opposite bank. They had nearly crossed to where I was, when the Yankees saw them & poured in a terrific fire upon them. The two soldiers immediately pulled for the bank from which they had started and reached it through a tempest of balls without injury. By this time the Yankees were within 100 yards of me, though they did not see me. For the next half mile, we "skedaddled" at a gallop, and at length came up to our main body, which was by this time in good fighting humor. We now prepared for fight[ing] in good earnest, planting our two little pieces of artillery, and throwing up some rail breastworks. We awaited the onset.

But the Yankees were now schooled to caution, and the onset did not come. After we had lain in wait about an hour, the 36th & 60th Regts. came from Winfield, 9 miles, double-quick to our assistance. We now assumed the offensive and advanced with thundering artillery and such hostile demonstrations that the Yankees fled in the utmost consternation. Unfortunately, the cavalry had been dismounted to fight on foot, and we consequently could not pursue them more than two or three miles. The force of the enemy was 1756 men, consisting of two regts. of inf., one of 600, the other of 800 men, and a regt. of cavalry of 356 men.[46] Our force after the 36th & 60th came did not amount to more than 1500 men. But we gave them such a fright that we have not been troubled since by them.

The next day, Sunday, we brought 60,000 lbs. [of] Bacon up the river and scouted to within five miles of Pt. Pleasant. We are now 8 miles above Buffalo and about a mile below Red House Shoals, which are opposite Winfield, the county seat of Putnam.

I wish I could have given you a detail of our expedition through the northwest, as it was full of incident, but I will not have time to give you more than a general outline. I gave you in my last letter, an account of it up to the taking of Buckhannon Aug. 30th.

After completing the work of destruction at Buckhannon, we set out upon the night of the 30th Aug. Three shots were fired at us that night by bushwhackers. The next morning we stormed Weston, the shire town of Lewis Co. at daylight but met with little resistance. Paroling our prisoners and destroying the tents and stores at Weston, we set out on the evening of the 31st for the Ohio. The Yankees were preparing for us at Clarksburg and Parkersburg, but we chose another and to them altogether unexpected route.

46. The *Official Records* contain no mention of a Union force of that size operating in the Buffalo area.

We struck across into Calhoun and through the insignificant little town of Arnoldsburg. Here we found a singular fortification in the shape of a square, upon the top of a round hill, built with logs and stakes & a parapet breastwork strengthened by palisades. But it was like a "banquet hall deserted" in one respect, viz, that it had no one in it. That night we jogged along through thunder, lightning and in rain till late, then bivouacked in the very playground of the storm. Supperless, shelterless, we lay down in a bottom and the waters arose around us as they did around the heathen in the moist old days of Noah.

The next morning, Sept. 1st, we dashed forward to attack a body of the enemy at Glenville in Gilmer Co. We found them strongly posted upon a hill near Glenville, but after firing 30 or 40 shots they took to their heels and left us in a peaceable possession. We remained at Glenville till evening, then crossing the Little Kanawha which runs through the town, we went our way. After traveling nearly all night and setting out at sunrise in the morning, Sept. 2, we sat down before Spencer, the county seat of Roane, and demanded its surrender.

The cowardly Col. Rathbone, who was in command of the post with a force of 300 well-armed men sufficient with their position to have slain half of us, surrendered unconditionally.[47] Seventy odd of his men ran away. We paroled 218 besides Col., Lt. Col. and Major. The celebrated Snake-Hunters, whom our men had fought from Cheat Mountain to the Ohio—now reduced to 45—were among the number, and bitterly did they curse their cowardly colonel. Here we destroyed a large number of guns, tents, commissary and Q[uarter] Master Stores.

The next morning, Sept. 3, we set out with the Yankees for Ripley in Jackson Co. Here we met with no opposition—captured some prisoners among whom was a Qr. Master with $7000—Yankee money, so that we had plenty

---

47. Few actions of the Civil War were more lopsided than the "engagement" at Glenville in Gilmer County. Five companies of the 11th West Virginia Infantry were stationed there when Jenkins's men approached. The Federals "fled after a single fire" without so much as a single shot in reply. *Official Records,* 12, pt. 2:759, 764. Union general Jacob Cox, commanding the District of West Virginia, was livid. "The whole affair was a burlesque upon military operations, without one redeeming factor," he declared. Ibid., 762–63. Col. John C. Rathbone and Maj. George C. Trimble of the 11th West Virginia were dismissed from the service "for cowardly conduct." See *West Virginia History* 23 (1962): 205–18, 269–81. Lt. Col. Daniel Frost took command of the regiment and led the unit gallantly until his death in July 1864 at the battle of Snicker's Ferry. Theodore Lang, *Loyal West Virginia from 1861 to 1865* (Baltimore, 1895), 278.

of "Green Backs."[48] The Yankees quartered that night in the Ct. House at Ripley. The next morning we dashed on toward Ravenswood at a regular sweeping Jehu charge. But the Yankees, of whom there were about 250 there, were too quick for us, and most of them got across the Ohio. The rest we captured.[49]

From the Ohio side, they kept up a constant fire upon us for awhile, but we soon made them run back among the hills. By this time we were clothed splendidly & fed sumptuously. All day, while we remained in Ravenswood, the Yankees kept up a fire upon us from the Ohio hills. One of our men was wounded quite seriously. Accordingly, we determined to drive them from their position. Flushed with victory, fat & hearty, we were conceited enough to attempt anything, so we bade farewell to our 200 or 300 Yankee Prisoners, who by this time had got to Ravenswood and started to ford down the river.

The General, with Capt. Preston's command, and Capt. R[ichmond] G. Bournes, Capt. G. W. Spott's and my companies of this Regt., crossed. One of Capt. Armersy's men drowned in the crossing.[50]

The remainder of the Regt. was ordered down the river on this side under command of Col. Corns. He was bushwhacked the whole night and got lost besides. But we, the invaders, with colors flying, marched through the land of the Philistines in triumphal procession.[51] The Yankees who had been shooting at us from the Ohio hills, fled as soon as we entered the water, so that we were not troubled by them.[52]

Ohio is a beautiful land, and well is the river that rolls there, called *"La Belle Riviere."* Now along the splendid turnpikes of Miegs[53] we cantered gleefully. On every side were the evidences of prosperity and affluence. The elegant mansions, the wildernesses of corn, the immense wheat-ricks, the

48. Jenkins placed the amount of money confiscated at $5,525. *Official Records*, 12, pt. 2:759.

49. For more on this action, see "War-Time Reminiscences of James D. Sedinger," 64.

50. B. F. Romme had enlisted in the Confederate army only ten days earlier when he drowned in the Ohio River. Nelson Harris, *17th Virginia Cavalry* (Lynchburg, Va., 1994), 82.

51. In the times of Samson, David, and other Old Testament heroes, the Philistines were the inveterate enemies of the Israelites.

52. Jenkins wrote of the Ohio River crossing: "In a short time all were over, and in a few minutes the command was formed on the crest of a gentle eminence and the banners of the Southern Confederacy floated proudly over the soil of our invaders. As our flag was unfurled in the splendors of an evening, cheers upon cheers arose from the men and their enthusiasm was excited to the highest pitch." *Official Records*, 12, pt. 2:760.

53. Return Jonathan Meigs Jr. was a leader in the building of post roads and turnpikes in Ohio. He also served as state governor and U.S. senator.

tremendous oat-stacks, and the barns crammed with the golden treasures of harvest, all told us how little that country had suffered from fire or sword or any of the "dogs of war."

The meadows were filled with heavy cattle and with horses sinewy, symmetrical, beautiful as Arabians. The exciting chases after the latter, for we took them wherever we could catch—they were wild as Irving's hunt after the untamed steeds of the prairie.[54] Best of all, the women waved their handkerchiefs and shouted "Hurrah for Jef."

A little before midnight, we reached the town of Racine. Here our advanced guard killed two Yankees & took five prisoners. One of our men was dangerously wounded. A little after midnight [September 5] we recrossed the Ohio at Racine. This at least no other Southern troops have done. The wildness of this rough crossing was heightened by the occasional flash of an Enfield on the Ohio bank, and the singing of the ball as it whistled over our heads, or skipped across the waters. They were very careful not to fire at us until all our men were in the water. Passing Letart, we went into a field, fed and slept [until] 3 o'clock AM Sept. 5.

At about 8 ocl., we set out again and met Col. Corns towards evening. We were now in Mason Co. At Pt. Pleasant, a heavy force was awaiting us. Dashing on to within 8 miles of the Point, near enough to put the blue watchdogs there into a regular furore, we whipped to the left, and swept down [to the] thirteen helter skelter, pell-mell.[55] At 9 ocl. we were at the Mouth of Thirteen on Kanawha, a creek so called because the mouth of it is 13 miles from the mouth of Kanawha at Pt. Pleasant. The next day we came to Buffalo. I will not trouble you with a further account, tho' the remainder of the expedition is as full of incident & much more hardship than the other.

Leaving Buffalo, we crossed the Kanawha—in which crossing I narrowly escaped drowning—and swept across the mountains to Jenkins' Farm on the Ohio, thence down the river thro' a raining fire from the Ohio side to Barbourville,[56] thence to Wayne Ct. House, thence up Twelve Pole and down

54. Sheffey was referring to Washington Irving's autobiographical work, *A Tour of the Prairies* (1835).

55. No Confederate attack was made on Point Pleasant. Jenkins explained why. "The enemy was in force superior to my own, but his troops were green, and I felt confident I could drive him from the field; but I know that seeking shelter, as he would, in the large court-house and other solid edifices in which the country abounds, I could not dislodge him from these without artillery. Unfortunately, I had none." *Official Records,* 12, pt. 2:761.

56. The 8th Virginia Cavalry galloped into Barboursville with guns blazing on a Sunday morning. A member of the regiment noted that a service was taking place at the Methodist church. "Three or four bullets struck the building. The preacher did not have to dismiss the

Fourteen into Logan, thence into Wyoming, thence on to the Marsh Fork of Coal in Raleigh, thence down Coal about 60 miles to Peytona, thence across to Malden, & Brownstown, thence down to Charleston & via Camp Tompkins & Coal Mouth to Buffalo, to which place we returned Sept. 21.

I have now given you a summary of our expedition. Our whole loss amounted to only about ten men wounded. We also lost about 500 horses. We captured about 700 horses & very nearly $2,000,000 worth of ordinance, commissary & Qr. Master Stores. We brought out about 600 recruits and paroled about 500 prisoners.[57]

> *Col. Alderson's,*[58] *Greenbrier Co., Va.*
> Nov. 8, 1862

Dear Josie,

I received your last letter while yet in Kanawha Valley. The Valley is now in possession of the enemy. We had several skirmishes with the enemy in the valley.[59] In all but one of them, the Cavalry only were engaged. None of them were of much importance. The cavalry is now scattered over Greenbrier and men and horses are suffering very much.[60] It is supposed that we will winter at Salem, one thing is certain, that we cannot winter here.

I have been thinking somewhat of coming home soon, but that will depend upon what conclusions you have come to. The time for our marriage

---

congregation. It was found getting towards home as fast as they could possibly go without waiting for the benediction." "War-Time Reminiscences of James D. Sedinger," 65.

57. Officially Jenkins and his 500 horsemen killed, wounded, or dispersed some 1,000 Federals, captured 300 horses, and destroyed a cannon, 5,000 stands of small arms, plus immense stores that could not be taken back to Confederate lines. While the raid did not "reclaim to the Government about 40,000 square miles," as General Loring asserted, Jenkins's foray did show how vulnerable the future state of West Virginia was to Confederate incursions. *Official Records*, 12, pt. 2:756.

58. John Marshall Alderson, listed in the 1860 census as a forty-six-year-old farmer, was one of the wealthiest men in Greenbrier County.

59. For typical cavalry movements taking place in the northwestern counties of Virginia at the time, see *Official Records*, 12, pt. 2:9, 463, 530, 635, 661, 685, 690.

60. In November 1862 Brig. Gen. John S. Williams took temporary command of the Confederate Department of Western Virginia. From Narrows on November 19 he wrote the War Department: "The army is little better than a mob, the country almost a desert, and the business departments require a complete overhauling. I found General Jenkins' mounted men at Lewisburg in a perfect state of chaos, but the general is not to blame, as he had no chance to organize or discipline his men." Williams added that 4,869 men were present for duty, while 2,707 were absent with or without leave. Ibid., 21:1024.

has long since passed and yet we draw no nigher to the end of this indefiniteness. Why not put an end to it at once? It is the most unsatisfactory relation that can exist between man & woman. Will you not marry me if I come home this winter? If so when shall I come? If not—but I need not look to the other side of the question.

Present my kindest regards to all. Answer the above questions as soon as possible please and believe me as ever, Yours.

Camp Stuart, Nov. 25, 1862

J. P. Sheffey, Captain of Co A, 8th Va Cavalry, Jenkins Brigade is hereby granted a leave of absence for Thirty Days beginning on the 1st Day of December 1862 and ending January 1st 1863. At which time he is expected and required to report himself to the regt. for service.

Approved:
Thomas P. Bowen
Major, Comdg.
8th Va. Cavalry

CHAPTER 6

OBSERVATIONS FROM CAMP

Dull and quiet duty occupied the next several months for Sheffey. He and the 8th Virginia Cavalry divided their time on picket at Newbern, Central Depot (present-day Radford), and back again at Lewisburg. The captain now began making acquaintances with the region's prominent Confederate generals: Samuel Jones, John Echols, John McCausland, and Gabriel C. Wharton.

Sheffey achieved a major personal triumph during this period: he secured a wife. In letters to Josie Spiller, he had continued describing the beautiful young ladies he was meeting on his travels. If this was not an ongoing effort to exert marital pressure on his fiancée, it gave every indication of being so. On June 9, 1863 (the day the Western Hemisphere's largest cavalry battle was fought two hundred miles to the east at Brandy Station), John Preston Sheffey and Josephine Spiller were married.

The 8th Virginia Cavalry remained in the southwestern Virginia area. Isolated from the major military theaters, Sheffey could only speculate on the big picture of the Civil War. For the first time he began to feel pangs of anxiety. He wrote of the prospects for peace and the fallacies of conscription. Comments on skirmishes, friends, and compatriots became more serious. Sheffey began expressing concerns to his bride about Union successes in Pennsylvania, Maryland, and Mississippi. Then, almost without warning, a Union threat appeared in Sheffey's own backyard.

> *Marion, Va.*
> DEC. 26TH, 1862

Dear Josie,

Your kind letter announcing your determination to seek refuge in Montgomery [County] was received and read with that delight with which your letters are always welcomed.

On the morning after you went to Montgomery, I set out for Bedford with Col. Peters[1] He is still unable to straighten his leg but is otherwise quite well.

---

1. Largely because of his crippling wound, William E. Peters had been dropped as lieutenant colonel of the 45th Virginia Infantry in the May 1862 reorganization of the regiment. A few

We made the trip safely, and I spent the 24th at Dale-Carlia, the residence of the Col.'s mother.[2] It is his patrimony, and quite a magnificent estate. The house is old, but commodious and filled up with much neatness and elegance. Old trees adorn the spacious yard, and it would be a delightful residence for a poet or a dreamer or anyone who loves the *otium cum dignitate.* "In the calm evenings mild and sweet," he could be happy under those old trees as the ancient Tityre under the shade of his wide-spreading beach."[3]

I returned to Marion yesterday to prepare for removing my company to the regiment. I was not aware when I saw you last that our Regt. would winter at the Central.[4] I am glad of it, however, as it will afford me an opportunity of being near you again and you an opportunity of becoming acquainted with the wild scatter-brains of the 8th—if you desire such an exalted privilege.

I will be with my Regt. on the 5th or 6th of January. I have not seen much Christmas yet. One or two of my men have taken wives but I was not at the weddings. I spend my time at home among books, but I have a great disposition toward vagrancy. I may take a flying trip to some tumultuous quarter of the globe yet before I return to my Regt., but it isn't probable.

The prospects for peace are more flattering now than they have ever been, but we will not yet gain it without hard fighting. The ball is still rolling, and though it will run slower, it will not pause until the explosive force which gave it its impetus is completely exhausted. I am not sanguine as most men about anything.

Goodbye. Write to me as soon as possible. I am never really content except when I am near you, or reading one of your letters. Time flies very sadly and slowly, and I sometimes dread that he will break down entirely ere he brings me to that goal of perfect happiness of which I have often dreamed. He whose happiness is in Hope, is little better than one of the miserable.

---

months later he became colonel of the 2d Virginia State Line. This regiment, one-third infantry and two-thirds cavalry, had the primary responsibilities of recovering the western part of Virginia under Union control and of protecting the salt works in that region. Peters was wounded three times during the war. Undated newspaper clipping, John Preston Sheffey Papers, Virginia Tech, Blacksburg.

2. Elisha and Cynthia Turner Peters were the parents of Colonel Peters. The father had died sometime in the 1860–62 period. The family landholdings were among the largest in Bedford County.

3. "Tityrus" is a poetical surname for a shepherd. It appears in Greek idylls and works by Virgil and Spenser.

4. Central Depot is now Radford, Virginia.

Marion, FEB. 11TH, 1863

My own dear brother,[5]

I intended writing yesterday, by John, but as usual we had company until the last hour, which compelled me to defer that pleasure until today. The Board of Exemption composed of Dr. [James Preston] Hammet,[6] Major Terry, Lieutenant A. Moore[7] and Mr. McGavock[8] has by Pa's invitation made our house headquarters, and we have enjoyed the visit very much indeed.

I do not think I ever met with a more agreeable gentleman than Dr. Hammet, one who conversed more fluently upon every subject, or one who came up so nearly to my idea of a real Virginia gentleman. He is very much like our Preston uncles in manner, appearance and to a certain extent disposition, though I think his is much more gentle and pleasant than theirs. Ma and Pa could scarcely resist his eloquent entreaties to allow us to go down to the Central; he refuted all their arguments by a single word and it was not until we came to their assistance with Miss Flora McFlimsey's[9] unanswerable plaint, that he would listen to reason at all. He offered us every inducement to go.

The pleasure of seeing and being with our dear brother, various little rides and excursions he would plan, and a regular *romp* at his house, besides a number of other agreeable pastimes, all of which he urged with all the eloquence of which he was master. Ma and Pa promised him that we should certainly go whenever the blockade should be raised. The whole party went to Abingdon on yesterday evening's train, where they expect to remain until Sunday.

The "Conscript-Fathers"[10] have almost depopulated our country since

5. Ellen White Sheffey was eighteen when she wrote her brother. The letter is included here because of the views it provides of Captain Sheffey's home front.

6. James Preston Hammet was a physician and farmer in Montgomery County.

7. The lieutenant was likely Andrew Moore, an attorney who served briefly in both the 22d Virginia Infantry and Imboden's partisan rangers. After the war Moore made his home in Pulaski. Terry D. Lowry, *22d Virginia Infantry* (Lynchburg, Va., 1988), 178.

8. Major Terry of the 4th Virginia Infantry was recuperating at Wytheville from a battle wound received the previous summer. Ephraim McGavock was one of Wythe County's most influential citizens.

9. Flora McFlimsey was the heroine of William Allen Butler's humorous 1857 poem, *Nothing to Wear*. The work recounts the subject's three journeys to Paris for continuous rounds of shopping. Each trip proved fruitless.

10. In mid-April 1862 the Confederate Congress enacted the first national conscription measure in the history of English-speaking peoples. A series of exemption acts passed steadily

their appearance and have lengthened considerably some visages not very pleasant before but which are now hideously elongated. Pa's overseer at the "Bowen Farm" was exempted, much to the relief of both persons interested. The only way in which Pa could get him off was to promise to make him general overseer of his negroes and stock.

Jesse Roland[11] was sent off rejoicing, although the reasons for exempting him were of a most uncomplimentary nature, the first being that he was mentally inept for military duty. The opinion of all, as expressed to us, was that he was constitutionally a coward. Jesse doesn't care, though, what the reasons were for releasing him just so he can remain at home and take care of his "fambly."

There is a perfect dearth of news now and nothing of interest from the United States except Vallandigham's speech,[12] which is exciting much attention both North and South. Major Terry had a *Cincinnati Enquirer* here with him which contained the speech in full, with many interesting comments upon it. It is evidently creating great excitement in the North and will ultimately render Vallandigham the greatest of men in that section. He has been the most conservative and consistent man in the North, and his speech indicates a mind of the highest order, richly stored, and a heart whose every throb is a desire for the good of the South as well as the North.

His mistake is his blind adherence to the thought that peace will be the signal for the return of the seceded States to their allegiance and his idea evidently is that the North will have the power of proposing the terms of peace. Wait, Mr. Vallandigham, there are a few things you do not know yet, though I think you will soon be able to see a little farther in advance of you than you do now! I think his influences will tell greatly upon the future course of the North, and his speech will assist in hastening the revolution which is just beginning in Abraham's home.

I hope the contents of the box we sent by John will keep you off the starv-

---

thereafter provoked loud outcries from those who did not qualify. The forcible drafting of men into the Southern armies produced far more discontent than reliable soldiers.

11. No such person is listed in the 1860 Smyth County census. Sheffey may have been referring to Philip J. Rolen, then an eighteen-year-old laborer.

12. Ohio congressman Clement Laird Vallandigham was the leader of the Northern Peace Democrats (contemptuously dubbed "Copperheads"). In a January 14, 1863, speech to the House of Representatives, he warned that a prolongation of the Civil War could lead to a merger between the Midwest and the South. The time was critical and opportune, Vallandigham said, for a negotiated peace.

ing list until we are able to get something out of which we can make up a nicer box. Eggs, butter and sugar have become very scarce, but we hope to get a new supply soon. Brother Willie [Peters] is at home now, very impatient to take command of his regiment again but still too lame to go to camp. He has had a very high heel put on his boot and we have been begging him to have it taken off. Dr. Cleaves[13] told him that he must do it or be permanently disabled.

We scan the papers eagerly every day for Christopher Waife's[14] reappearance and hope to greet him soon again. The "White Eagle" was beautiful. The "Southern Illustrated" could be *improved* without any injury to its popularity. All send much love. Write as soon as possible.

Your own loving
Nellie

Camp Radford,[15] *Va.*
FEBRUARY 15, 1863

Miss Josie,

I am very glad to learn that you are better this morning. I send some sugar, (not very good but the best I have) by John, which I promised last night to Willie. Tell Will, whenever he is hard run for *"sweet-nin,"* to apply to me and I will supply him.

I extended an invitation last night to Mrs. Hammet,[16] Miss Lucy [Spiller] and through them to all my other lady friends in this section to dine with me tomorrow. On consultation with my *aide-de-camp,* John, I find that the said invitation is impolitic, and it is hereby respectfully rescinded. The fact is that John is something like Caleb Bolderstone, the old butler of Wolf's Crag, in the "Bride of Lammermoor,"[17] willing to resort to almost any means to prevent the poverty of his establishment from becoming manifest. Mrs. Hammet

13. Surgeon Samuel Crockett Cleaves of the 45th Virginia Infantry was then on duty at the military hospital in Dublin.

14. Christopher Waife was a journalist whose writings included "White Eagle."

15. Dr. John B. Radford was one of the most prominent citizens of Central Depot, a railroad town founded in 1856. When Central underwent incorporation as a city in 1892, its name was changed to present-day Radford.

16. The 1860 Virginia census lists the physician's wife as "C. Markham Hammet."

17. Sir Walter Scott's 1819 historical novel, *Bride of Lammermoor,* is the story of two lovers who, their marriage plans ruined, each die tragically.

indeed promised me a turkey in the event of the aforesaid dining, but as that is effectually prevented by *John's* arguments, I hope the *bird* will remain in *status quo*. (I was just about to write *poor bird* from sympathy but was afraid it might be construed to have reference to a want of fatty matter.) *I don't like turkey*. Besides, the Bedfellows here would gobble at me for a week if I were to receive so munificent a gift. Such would be the result of envy. I am surprised at my own impudence, but hope I shall be foregiven.

I trust that you will soon be well.

Camp Radford, near Central Depot, Va.
MARCH 7TH, 1863

Dear Josie,

I returned yesterday morning from Newbern, that delightful city set upon a hill within whose precincts I had been "dancing attendance" for nearly a week as witness before a general Court Martial. It is indeed a delectable place, for its people seem to be in a worse condition even than Miss Flora McFlimsey for they complain that they have "nothing to eat." While there I met for the first time our Major General,[18] though I had indeed seen him before. He is about 45 or 50 years of age, I should think, about 5 ft., 10 inches in height, slightly built, light hair & sandy moustache and whiskers. His expression is care-worn, and colorless. He is said to have distinguished himself by his bravery at the first battle of Manassas, and as he is a sensible man and understands his business, it is a pity for him that he should have been sent to this great western burial ground of military chieftains.

Before I went to Newbern, we had a review of our Regt. at which Col W. H. Jenifer, Major Widney,[19] & Lt. Col. Wm. Mumford[20] and Dr. Hammet were present. We did remarkably well and were highly complimented by the

18. Maj. Gen. Samuel Jones was an 1841 graduate of West Point and former instructor at the U.S. Military Academy. He won fame at First Manassas while chief of artillery under Gen. P. G. T. Beauregard. Jones's Civil War service thereafter was in overseeing departments and districts. In December 1862 he was appointed commander of the Department of Western Virginia. Sheffey would acquire an increasing dislike of the general.

19. C. T. Widney served as an aide and a surgeon before his assignment as major of the 37th Virginia Cavalry.

20. William Mumford had formerly been lieutenant colonel of the 24th Virginia Infantry but was dropped from the ranks after what Maj. Gen. Jubal Early termed excessive absences without leave while "laboring under the effects of intemperance." Krick, *Lee's Colonels*, 244. At the time of Sheffey's letter, Mumford held neither rank nor a command.

visiting officer, but some stultified fellow in the Regt. ruined the whole thing by publishing a fulsome account of the review in the Lynchburg Republican. The account, I understood, for I did not read it, was highly eulogistic and ventured the opinion that this remarkable regiment was the equal of Napoleon's Old Guard,[21] or something after that fashion. It was written, I have been told, by a Mr. Lewis in the Kanawha Rangers.[22]

At Newbern I met Mrs. Tiffany, the dashing widow from Union. She was surrounded as usual, by a host of admirers, "one of whom I was which," as a matter of course, since I have a *fondness* for widows. She introduced me to another young madam, the widow of Dr. Withers of worthy memory.[23] I spent two very pleasant evenings at her father's, Mr. Alexander's.[24] Had it not been for the kindness of these people, I should have been possessed with "Caerulean demons" worse than old Legion during my stay at Newbern.[25]

The Court Martial was composed of Cols. Norris,[26] Moore,[27] and Rust.[28] Col. Norris is a distinguished lawyer from Maryland. All three are very gentlemanly and very kind except to the Judge Advocate, Capt. Wall from Kentucky,[29] who, being slow and not well-suited to his position, seemed to be *the* object of their pique, and regarded by them as at all times a proper subject

21. Napoleon Bonaparte won his greatest empirical victories with his Old Guard, consisting of the forces of Marshals Ney, Davout, Murat, and others. The army's exploits not only maintained Napoleon's reign but also made him a living legend.

22. Four soldiers named Lewis were in Company I (Kanawha Rangers) of the 8th Virginia Cavalry.

23. Robert W. Withers was a farmer and physician in Campbell County prior to his family moving to southwestern Virginia. His wife was Susan Dabney Alexander.

24. It was fitting that Jabin B. Alexander was listed first on the 1860 Pulaski County census. This farmer had assets of $100,000, a gigantic sum in that day.

25. In Lord Byron's 1818–23 satire on English society, *Don Juan,* he writes in Canto 4: "Oh ye, who make the fortunes of all books, / Benign ceruleans of the second sex! / Who advertise new poems by your looks, / Your imprimatur will ye not annex?"

26. William Henry Norris was a prominent Baltimore attorney who became a colonel and judge advocate in the Confederate army.

27. An Irish immigrant and successful Richmond merchant, Patrick Theodore Moore was colonel of the 1st Virginia Infantry until severely wounded at First Manassas. He resigned from field service in April 1862 and for a period thereafter served as presiding judge of courts-martial in Samuel Jones's department. See *Official Records,* ser. 4, 2:248.

28. Armistead Thomson Mason Rust, a native of Loudoun County, graduated from West Point and was the first colonel of the 19th Virginia Infantry. He was not reelected in the spring 1862 reorganization. On December 20, 1862, he became a judge advocate in the Department of Western Virginia.

29. The 1860 census for Kenton County, Kentucky (directly across the Ohio River from Cincinnati), lists Garrett S. Wall as a forty-year-old attorney. On the same date that Rust re-

for their sarcasm. I felt sympathy for him as he is a very clever man, and would now be a match for the best of them, if he were what he seems once to have been. But he is a wreck physically, and perhaps mentally. His exposure during his escape from Island No. 10[30] was, he told me, the cause of it.

I was thrown frequently in company with Mr. Wysor,[31] whom I found to be a much more pleasant companion than I had ever imagined him to be. He is a man of wonderful information, but he resorts as often to sophistry as to reason to bring on his conclusions. This is not from want of depth but from love of debate. It is the characteristic of most old lawyers. The quaintness of some of his ideas added not a little to the interest with which I listened to some of his conversations. He seems, like Patrick Henry, to have studied men rather than books, and is delighted to sit or stand in a barroom and hold forth to a gaping auditory.

He ventured the opinion, groundless I think, that within 3 weeks we would be recognized by France, and that this war would eventuate in a general war between England and the North on one hand, and France, the South, Mexico, and Spain on the other. That would give us a strong hand and, I think, would be sufficient to bluff John Bull and Jonathan.[32] Though he believes in recognition by France, he does not believe in speedy peace. There I am with him. "Gentlemen may cry, Peace, Peace, but there will be no peace,"[33] until many more of us have learned, like stormy petrels, to love the billows and breakers and make ourselves at home in the midst of the tempest. Our soldiery can do that already if the government will see to it that we do not starve.

---

ceived his appointment, Captain Wall was assigned as a judge advocate. Joseph H. Crute Jr., *Confederate Staff Officers* (Powhatan, Va., 1982), 107.

30. Confederates had fortified Island No. 10 in the Mississippi where the river made a sweeping curve above New Madrid, Missouri. On April 8, 1862, a combined force of Union gunboats and troops seized the island and its seven-thousand-man garrison.

31. Benjamin Franklin Wysor was commonwealth attorney for Pulaski County and one of the area's most influential figures. He had represented the county in the Virginia State Convention, where he voted for secession. William H. Gaines Jr., *Biographical Register of Members, Virginia State Convention* (Richmond, Va., 1961), 83.

32. John Bull is the national nickname for Great Britain. Once during the American Revolution, George Washington was in need of ammunition. None of his officer had a practical suggestion. "We must consult Brother Jonathan," Washington then said, with reference to Connecticut governor Jonathan Trumbull. "Brother Jonathan" has become a cognomen for the United States.

33. Sheffey was quoting Patrick Henry from a 1775 speech. Henry extracted the phrase from Jeremiah 6:14.

I understand that with *tableaux, et cetera* you are having a gay time in Wytheville. I suppose Miss Lucy has given up her Quixotic expedition to Charleston. How do you like Miss Jennie Stuart, or have you become acquainted with her? We are told you have a formidable array of beauty in your college this session.[34] I doubt whether it holds any "gem of purer ray serene," or any young lady of more sweetness and *naivete,* than this same Miss Jennie Stuart. She reminds me of the bonnie Katie Stewart of the old Blackenod tale, who grew up so artless and sweet by thy burn of Klellie, and watched so long and anxiously for the coming of Willie Morrison.[35] But you have not read the tale, I think, and your opinion of Miss Stewart will not perhaps coincide with mine. But Dr. C. H. Baker's does and he is *more* interested than you and I. I look upon these girls and widows from a disinterested standpoint, yet with the eye of one who thinks he is *a* connoisseur. (How vain, how foolish, how fallible is man!) None of them comes up to my standard save one, and she . . .

I am going up to Dr Radford's this evening.[36] The two younger ladies have come home. Miss Nannie [Radford] is over at Rockfort. We also are to have tableaux *ad infinitum,* I hope not *ad nauseam.*

P.S. I would have finished the sentence above but I have already told you too often. Are you not going to invite me to Wytheville?

> *Camp Radford, Va.*
> MARCH 27, 1863

Dear Josie,

Your letter was received this morning and I cannot perhaps better employ a portion of this day set apart for good thoughts and deeds than in writing to you. I do not find fault with you for not writing earlier, for I am aware that you have much to occupy your time. Besides, if you were ever deserving of "reproaches," I would be the last to give you your desserts. I think you are only deserving of commendation and devoted, ceaseless, boundless love. In

---

34. For the several schools in Wytheville during that period, see Mary B. Kegley, *Wythe County, Virginia: A Bicentennial History* (Marceline, Mo., 1989), 143–44.

35. Margaret Wilson Oliphant's *Katie Stewart* was published serially in the 1852 issues of *Blackwood's Edinburgh Magazine.* It is a love-tale set amid Scottish life in the early nineteenth century. Katie rejects wealth and position by remaining true to her heart and lives happily ever after.

36. John Blair Radford was a physician and principal figure in the establishment of the city that now bears his name.

those whom I love, I see only the perfection of purity, beauty, goodness, and truth. To love you was an instinct of my boyhood; it is a part of my second nature now. The loves of most men like those of most women are ephemeral. In me there is no change, neither the "shadow of turning."

As long as you love me, this will continue, and as long as I am confident of your love, my own heart would find a ready excuse for whatever you might do. This is no ordinary affection. If you appreciate and cherish it, it will not be my fault if your life does not pass like one long, cloudless, sunlit summer day. The years that are past bear witness that this is truth. Were you tomorrow to be stricken deaf and dumb and blind, or become an object hideous to all other eyes, to me you would be the same impersonation of the beautiful and your love would be as necessary to my happiness as now. When I change, the change itself will be a convulsion, a convulsion you alone can ever have power to effect.

Thus vested with absolute dictatorial powers, like Lincoln, you must use them with more discretion than he, or you may sometime get up a rebellion in your dominions.

The most loyal subjects become the most uncompromising rebels when they are intentionally neglected or oppressed, and the most absorbing, devoted and enduring love may become the most jealous, most exacting, and least to be trifled with. But this is *mal a propos.*

In your letter you say that your habit of procrastination has become so confirmed that you fear it will influence you in "more important matters than letter writing." I trust this is merely a general remark and has no application to our approaching marriage. You will recollect that this is the third time you have promised. But I regard such remarks as only general, since I feel assured that you would not hesitate to inform me definitely of any change you desired to make in your plans.

Ondits: Genl. Jenkins has captured "Col. Dills," 14th Ky. Regt.[37] Rad and Rob Hammet are at home.[38] Miss Lizzie Radford,[39] riding home from church

---

37. This report was both unfounded and garbled. On March 22 Jenkins and four hundred cavalry left on a raid to Point Pleasant. The Confederates saw no action until the day after Sheffey's letter (March 28), and that was a brief skirmish with the 13th West Virginia Infantry. Dickinson, *8th Virginia Cavalry,* 37. Col. John Dills Jr. then commanded the newly formed 39th Kentucky Mounted Infantry (U.S.). In mid-April he was victorious in an action at Piketon, Kentucky. *Official Records,* 23, pt. 1:240–41.

38. John Radford Hammet led a company in the 54th Virginia Infantry. Robert C. Hammet was adjutant of the regiment.

39. Lizzie Campbell Radford was then the fifteen-year-old daughter of Dr. and Mrs. John B. Radford.

today, fell off into the only mud hole there was on the road. Miss Nannie[40] sat in her parlor window yesterday looking afar to where she thought "her lover's stead kept pace with her expectancy and flew," but disappointment "like a worm in the bud, preyed on her damask cheek."[41] I took the Scottish Chiefs down to her last night in the hope that William Wallace might supplant him.[42] *Entre nous,* when I knocked she thought I was the Col. And as I came in at one door, she "vamoosed" from the parlor through another intending to primp. She came back without primping but I knew nothing of it until afterwards, and you mustn't tell, for she would be as mad as a whole nest of hornets at my informant. I am a little afraid of her myself.

I was not at church today for the simple reason that it was too far to walk, but I understand that our Chaplain preached one of his great big sermons. Miss Sue Hammet[43] and Miss Lizzie Radford, nothwithstanding the solemnity of the occasion, laughed when two dogs commenced fighting in the aisle. The golden haired Sue went there on horseback accompanied by her handsome brother Rad; and during the services, some scamp stole her bridle and substituted one instead which seems to have been peculiarly the property of this "Rope Cavalry." I think they will have to be called *Cavaliers d'acier* since "steal" seems to be the watchword, countersign, shibboleth, and slogan of a majority of them.

I made an agreement with Dr. Hammet some time ago to go with him over to Col. Robt. Preston's[44] but hitherto the "clementhy of the weather" as Fred Collup[45] in Smyth would say, has prevented. Fred was a great exhorter. He carried a bible in one pocket and a half-filled whiskey bottle in the other. He arose one day in Smyth in all his majesty and splendor and glory, like the sun from behind a cloud, and with all his woolgathering wits about him, led off in the following exordium: "Brethring and Thithters." Here he paused,

40. Eighteen-year-old Nannie Radford was the third of seven children of Dr. and Mrs. Radford.

41. The quotation is from Shakespeare's *Twelfth Night.*

42. *The Scottish Chiefs,* by Jane Porter, is an 1810 novel that was set in 1296 Scotland. Robert Bruce and William Wallace are the principal characters.

43. Susan Hammet, the last of five children to prosperous Montgomery County farmer Edward Hammet, is listed on the 1860 census as then being fifteen years old.

44. Former colonel of the 28th Virginia, venerable Robert Taylor Preston became colonel thereafter of the 4th Virginia Reserves and the 5th Virginia State Line. He constructed "Smithfield," the family estate in present-day Blacksburg.

45. Sheffey in all likelihood is referring to Frederick Cullop, who was active in the Lutheran faith in Smyth County at the time of the American Revolution. See Goodridge Wilson, *Smyth County History and Traditions* (Marion, Va., 1932), 122, 133.

that his silvery tones might have their full effect (or more probably to see if his bottle was all O.K.), and when he proceeded, the effect was such as would have gratified Whitfield or Bascom,[46] or even the old blind James Waddell, Wirt's favorite, in his palmy days.[47] "I hathe been kept from you by the clementhy of the weather, but I hathe come now, and you mutht come up an feth your thinth now, far ef you don't come up an feth, you'll never be thaved in thith worle, no nor in the New Nited Sthateth."

He was a real *bona fide* exhorter. But I mustn't talk about the people of Smyth. I am afraid you already have a horrible idea of it and, like Juan Fernandez,[48] had rather "dwell in the midst of alarms than to reign in that horrible place." But the world will be open to us and, though the people of Smyth are very clever people, I do not think it will suit me to settle there for life. We can go where we please, so soon as Abraham [Lincoln] is whipped.

But I have written enough nonsense to horrify you.

Camp Between Lewisburg and Frankford,
MAY 11, 1863

Dear Josie,

I reached this point day before yesterday with 52 [men].[49] Am in bivouac with a great blue grass pasture, tentless and houseless. I have neither cooking vessels nor axes, but the people are kind and General Echols[50] seems disposed

46. Along with John and Charles Wesley, English evangelist George Whitfield founded the Methodist denomination. George Bidleman Bascom achieved success as a Methodist bishop and president of Transylvania University in Lexington, Kentucky.

47. James Waddel was a renowned Presbyterian cleric in Virginia. He did not let blindness in his mid-forties deter his efforts. For eighteen years thereafter, Waddel was known reverently as the "Blind Preacher." Among his strongest supporters was William Wirt, lawyer, essayist, and attorney general in the administration of Pres. James Monroe.

48. Jose Joaquin Fernandez won high praise as a Mexican journalist and novelist. In his writings Fernandez stressed morality and patriotism.

49. On May 5 Maj. Gen. Samuel Jones sent a message from his Dublin headquarters to Brig. Gen. John Echols at the Narrows: "Captain Sheffey, Eighth Virginia Cavalry, has just arrived with his company, and will be pushed on to you as soon as his horses are shod. Captain Sheffey's company is small at present; many men are absent collecting their horses. They will be sent forward as soon as they come in." *Official Records,* 25, pt. 2:779.

50. Lynchburg-born John Echols had studied law at Harvard and established a successful legal practice in Union. He was Monroe County's representative to the Virginia Secession Convention. Appointed lieutenant colonel of the new 27th Virginia Infantry, Echols won promotion to brigadier general in the spring of 1862 for gallantry at the battle of Kernstown. He commanded forces in and around the Narrows during the first months of 1863; but when

to render me every assistance in his power. The labor thrown upon my company for the present is immense, but I will be relieved of the greater portion of it in a few days. The rest of our Regt. will soon be with us in Greenbrier.

Col. Edgar's affair here was quite a brilliant little success. With a force of 300 he repulsed 500—killing and wounding 75 and not losing a man. One of the Yankee Lieutenants died day before yesterday at [Joseph M.] McMillon's near Lewisburg.[51] I came to Lewisburg yesterday upon business. The sound of the church bells, however, soon notified me of a fact which I was completely ignorant, that it was the Sabbath. I think I never saw so many pretty ladies together. Indeed there is quite a super abundance of the sex in this country.

That matrimonial affair in June is now, I think, reduced to a moral certainty. At least we may safely regard it as such. I have little else to write. This country is absolutely magnificent, and the slavery which ties me down by this spring and under this tree on this delightful day is almost intolerable. But I have been married to my company until I have learned patience and endurance as Socrates did by his marriage with Xantippe.[52]

The love-affairs of some of the men are amusing. One of them began a flirtation here last fall with a lady several years his senior. I think he had the advantage until our return, but she is very sensible and is already drawing her coils well and warily around him. She will soon have the vantage-ground, and if he does not "crawfish," he will be forced either into an interminable engagement or an unconditional surrender. What woman ever failed? I know perhaps one or two, but they are all. But I will write no more at present.

Southern troops took the offensive in May, Echols shifted his headquarters to his adopted hometown, Union. Ibid., 640, 751, 773.

51. This engagement on May 2, 1863, two miles west of Lewisburg was unique in that it was waged in the middle of the night. A year earlier Lt. Col. George Mathews Edgar had been defeated and captured in fighting at Lewisburg. Redemption came when he and 250 soldiers of his 26th Virginia Infantry Battalion ambushed 700 Federals of the 2d West Virginia Cavalry. The "fight by starlight" began at 1:00 AM and lasted no more than twenty minutes. The Federals were so startled that their erratic return fire failed to hit a Confederate. Union losses were 4 killed (including Lt. George B. Shoemaker), 8 wounded, 4 missing, and twenty-eight horses slain. Edgar lost 4 men captured. Ibid., 25, pt. 1:1099–1102; Sutton, *Second Regiment, West Virginia Cavalry,* 76–79, 81.

52. The wife of Socrates exhibited such a bad temper toward him that her name has become synonymous with scolding.

Camp Stuart, Va.
MAY 25TH, 1863

Dear Josie,

I received your letter when I reached this camp yesterday. I scarcely know what to say about the five groomsmen. It is almost impossible for men of this Regt. to obtain leaves of absence. Maj. Bowen will make an application for leave today, and will accompany me if he succeeds in getting it.

I do not know where Will Tate is.[53] I enclose a note to him in this which you will please send to him. Frank will, of course, regard himself as first groomsman.[54]

I will leave Greenbrier on the 1st of June. If it is necessary to write to Frank, I will do so, but as I will probably see him very soon, I do not think it is necessary.

I shall write to several gentlemen by today's mail, Major James H. Nounnan,[55] Col. David Edmundson[56] and Rob Hammet. I will be compelled to apply to one or two more than the number, or I will not succeed in getting them.

I hope that invitations will be extended to C. H. Baker, Surgeon 8th Va. Cavalry, Central Depot, and to Lt. Col. George Edgar, Lewisburg, Va., and Lt. Col Cook, Adjt. Stratton and Dr. Timms,[57] 8th Cavalry, Lewisburg, Va. These are merely honorary invitations. None of them will be able to obtain leaves of absence. The same will be the case with many others whom I would have liked to have had invited under other circumstances. I have been treated so kindly by the Stuart family in this County that I hope Miss Virginia Stuart,

53. Wythe County's William Hanson Tate originally enlisted in the 4th Virginia Infantry. By 1863 he was a captain in the 51st Virginia Infantry. Tate was killed at the May 1864 battle of New Market. Robertson, *4th Virginia Infantry*, 76; Davis, *51st Virginia Infantry*, 92.

54. Francis Smith Spiller was Josie's brother. He served the first year of the war as a sergeant in the 4th Virginia Infantry.

55. James H. Nounnan rose to the rank of major in the 16th Virginia Cavalry, serving in that unit throughout the war and becoming its second in command.

56. A Montgomery County farmer who attended VMI, David Edmundson was a captain in the 4th Virginia before appointment as lieutenant colonel of the 21st Virginia Cavalry. He was captured at the battle of Fisher's Hill in September 1864. Before his release five months later, Edmundson alternated between Fort Delaware in Delaware Bay and Old Capital Prison at Washington, D.C. John E. Olson, *21st Virginia Cavalry* (Lynchburg, Va., 1989), 65.

57. Ajax M. Stratton was a lieutenant in Company B of the 8th Virginia Cavalry. The surgeon of the regiment was Dr. Charles W. Timms.

who is at school in Wytheville, will be invited. That, however, is, of course, just as you think proper.

My grandfather, Col. John Preston, and my uncles and aunts, Mr. and Mrs. Henry Preston, Mr. and Mrs. James L. Preston, Mr. Frank Preston, and Miss Elizabeth Preston, and Dr. and Mrs. Robt. F. Preston, Goodson, Va., will, I know, not be able to attend, but invitations will be expected by them, as a tribute of respect to them. My uncles and aunts, Mr. and Mrs. Hugh W. Sheffey, Staunton, Va., Dr. and Mrs. Lawrence Sheffey, Huntsville, Alabama, and Daniel Sheffey, Emory & Henry College, I would like to be invited for the same reason. My other uncles are at points where invitations would not reach them. I think none will be present but my own immediate family. I believe you know their names.

I will be unable to write to Robt. Hammett from ignorance of his address. I suppose he and Rad will be invited by you and I can write to Rob when I reach home.

Marion, Va.
June 3rd, 1863

Dear Josie,

I found a note from Lieut. Tate awaiting me at home. He will be present on the 9th. In a postscript he says that Frank also will come "Deo (and the military authorities) violente." Yesterday evening a note of acceptance came from Capt. Halsey.[58] He says he thinks Col. Edmondson will return in time— but his whereabouts are at present unknown. He is with Col. Peters, however, and I think he will be here in a few days.

Please let me know if you hear from Rob Hammett.

I have heard nothing further from Maj. Bowen & Dr. Baker, but I think their coming is certain. I wrote to Mr. Leftwich yesterday. He is in Radford but will be here, I think, on Saturday.

Old Time[59] has lost his wings and walks wearily. *With* the girls, however, he seems to travel fast enough.

I hope Mrs. Brown and Mrs. Carrington will defer their Charlotte trip for a while and come with us to Marion. And your mother and Dr. and Mrs. Hammet will be expected to come with us.

58. Stephen Peters Halsey was then a captain in the 4th Virginia State Line. He later would be major of Col. William E. Peters's 21st Virginia Cavalry.

59. This was the name of Sheffey's horse.

My mother will probably not be able to go to Wytheville. She prefers to receive you at home, where she can take you to her heart at once. She says she intends to take your part on all occasions. Really I shall become very jealous, for I flattered myself that I alone would always be her idol. My uncle, Hugh Sheffey of Staunton, has decided to come. He is one of my favorites and I am glad you will have an opportunity to become acquainted with him. He will not be at Wytheville, *however,* I think. The bridal party will remain with us for seven days.

My little sisters, when they write to me, always close with sending "bushels of love." In imitation of them, I would close by sending "bushels of love" from all but I don't think the illimitable love all are prepared to shower upon you can be reduced to measure. We will not disturb ourselves about the future, until the clouds have passed away. Darkness cannot endure forever, and we must look only at the silver lining that gilds the cloud.

Camp at Lewis' Church[60] *Greenbrier Co., Va.*
JUNE 30TH, 1863

My dear wife,

I reached Camp safely yesterday evening a day sooner than I intended. But it is perhaps well enough as the affairs of my company needed attention. I have a splendid company now, having recently received an addition of eighteen men. My aggregate no. now is 96, and most of them are large stout healthy men. I will be able to make my mark, if an opportunity occurs, though I think it probable that we are doomed here to a life of inglorious ease.[61] My men say they have almost forgotten that they belong to the army, and regard themselves merely as spectators. It is not a pleasant life to me, now especially, unless you could be here with me.

Some gentlemen are endeavoring to establish a line of stages from Dublin to the Salt Sulphur.[62] When they succeed, if they do, I think I will send for you, though that will depend considerably upon our movements and the movements of the enemy. The roads towards Gauley are all blockaded, though our

60. Sheffey's location at the time cannot be determined. No church or pastor of note named Lewis was in the county. Rice, *Greenbrier County,* 181–219.

61. When General Jenkins departed to join Lee's Army of Northern Virginia for the invasion of Pennsylvania, Sheffey's regiment was left behind for scouting and screening duties in the eastern panhandle of what was to become West Virginia.

62. Salt Sulphur Springs is two miles south of Union in Monroe County, West Virginia.

officers are still anticipating a raid of Yankee Cavalry.[63] I do not myself regard such an event as among the probabilities. The last Yankee raiders fared so badly in this country that I think they will not attempt it soon again.

I hope you are very happy and very well. I am already intensely *homesick*, but if you only keep well, I will be patient.

My men for the first time have had an opportunity to try other officers, and I think they like me much better than they did before I left. They find that others are hard upon them as well as I. The married men too think that I will have an immense amount of sympathy for them now. I doubt whether I will be much improved in that respect. I have been congratulated, to an *enormous degree*. I do not think that a young man forced away from a wife, who is dearer to him than every thing else on earth, is an object of congratulation. It is reported here that Jenkins is very near to Harrisburg in Pa.[64] I hope that is true and that he will succeed in taking and burning that hotbed of abolition.

Genl. Echols asked one of my men recently if he had ever seen my wife, and if she was sweet and beautiful as he had heard. The fellow told him, yes, she was everything that heart could wish. And the Genl. said that I *deserved such a wife*, and that he was very glad indeed that I had been so fortunate. So you can perceive the estimation in which you are held in Greenbrier already, and you can also perceive that some of our officers have a talent for buncomb speeches, which they know will reach the ears of those for whom they are intended.

Today is our muster day, and I must close this note to attend to that. I will write to you very frequently.

Love to all.

May He who doeth all things well, keep you from all harm, and lead us rapidly on to that future of love and joy & happiness which we may so confidently anticipate.

63. Earlier in June, departmental commander Samuel Jones informed General Echols in Union, "If the enemy has obstructed the main road from Lewisburg to Gauley Bridge, it indicates that they do not intend to advance by that route, unless they have obstructed it but slightly; in that case, it may be intended only to mislead us." *Official Records,* 27, pt. 2:870.

64. Jenkins was commanding a cavalry brigade consisting of the 16th, 17th, and 24th Virginia Regiments, plus the 34th and 36th Virginia Battalions. His troops pushed to within three miles of the Susquehanna River—the farthest advance north by Confederates in the eastern theater during the war. At Gettysburg Jenkins was wounded seriously enough to have to relinquish command to Col. Milton J. Ferguson.

Camp at Lewis
JULY 8TH, 1863

My dear wife,

As I am sending home several of my Smyth County men this morning, I have determined to write to you by one of them, or at least to get him to convey this note beyond the influences of the high waters which for some time have stopped all my mails. I have not heard from you or from Smyth since I came here. Can I presume you are all well? I am sending home twelve of my men for the purpose of gathering in their wheat-crops, and they are jubilant over the prospect. I send a Lieutenant with them, by permission.[65] However homesickness is a weak ailment, and I would not acknowledge it to anyone else than yourself or some body—which is a Magician.

I send one man home to get married. His name is Smith from Smyth,[66] and he is to marry a Miss Snavely. You can see the effect of a good example. It is better than precept. I have another man who will be married in this neighborhood ere long, and Major Bowen is ah, but that is a secret which I am not allowed to tell even to you.

It has rained here fourteen days in succession, and still the eternal drip-drip, drop-drop, drizzle, drizzle is tormenting us.

> Besides that all is quiet on Muddy Creek.
> All quiet along Muddy Creek this week
> Except here and there a stray picket
> Shoots a crow as he walks on his beat to and fro
> Or a squirrel or a hare in the thicket
> Or some other of the "brutes that perish"
> Which however does not mean yankees as they are scarce.[67]

Our scouts have killed four of Ramsay's men recently.[68] *It is said* that each man who brings in one of their scalps, or more properly according to the

---

65. The two 8th Virginia Cavalry lieutenants from the Wythe-Smyth area on duty at the time were William C. Copenhaver and Hezekiah Harmon.

66. Thomas F. Smith enlisted in the Smyth Dragoons in July 1861, was absent without leave for a month in 1864, but surrendered at Appomattox at war's end. Dickinson, *8th Virginia Cavalry*, 107.

67. These lines are a parody of the well-known Civil War song "All Quiet along the Potomac."

68. Capt. James R. Ramsay led a company of West Virginia partisan rangers whose reputation seems to have been more harsh than its deeds.

dialect of this country, *"sculps,"* gets a furlough for thirty days. This stimulates the business very considerably. But I do not vouch for the truth of the report.

Beyond the River our cavalry under command of Capt. Lewis[69] have been making some important captures. So has Thurmond's Co. of Partisan Rangers.[70] They are having a merry time and if it were not such a desolate country where they are, I could wish for the sake of a little excitement to be with them.

Genl. Echols has resigned. This I regret exceedingly. We will not get another commander as kind and amiable as he. Col. Patton however, it is said, will succeed him and he is a fine officer.[71] If McCausland succeeds Echols, I shall want to be sent to Maryland for he is our very particular destestation.[72] Wharton could give better satisfaction than either.[73] The cause assigned for Echols' resignation is ill-health.[74] He has been suffering with what he thinks is a disease of the heart. I hope he is mistaken. He is one of the kindest officers and most amiable of gentlemen.

I suppose Frank has returned to his post,[75] and you are left alone to enjoy your *dium cum dignit* without fear of molestation from any of our charming sex. This is perhaps an unjustifiable supposition for these majors cannot stay away long from "Madam Brown or [Emma] Brown." I beg her pardon for quoting from Frank and Major King.[76] And Lucy Spiller too has, I doubt not,

69. Charles Irvine Lewis then commanded the Kanawha Rangers (Company I) of the 8th Virginia Cavalry.

70. Capt. William Dabney Thurmond led an undersized company of irregular troops. Their duties ranged from scouting to pillaging.

71. George Smith Patton, former colonel of the 22d Virginia Infantry, was the grandfather of the famous World War II army commander. He temporarily took charge of Echols's brigade during the latter's absences.

72. Known as a humorless, hard taskmaster, John McCausland had a personality in sharp contrast to that of Sheffey's congenial friend John Echols.

73. On the day that Sheffey wrote this letter, Col. Gabriel Colvin Wharton of the 51st Virginia Infantry was promoted to brigadier general and assigned temporary command of the Shenandoah Valley district.

74. Echols was frequently on leave during this period because of what was termed "neuralgia of the heart." Richard M. McMurry, *Virginia Military Institute Alumni in the Civil War* (Lynchburg, Va., 1999), 120.

75. Following discharge from the 4th Virginia Infantry, Francis Spiller had joined Capt. Napoleon B. French's artillery battery. Later it and Spiller were made part of the 30th Battalion, Virginia Sharpshooters.

76. Probably Maj. John Floyd King, who shortly thereafter organized and led the 13th Battalion, Virginia Light Artillery.

her train of lovers "sighing like furnaces, with woeful ballads made to their lady's eyebrow," as that *Rara avis* Bartley used to make to the eyebrow of a certain old lady, I toot of.[77] This pays you back for calling me "old man." Never mind, I shall myself have business in SW Va. some of these days.

Is Rob Crockett married yet?[78] Are you going to the Central [Depot] this summer? You must not sit idly in the house and get blue. When you get tired of Wythe, you must go to Smyth, and when you get tired of both you must go to the Central, or if you can make up a *large* party to the Salt Sulphur, which is receiving visitors this season by a hack line from Christiansburg. It is 17 miles south of my camp, and is now Genl. "Jones" hdqtrs. Such a trip at present, however, is too much for you to undertake on account of the bad roads and the desolate condition of the country. The high waters have washed away pikes and dykes and fences & bridges with a vengeance. Indeed, in some places they have washed away everything except the mud holes, so I have heard.

You will please overlook this bad writing, and in overlooking it you will, I trust, find in your heart an excuse for it. If you could have seen the superannuated new and the attenuated drop of ink with which I undertook this missive, and the position *a la Turque* which I have maintained since I commenced writing, you would acknowledge that my self-confidence was commendable, that my ingenuity and my fortitude are remarkable, and my energy and perseverance indomitable.

Camp at Lewis Church
Greenbrier Co., Va., JULY 14, 1863

My dear Wife,

Your dear letter of the 6th inst. was received yesterday. I cannot describe to you the sunshine it brought with it. I thank God for your love, my darling, and fervently pray that each recurring year may make me worthier of you, and cement more closely the bonds of affection and mutual confidence which have bound us together. Your letter was brought to me last night by

77. The poetic phrase is from Shakespeare's *As You Like It.* James A. Bartley was a well-known teacher in the Wythe County area. See Kegley, *Wythe County,* 144.

78. Wytheville attorney Robert Crockett Jr. had been a captain in the 4th Virginia Infantry until wounded at Second Manassas. He was at this time acting as an enrolling officer in Wythe County. Robertson, *4th Virginia Infantry,* 46.

courier. The rain was pouring down in torrents, and the night was "dark as Erebus,"[79] or "Old Night," or any other night that history or poetry gives an account of. I was out of candles, and you would have been amused to have witnessed the strenuous exertions I made to get a light. Our fires were all out, but I managed to find a match or two, and a flickering taper which I prized as highly as even Aladdin did his "wonderful lamp."[80]

Since I wrote last, the disposition of our forces has been materially changed. The 22nd Regt. and Derrick's Battalion[81] were sent two-or-three days since from Lewisburg towards Pack's Ferry,[82] it is supposed, to reinforce McCausland but we know little of their destination. McCausland is still at Piney Creek[83] in Raleigh unless he has been sent after the Yankees, who are said to be making their way towards Saltville. We learn from our scouts that 4000 Yankee Cavalry started recently up Sandy for Saltville, but they are now said to be retreating.[84] I hope so sincerely. The 45th Regt., which was camped within three miles of me at Aldersons Ferry, has been sent to Lewisburg.

My company is now fifteen miles from any other force and my picket duty is very much increased. But we have a delightful camp and are getting along amazingly. It is too exposed a point, however, for me to think of bringing you here. The people would welcome you with the utmost cordiality, for I flatter myself that I am quite popular with them; but my anxiety for you would make me miserable. Even the Salt Sulphur is at present an exposed point, on account of the removal of the 45th. My pickets at Hayne's Ferry, 10 miles below this on the Greenbrier, are its only guards. And they can only give notice to the Genl. of an approach of the enemy from that direction. It

79. In Greek mythology Erebus was the son of Chaos and the brother of Night. Hence, he was darkness personified.

80. *Arabian Nights Entertainment* is a collection of ancient Oriental tales first translated into French and English in the early eighteenth century. One of the most celebrated characters in the series is Aladdin, whose lamp was the source of wealth and good fortune.

81. Lt. Col. Clarence Derrick commanded the 23d Virginia Infantry Battalion, which was but two companies shy of regimental size.

82. These two Virginia units were part of Echols's brigade and spent the summer at camps in and around Lewisburg.

83. Piney Creek (or Piney, as some contemporaries called it) is midway between Fayetteville and Princeton in Raleigh County, West Virginia. David L. Phillips, *Tiger John: The Rebel Who Burned Chambersburg* (Leesburg, Va., 1993), 155–56.

84. A Union cavalry force of thirteen hundred men was moving eastward on a raid to sever the Virginia and Tennessee Railroad. The Federals advanced on Wytheville rather than Saltville. William Marvel, *The Battles of Saltville* (Lynchburg, Va., 1992), 50–60.

is possible that Derrick's Battalion may have been stopped at some point in Monroe. If not, the Genl.'s Hdqrs. are very unprotected.

I have received no letter from Smyth since I left Wytheville. I suppose they are all well there or they would have written. I wrote to you four or five days ago, and presume you have received that letter ere this. I will write to you very frequently. I am glad Wytheville has been gay, and hope that you will mingle as much as possible among the "young folks" in their amusements. It is indeed useless to give ourselves up to vain regrets; and while we will cherish for each other that sincere affection whose continuance is so indispensable to our happiness, it is still our duty to feel that God orders all things aright, and to keep as much sunshine as possible with us, wherever we may be.

It is preeminently our duty now—more indeed than ever before—to look to Him "Who so loveth us," for strength to bear whatever of sorrow may be mingled in our cup of blessings. Under His guidance alone can we set our feet aright in the new path we have undertaken to travel, and by His strength alone can we be sustained under such afflictions as may now befall us. May He, as we pass through the lights and the shadows that are before us, bind our hearts, if possible, more closely together, and lead us as with one heart and one mind to Himself, Who alone is the "Giver of every good and perfect gift."

In your choice of a church, if at any time you should think proper to connect yourself with one, I trust you will not allow any predilections of mine to influence you. Wherever your inclinations lead you, there will I follow, for I do not regard the differences between the Protestant Churches as at all important, certainly not so essential as that you and I should be of one mind in a matter of as much importance as this.

I am grateful for the kind messages from our friends in Wytheville, and regret sincerely that I could not be present during the gayeties succeeding Rob Crockett's marriage. I hope sincerely there is much happiness in store for him and his beautiful wife.

The news from Vicksburg & from Maryland is very conflicting.[85] I hope it will turn out to be not near so bad as the papers of the 9th and 10th represent.

I, too, count the hours and the days that keep your letters from me. I hope you will write as often as possible, if it be but a line to tell me that you are well and happy.

85. Vicksburg, the last major Confederate stronghold along the Mississippi River, surrendered to Union forces on July 4, 1863—the day Robert E. Lee began retreating after his defeat at Gettysburg.

Whenever my company is thrown to a point to which I can bring you without endangering your safety, I will avail myself of the opportunity, but this I fear will not occur before Nov. or Dec. and I hope to be allowed to visit Wytheville before that time. In the meanwhile, I hope you will find it pleasant to spend much of your time in Smyth. The dear ones there have indeed taken you to their heart. Long ago I knew that their love was a priceless and an exhaustless treasure. As it has been lavished upon me, so it will be upon you.

The courier is waiting and I must close. Best love to your dear mother and sisters & Rob & all and may the all Merciful Father keep you from all harm is the prayer of your devoted husband.

Camp Stuart
JULY 21ST, 1863

My dear wife,

I would have answered your letter of the 16th inst. day before yesterday, but have been engaged in moving camp and settling up my affairs on Muddy Creek.

I have been in an agony of anxiety for two days on account of the report that 1200 Yankees had burned Wytheville, and committed immemorable other acts of cruelty and vandalism.[86] I have consoled myself by disbelieving the whole thing. Yesterday evening we heard that the militia at Wytheville had put them to rout, but that they had succeeded in burning the bridge across Reed Creek.

The very idea that you may have been in so much peril is an agony to me. I hope I shall hear certainly this evening.

I think I will bring you to Greenbrier. You would be as safe here, if not safer than anywhere else, as this country by a singular folly of our genl.[87] is well protected while the [Rail] Road, Salt Works & Lead Mines are almost at the mercy of the enemy. It will be difficult, however, for me to make suitable

86. On July 18, 1863, Col. John T. Toland and 1,300 horsemen arrived in Wytheville near sunset. Concealed home guards and civilians opened fire with effectiveness. Union casualties were 14 killed, 32 wounded, and 43 captured or missing. Brig. Gen. E. P. Scammon officially reported that his Federals "totally destroyed the town" in their anger over high casualties. That was an exaggeration, but a West Virginia soldier observed that "quite a number of homes" were burned. *Official Records,* 27, pt. 2:941–63; Sutton, *Second Regiment, West Virginia Cavalry,* 88–101; Kegley, *Wythe County,* 195–98.

87. This is a reference to the departmental commander, General Jones.

arrangements quickly, as I shall have to purchase a carriage and horses, and they can scarcely be procured for love or money. If you were here, Ellen Ross, who is an excellent servant, could be your waiting-maid, an institution you could not get along without, and John [Ross] could be your Carriage driver. By them you would be as well cared for as any one could be under such adverse circumstances. You could not bring a slave here without imminent danger of losing her, and though free, John and Ellen are the most faithful of servants. You could not get along on horseback and there are no public conveyances here. In an open buggy, you would be too much exposed, and indeed, it would soon be broken to pieces. The only feasible mode of conveyance for you is by strong covered carriage drawn by two strong horses.

If I can get another riding horse, the two horses I have here will answer perfectly as they are very strong and very gentle. The carriage will be the most difficult to get. I can, I think, get boarding for you at Mr. [William] Robinson Stuart's, whose house is in sight of our camp. If not, there are plenty of hospitable people between this and Lewisburg, and your kinsmen do not live far away.

Since writing the above, Mr. Stuart has called on me at my tent. He has gone to see his wife upon the subject and will let me know tomorrow. At present Capt. Ruby's wife & family are boarding there, but they will leave in a few days.[88] At Mr. Stuart's, you would, I know, live very happily, for there is no family of more kindness or true genuine refinement anywhere.

All these arrangements will depend of course upon your own wishes. If you still wish to come, I will certainly make the arrangements. You will of necessity be compelled to trust yourself to the care of John & Ellen Ross in coming here, but they are perfectly trusty, and will be eager to obey you in everything. It will be impossible for my father to leave home & still more impossible for me to get a leave to come for you.

I am very anxious that you should be as near me as possible, particularly so since it is your own wish. But you must make up your mind to endure some privations and to be occasionally lonesome, and sometimes frightened. Even when you are close to me, I will be required to be in camp the greater part of my time. Still I believe such a life would be a much pleasanter one, than a life of solitude and anxiety at home. So far as I am myself concerned, I would make almost any sacrifice to have you with me. The only drawbacks

88. Capt. John C. Ruby served as an aide on the staff of Colonel McCausland. *Official Records*, 12, pt. 1:495.

are the difficulties of procuring a conveyance and the fear of bringing you into danger.

I think it very probable that we will be left here for the balance of this year, but if we were ordered to a place where you could not go, I could easily send you back home. If you come to Greenbrier, you will of course have to bring a trunk well-filled and among other things: a few pr. of *yarn stockings* and a pair of rather thicker shoes than you are fond of, for it rains here sometimes. Besides, it is the *fashion* for travellers to dress their feet very warmly. This is cruel, tyrannical and oppressive, is it not?

A dispatch has been received today that the militia whipped the Yankees at Wytheville. I am very grateful to them, but as the fight seems to have been in or near the town, I am still very uneasy about you. You will write to me immediately, will you not? and give me a full account of this wonderful Yankee visitation, and the gallant stand of the brave fellows who fought them.

Oh, how very much I wish our Regt. could have been there. It is in better condition than it ever has been, but it is doomed to a life of inaction. The Yankees have effectually blockaded all the roads leading from here to Gauley. In some places they have dug deep ditches across the roads, and in others the roads have been entirely dug away so that even infantry can only pass by climbing around the hills. At present I object to so much security. If you were here, I should think differently. Miss Jennie Stuart and her brother Charles are expected to reach home tonight.[89] I wish very much you could have come with them.

I went to church last Sabbath on Muddy Creek. I mention it because the sermon was the most "lonesome" I have ever heard. Almost all but I went to the land which Cain visited,[90] and I was compelled to amuse myself for the first time in my life by scribbling epigramatically on the back of our old bench.

Poor Houston[91]
Though to sin-stricken souls
Thy words seem terrific

89. Charles A. Stuart was clerk of the Greenbrier County Court. His sister Jennie was the Virginia Stuart mentioned several times in Sheffey's letters.

90. In Old Testament history Cain was the son of Adam and Eve. He murdered his brother Abel in a fit of jealousy. God condemned Cain to a life of continual wandering as a vagabond on earth. Here Sheffey is referring to mindlessness.

91. Houston was doubtless the name of the minister at that service.

> To sleep-stricken eyes,
> They are quite soporific.
> And though sleeping churches
> Soon fall to the ground
> Thy church will last long
> For its sleepers are sound.

This poetry is as good as the commencement of John Rowsy Peyton's[92] "discovery of America" to-wit:

> Columbus he did went
> For to see the Continent

Or of Sam Cox's[93] "Chatham Hill" to-wit:

> Two old stores & one old Mill
> A brand new church & Harman's still
> Jackson Snavely and a dollar bill
> Is all that's left of Chatham Hill

Such a thing as metre was not counted upon and, indeed, as I was bored beyond *measure*, could not be expected. This poem, if completed, would have been worthier of the inspiration which caused it than that parody you admired so much, but you must not be so enthusiastic in your applause lest your friends should think that your education in the Bartley school had—the dim shadow of a descending broomstick—one of those "coming events" which "cast their shadows before" warns me to desist.

When we left Muddy Creek, an old man with whom I had been boarding actually shed tears like a child, but that was because we were relieved by *Dunn's Battalion,* the worst curse ever inflicted on a people, and not I suppose from sorrow at our departure.[94] There was sorrow among the lasses

92. A patriot in the American Revolution, John Rowze Peyton became known as the "Hero Boy of '76."

93. The 1860 census for Smyth County lists Samuel A. Cox as a twenty-nine-year-old merchant. The lines quoted by Sheffey are more doggerel than poetry. Chatham Hill was an early community in Smyth County.

94. Ambrose C. Dunn's 37th Virginia Cavalry Battalion was basically a partisan ranger command that often did not obey to the letter the rules of war. As the unit's historian notes, this battalion contained "men known for their ability to ride and shoot, but who preferred the life of a guerilla fighter to that of the more disciplined regular military personnel." J. L. Scott, *36th and 37th Battalions Virginia Cavalry* (Lynchburg, Va., 1986), 49.

though, for the "Dragoons" had improved their time, and more than one Muddy Creek maiden had lost her heart and pledged her hand to these invincibles.

But all this is very interesting to you, I doubt not. I rather think your heart will fail you, when you contemplate more closely your trip to Greenbrier. Still its difficulties are rather imaginary than real. Courage & determination can easily surmount them. I am afraid your mother will think it a very perilous undertaking, but Wytheville, it seems to me, is less secure than Lewisburg. I will write home immediately to let them know my intentions, and to get my father to procure a carriage for you if possible. If he can do so, I will start John with two horses as soon as I hear.

The time seems very long which separates me from you. The days seem weeks, the weeks are lengthened into weary months. If there were any hope of speedy peace, we might endure this separation, but with interminable war staring us in the face, and danger at home as great as at the outpost, I can see no good reason why we should not be nearer to each other at least during the summer and autumn.

I know that many will think me rash, and I know too that I should never cease to reflect upon myself if any evil were to befall you upon such a trip, but I do not apprehend any. Even if by an advance of the enemy you were to fall within his lines, it could only be temporary and you would be in no danger. The enemy has been all over Greenbrier several times and no woman has ever yet been interferred with. Still if you come, such chances will be vigilantly guarded against. I would willingly lay down my own life at any time for your protection, and I doubt whether any one else would. I am therefore the best judge of how far I can risk one without whom my own life is a dreary blank.

Best love to all. Write as soon as you can and may God bless & guard you from every peril and every grief, my dear wife, is the fervent prayer of your devoted husband.

Marion, JULY 22D, 1863[95]

My dear sister,

Upon hearing of the occupation of Wytheville by the Federals, our anxiety was intense and I verily believe Pa would have left us to take care of ourselves,

95. This letter to Josie Spiller Sheffey from her sister-in-law is included to provide a glimpse of elusive home-front feelings and activities during the war.

if there had been any possibility of his getting to you. Although we anticipate an attack from the Yankees hourly, yet the wish that "Josie was here" was expressed at least a hundred times. Mr. Venable[96] came from Wytheville yesterday evening, bringing the full particulars of the fight and retreat of the enemy—also a message from you.

We had heard nothing directly from you before that and felt quite relieved and grateful to Mr. Venable for the information he brought. He had heard a great deal of the heroic conduct of the ladies, and was so completely over flowing with news that the words tumbled out, rolling over and over each other, until I was in mortal fear of his *shaking* to death. However, he gave us a better idea of the result of the raid than we had had previous to his coming, so I can very readily forgive him the terror he kept us in, of the occurrence of the sad event above mentioned. I presume the Yankees are perfectly satisfied with the cordiality of the reception they received in Wytheville, and I know that *we* are perfectly resigned to wait a while longer before they extend their visit this far.

Last Sabbath will never be forgotten in Marion, for it was one of intense anxiety and suspense from daylight until dawn. Our usually quiet little village was completely metamorphased, and the hurrying to and fro of soldiers and citizens, preparing for the expected engagement, really possessed a fascination for me which was wholly inexplicable, for I dreaded the occupation of the town by the enemy and I feared the small force we had could not withstand the attack of such a superior number. All the ladies in town, nearly, came in to know what Ma intended doing with china, silver, piano, furniture, carpets, flour, bacon, servants and everything else, and when Ma with unperturbable coolness and composure told them she intended letting them remain where they were, they seemed to imbibe a portion of her calmness and concluded to let everything alone but such articles as they could hide on the premises. We concealed our jewelry about our persons, packed a few necessary articles of clothing that could be moved, in case the house should be burned, and then seating ourselves on the *front porch* calmly awaited the coming of the Yankees.

The nearer the danger came, the less fear and excitement were exhibited, and I believe if the Yankees had come, they would have suffered severely, for every man seemed determined to do his whole duty. Mr. Venable said that

96. Possibly Abraham B. Venable, an elderly Wytheville schoolteacher. See Kegley, *Wythe County*, 144.

he thought a wounded Yankee Colonel was at your house, but did not know his name. I presume it is the notorious Powell, as I see from the papers that he was dangerously wounded.[97] Have Mrs. Brown and Lucie been frightened out of all idea of going to the Springs? I think Lizzie has.

I have been suffering so much with the toothache recently that I have thought two or three times of going to Wytheville or Abingdon to have my tooth extracted, but I can't "screw my courage up to the sticking point."

Pa goes to Wytheville tonight to see about *"his daughter"* and his farm. We all hope you will come back with him. Can't you? I wrote to brother yesterday. He complains of our silence very much, but I have written repeatedly an[d] so have the other girls and we cannot account for his not receiving any of our letters. All send fondest love. Affectionate remembrances to Mrs. Spiller, Mrs. Brown and Lucie. Don't forget "Mr. Frank." Hoping to have you with us soon.

        I am, your affectionate sister,
        Ellen

97. Col. William H. Powell of the 2d West Virginia Cavalry fell wounded in the fight at Wytheville. According to several local sources, Josie Sheffey's mother, Susan Crockett Spiller, hid the injured Powell in a local hotel and tended to his injuries. Mrs. T. J. Morrison and a Mrs. Kincannon assisted Spiller in nursing Powell back to health. The Union officer was then handed over to Confederate authorities and incarcerated at Richmond's Libby Prison until his exchange six months later. Ibid., 197–98. Subsequently in the war, Powell repaid the kindnesses by interceding on behalf of then-captured John Preston Sheffey.

CHAPTER 7

AFFLICTIONS AND SUBSTITUTIONS

During the three-month period from the end of July through October 1863, Sheffey and his company were on patrol duty in Greenbrier County, West Virginia, and Tazewell County, Virginia. Confederates were continually moving to counter Union probes aimed at the Virginia and Tennessee Railroad and the vital works at Saltville. Even Sheffey's father was called to duty with the home guards to meet the enemy threats.

Sheffey mentions several undocumented clashes that occurred between opposing cavalry. Two letters from his sisters provide vivid pictures of the uncertainty and the cares of war behind the battle lines.

Dejection twice struck the captain that summer. First, and despite extensive preparations, Josephine Spiller Sheffey was unable to join her husband in the field. The captain even secured high-level permission for her to pass through the lines, but orders for the Smyth Dragoons to depart Lewisburg on scouting duty squashed his excitement at having his wife with him.

Commensurate with that disappointment, Sheffey contracted the most serious illness he had to endure during the Civil War. He thought it at first to be simple neuralgia. Time showed that a far more serious ailment was present, though. The likely diagnosis was an abscess in or under the skin near one of his eyes. A second possibility was an infection of the lachrymal drainage apparatus (tear duct), which can cause a lump at or near the corner of the eye—one of Sheffey's ongoing complaints. His symptoms are also consistent with shingles, which could trigger significant neuralgia as well as blisters around the eyes. Given the treatments administered, conjecture points to the first of the three suggested infections as the most probable.[1]

Through it all, Sheffey's spirits remained high. He was optimistic over the progress of the war. He joked about his servant's views of science and twice wrote at length of reported ghosts in Greenbrier County.

Then in mid-October the 8th Virginia Cavalry was ordered to Abingdon, Virginia. It was to become part of an active brigade led by Glade Spring's colorful but caustic Brig. Gen. William E. "Grumble" Jones.

1. J. Stephen Hudgins, M.D., to editor, Dec. 6, 2002.

Camp Stuart, Greenbrier Co., Va.
JULY 23RD, 1863

My dear Wife,

I cannot allow another day to pass without again writing to you. I have suffered more anxiety during the last few days than I have before [or] during the war. I have been relieved somewhat by letters received here today, and by the tidings brought by one of my men who left Wytheville the morning after the visit of the Yankees. From him I learn that your home is not burned and that you are all safe. I am therefore comparatively happy. Still I know you must have all been terribly alarmed.

Our Regt. has been in a perfect fever because they were kept here. We could easily from this point have intercepted the Yankees in Abb's Valley,[2] on their return if Genl. [Samuel] Jones had exercised the discretion becoming one in his position. It has been done, however, by Lt. Col. May[3] with his Battalion and two companies of our Regt. which were with Col. Mc-Causland. We are told that they intercepted the raiders in Abb's Valley and scattered them in every direction, killing and capturing many of them. It will be an everlasting disgrace to Genl. Jones, if a single one of them makes his escape.

I would have given my right arm to have been in Wytheville with this Regiment, and we might have been, for Genl. Jones knew of the Yankee approach forty-eight hours before their arrival, and an order from him could have reached us in three hours from Dublin, for there is a telegraphy line to Union. By constant travelling we could have made the trip in time.

I sympathize deeply with those whose property has been burned, and I understand that all the houses north of Crockett's Hotel and the Court House on the Tazewell road were destroyed. But oh! how can I be sufficiently thankful that you and your loved ones have been spared the horrors of a burning home! Still I fear it is not a Christian thankfulness, for with almost

---

2. Abb's Valley is an area between Tazewell and Richlands, Virginia. Initially settled in the early 1770s, it was named for its discoverer, Absalom Looney. William G. Pendleton, *History of Tazewell County and Southwest Virginia, 1748–1920* (Johnson City, Tenn., 1989), 411–12.

3. Col. Andrew J. May commanded the 10th Kentucky Cavalry. His pursuit of the Federals, Brig. Gen. John S. Williams reported, was "without parallel." In less than forty-eight hours, the small Confederate force "pressed and fought the enemy without resting." *Official Records*, 27, pt. 2:952.

equal fervor I pray that the hour may speedily come when we will be permitted to avenge ourselves to the uttermost.

Lt. Col. Powell is at your mother's, I am told. I have seen him, and hope that we may meet him some day where the rights of a prisoner, and the claims of a wounded man, will not prevent him from a short shift and a quicker trip than that to Wytheville. He has murdered our men who fell into his hands in cold blood. He has burned the homes of our people, and has added much to the horrors of this war as much as anyone. But though his heart were ten times blacker, and his hands ten times redder with the blood of his innocent victims, he would still have to be spared because he is a prisoner. With an unchristian wish, I hope that his wound will be as fatal as if it were "as deep as a well and as big as a barn door."

I hope to get a letter from you tomorrow. I purchased an additional horse today. And if you are still willing to come to Greenbrier, I will send John after you immediately. He will be able, I think, to procure a carriage in Wythe or Smyth.

I wrote you two or three days ago. Please write as soon as possible. I shall be very anxious until I can hear from you. Love to all.

Camp Stuart, Greenbrier Co., Va.
JULY 24TH, 1863

My dear Wife,

Your letter of the 21st inst. giving an account of your fright and terrible experiences during the fight at Wytheville reached me this evening. I am so rejoiced by the news of your safety that I can scarcely express my thankfulness to Him Who disposed the hearts of the Yankee marauders to mercy and kindness towards you and our dear ones.

It is now almost night and I can write but a few lines, but I could not let another mail go out without again writing to you. I hope very soon to be able to bring you to Greenbrier. I was at Mr. Stuart's last evening. Mrs. Capt. Ruby unfortunately is there with four children. If they were away, I could easily get boarding for you there, and it would be a very pleasant place for you.

As it is, there is no room, but when Mrs. Ruby leaves, which I hope will be very soon, you will be received there. Tomorrow I will send John to Capt.

Hugh W. McClung's[4] and Mrs. Tuckwiller's,[5] whose residences are about two miles off, to get boarding for you at one of those places. If he succeeds, I will start him for you in two or three days. I will trust to him to procure a carriage & harness in Wythe or Smyth, and will furnish him money for that purpose. He will take my black horse & bay with him and they will bring you in safety.

You had better bring Ellen Ross with you, as she will be of much service. It will also make John if possible more faithful, and he and she are both almost crazy lest this should not be the arrangement. It is the only feasible plan. You could not get along without some one to attend upon you, do your washing, etc. Ellen is an elegant seamstress & washer woman. The arrangement too will be so agreeable to her that she will, I am confident, use every exertion to please you. John, I can trust anywhere. Except Mr. Stuart's, there is no suitable place for you nearer than two miles.

You must keep your spirits up and not lose courage now when you have passed safely through the most terrible of dangers. Here, as well as at Wytheville, you *may* be called upon to exercise courage and coolness and fortitude under trying circumstances as well as at home, but I think you will be safer here. You will also, I doubt not, be occasionally very lonely, for from the very nature of the service I am compelled to do, you will be left alone with strangers and in the care of John & Ellen the greater part of the time. Still, I will manage to be with you very often and you will soon make pleasant acquaintances and fast friends, for this is a whole-souled people.

My entire company was sent out upon picket duty this morning except those left for camp guards. I am "field officer of the day" until day after tomorrow. Today I am confined closely to camp. Tomorrow I set out to visit all the outposts. It will require hard riding until day after tomorrow evening, as the pickets are scattered from the old State road near Blue Sulphur to Frankford and I have to ride over fifty miles.

My best love to all. Tell Aunt Betsy and Tom[6] that I too am very grateful

4. The only family by this name in Greenbrier County was that of Samuel McClung, a highly prosperous and influential farmer in the Lewisburg district. The 1860 census lists five children in the family, but none was named Hugh. Regardless, Capt. Hugh L. W. McClung commanded an unattached Tennessee artillery battery then on duty in the southwestern Virginia department.

5. In 1860 forty-seven-year-old Martha A. Tuckwiller was the wife of seventy-two-year-old David Tuckwiller, a well-to-do farmer. She is most likely the "Mrs. Tuckwiller" to whom Sheffey refers.

6. These were slaves or freedmen associated with the Spiller family.

to them. Write as often as you can and may God in His Infinite mercy and goodness continue to watch over and preserve you through every danger and every trial, my darling wife, is the constant prayer of your devoted husband.

Camp Stuart
JULY 29TH, 1863

My dear Wife,

I have succeeded in getting boarding for you at Mr. Robinson Stuart's. John will set out for Smyth with two horses tomorrow. If he succeeds in procuring a suitable carriage speedily, you will be able to get to Greenbrier in about twelve days. You may have some little trouble about passing the pickets, but I will provide against that as well as possible. Until you are safely here, I shall be very anxious. The only pickets that you will have difficulty in passing are those at the Narrows, and the Commander of the Post there will pass you through. John can easily arrange that.

This trip is still, of course, dependent upon your own will and discretion. You will, of course, if you come, bring Ellen Ross with you. If John fails to get a carriage, the whole thing will fail. In that case he will leave one of the horses at home and return to me with the other, but I trust there will be no difficulty of that sort. I send John rather at a venture in the hope that he may be able to make every necessary arrangement at home. If we are ordered away in the meantime, I will inform you of it immediately, but I do not apprehend any thing of that sort. I wish I could go for you myself. John will bring you direct to Mr. Robinson Stuart's, where every arrangement will be made for your reception.

I have had a terrible neuralgia for several days, but am now well with the exception of a slight swelling under the left eye and one or two ornamental blisters.[7]

Night before last I staid at Mr. Stuart's, where I was treated with great kindness. I was expected there last night but was so much better that I remained in camp, so they have avenged themselves by inviting me to dinner to-day with some others. Love to all. Please write to me what day you will start so that I may know when to look for you. With the fondest affection and the utmost anxiety I shall watch for your coming.

7. At the time of the Civil War, any facial pain was customarily termed neuralgia.

Camp Stuart, Va., JULY 29TH, 1863

Brig. Genl. Jno. Echols
Genl.,

My wife wishes to come, next week from Wytheville, to Mr. Robinson Stuart's in Greenbrier. I respectfully make application for a pass for her with two servants to that point. My servant, John Ross, will take it to her at Wytheville. I suppose a pass from you will be sufficient, as the Commander of the Post at the Narrows will, I think, pass her through, but she may be stopped by some of the pickets in this county.

Respectfully, Yr. Obt. Servt.,
J. P. Sheffey
Capt., Co. A
8th Va. Cavalry

Hdqtrs. Dublin,
JULY 31ST 1863

Pickets & Guards will pass Mrs. Sheffey to Greenbrier with three (3) servants.

By Com'd., Mg. Genl. Jones

Camp Stuart, Va.
JULY 31ST, 1863

My dear sisters,

I started John home day before yesterday to bring Josie to Greenbrier. I have just written to her not to come until she hears further from me, as it is very probable that we will soon be ordered into Fayette or Raleigh [Counties].

I have been suffering terribly with neuralgia, and my left eye is still a little swollen, but I think it will be quite well in a day or two. Neuralgia is quite a new disease for me.

I hope you are all getting along well. Your letters are like "angels visits" in more senses than one. Is Josie at Marion? I hope John will succeed in getting a carriage. If I were footloose for awhile, I would buy a good one. Josie could then come to see me whenever she felt so disposed, provided we were always in as safe a place as Greenbrier.

A hundred & fifty or two hundred of Morgan's men have passed through our lines. The others have, I believe, been captured. Quite an unfortunate result.[8]

I sat down to write you only a short note. I will try and write again in a day or two.

Love to all. Take good care of Josie and do not come to the conclusion that because I am always so anxious to hear from her, I am not as anxious as ever to hear from you. Write to me very frequently.

Since writing the above, I have received a letter from Josie. She has changed her mind about coming to Greenbrier. Please send John back to me as soon as possible. Tell him to bring both horses back with him. Josie says her mother has been in a very nervous condition since the visit of the Yankees to Wytheville. It is, of course, therefore proper that she should stay with her.

Camp Stuart, Greenbrier Co., Va.
Aug. 3RD, 1863

My dear Wife,

Your very welcome letter of the 27th ult. was received yesterday. The other two letters referred to in it have been also received, and I need not tell you what a source of pleasure they have been to me.

We leave this Camp tomorrow but for what point none but our superiors know. The Yankees are clearing away the blockades on the road from Gauley Bridge to Summersville. A considerable force is also advancing against Jackson at Huntersville in Pocahontas [County]. The 45th has orders, as well as we, to hold themselves in readiness for marching.[9] I do not think, however, that we the cavalry will go towards Pocahontas. If we are moved from the county at all, it will, I think, be toward McCausland. But of course we know nothing about it.

Mrs. Stuart and the Misses Gussie & Jennie [Stuart] were on our drill

8. During July 1–26, 1863, Kentucky partisan ranger John Hunt Morgan led 2,500 horsemen on a "Great Raid" through Indiana and Ohio. Initially the physical and psychological effects of the foray were enormous. Then large Union forces began a pursuit that drained the Confederate efforts and led to the disintegration of the raiding party and the capture of the general himself near West Point, Ohio. What Sheffey saw was a remnant of about 150 of Morgan's men who had fled to the safety of the Confederate lines in West Virginia.

9. The 45th Virginia Infantry, together with McClung's Tennessee battery, were also encamped in Greenbrier County.

ground today. I talked to them for some time. They are very much disappointed that you are not coming. It turns out all for the best, however, as we are going away. I sincerely hope that you received my last letter, as it would be quite a misfortune if you were to come to Greenbrier & find me gone. John, I hope, will return to me immediately, as I shall need him very much.

My eye which was affected by the attack of neuralgia mentioned in my last is improving. There is quite an ornamental lump on the side of my nose and at the corner of the eye. It has produced, I think, lumps & inflammation of the nasal duct, and Dr. Baker has thought that an operation would perhaps be necessary, but to-day it is suppurating slightly, and unless the duct proves to be permanently stopped, I think it will get well without. You must not be uneasy about it as it is a trifling affair and I no longer suffer with it. The eye ball has not been affected. I am attending to my regular duties and with the exception above mentioned am in splendid health.

Lieut. Vincent of the Sandy Rangers[10] in a scout he returned from yesterday captured six horses and killed two Yankees beyond Gauley. He made a narrow escape himself. Genl. Morgan & his captured officers have been imprisoned in Ohio and will not be exchanged. His escaped men are still in Greenbrier. The affairs of the Country are rapidly approaching a crisis, but we can stand several reverses. Yet may God strengthen our hearts, and give us victory! We will hope on. It is impossible that we should be subjugated. God will give us victory even when we are driven to the wall, which certainly is not yet. Our wives and sisters and mothers also must keep up their spirits and courage.

I hope Genl. Lee's army will be rapidly strengthened. Upon this success in the impending battle in the East hangs the answer to the question "shall we be slaves or free?" Still I do not think a battle will be fought there for several weeks yet. Do not look for me for some months to come. Already it seems that twelve months have passed since I saw you, but we must be patient and make our happiness a matter of secondary consideration to the claims-of-duty. If you were sick, I would come to you at every hazard, and I will come anyhow at the very earliest opportunity. Meanwhile I will write to you constantly. Your letters are my only source of pleasure. You will therefore, I know, write as often as possible. Give my best love to all. I hope your

10. This is probably Elias Vincent, who led a small detachment of partisan rangers before his 1864 appointment as a captain in Swann's Virginia Cavalry Battalion. Wallace, *Virginia Military Organizations,* 75.

mother & sisters are well as yourself, [and] have entirely recovered from the effects of the Yankee visitation.

Camp Stuart, Greenbrier Co., Va.
AUGUST 7TH, 1863

My dear Wife,

Since I wrote, the slight activity in military affairs in Greenbrier has died away, and we have returned to our wanted quiet. The party of Yankees which threatened Jackson at Huntersville seems to have been sent out merely for the purpose of reconnaissance. I think it is now tolerably certain that we will remain in Greenbrier for the remainder of the season. Though I have not recently been in a condition for anything else but rest, a little excitement would be infinitely preferable to this intolerable quiet.

Since the date of my last letter to you, I have suffered much with my left eye, but am now rapidly getting well. My whole face again swelled up, and I took refuge at Dr. Peyton's,[11] where for several days I have been cared for with the most considerate kindness. Yesterday morning the rising near the corner of the eye broke, and has since been suppurating profusely. Three or four weeks have passed since the eye first became inflamed, but the boil which has been developed by Mrs. Peyton's poultices has, I think, finally relieved it. Had I put myself under her care, I might have been well long ago. I am in camp during the day. I will sleep at Dr. Peyton's for several nights longer.

Yesterday Miss Jennie Stuart sent me quite a basketful of niceties. They are quite offended with me, I believe, because I did not go there and stay until convalescent, but it was a little too far from camp and there are too many young people there for a sick man. Mrs. Ruby with her family left there yesterday. It is quite an interesting family.

I suppose you received my last letter. Have you seen John yet? He is doubtless disconsolate because he couldn't have the honor of bringing you to Greenbrier. He was very homesick, almost as much, perhaps, as I am myself. His trip therefore will be of benefit to him.

I have written as much as I ought, with one eye. Do not be uneasy about me. I will be perfectly well in a day or two. Write as soon and as often as possible. Best love to all.

11. In all likelihood this was Charles S. Peyton, who classified himself on the 1860 census as a farmer. His wife was Agnes Stuart Peyton.

P.S. The above is very brilliant chirography but under the circumstances I think excusable.

Camp Stuart, Va., AUG. 10TH, 1863

My dear Wife,

Your last letter was received yesterday. You must not think of coming to Greenbrier. I would like for John, however, to return to me as soon as possible.

You must not think that I have been put to any trouble at all, and if I had it would be a pleasure to me. John was very homesick, and I would have sent him whether you were coming or not.

It is very difficult for an officer to get a leave of absence from this Department now. The powers that be are very tyrannical. Therefore, I shall not attempt it for some time unless I get sick again. The surgeon gave me a recommendation for a sick leave for 30 days which was approved by the Col. But I am getting well so rapidly that I will not forward it. I will not practice any deceit towards them to gain any favor. I will be well enough for active duty in two or three days.

Therefore we can only be patient under our separation. We change our camp this morning to Sinking Creek.

I am glad you have again had a pleasant visit to Marion. Hope you will frequently find it pleasant to go there. The family there keep up their spirits very well, and frequent visits to them will, I think, effectually exorcise the Blues.

I met the Misses Stuart at Church yesterday. Miss Mae Price was also there.[12] Mrs. Stuart was informed some time ago that you were not coming, therefore no harm done in that quarter, except that they are very much disappointed that you are not coming.

As we are about to move camp, I cannot write longer.

Write to me very often. Reading your letters is the only pleasure I have.

---

12. One of the wealthiest citizens of Greenbrier County at the time was Lewisburg attorney Samuel Price. In 1860 he had two daughters, twenty-year-old Mary and eighteen-year-old Margaret. Sheffey refers to one of them as "Mae."

Marion, Smyth County, Va.[13]
AUGUST 13TH, 1863

My dear sister,

Enclosed I send you a letter from brother brought to us a few moments ago by Jim Cooley,[14] who has just arrived from camp. Ma [Ellen Preston Sheffey] received one on yesterday but it contained no news of interest except that he thought his eye was some better. I hope he will come home as soon as he is able to stand the trip on horseback. Jim says that the motion of the horse causes a good deal of pain in his eye, and as long as this is the case, of course we do not want him to attempt to come. If his letter contains anything later, or more satisfactory, we would be very glad if you would let us know, as we have all felt and still feel, quite anxious about him.

After writing the above, Ma called me down to say that after a consulta-tion with Pa [James White Sheffey], they had concluded that it would be best for you to send John Ross back to Marion for the buggy, so that he could go for brother, if your letter confirms the statement brought by Jim Cooley with regard to his inability to ride on horseback. We are all very anxious and think it would be much better if he were at home where his eye could be properly attended to. He is, of course, entirely unfit for service in his present condition and might as well be at home inactive as to be in camp suffering with his eye and the "Blues." Poor boy, it is difficult to tell which causes the greatest amount of suffering.

Sister Maggie [Margaret S. Peters] went with brother Willie [William E. Peters] to the Saltworks on Monday to spend a week or two with him. We have not heard from her since she left home. I wish you could have been here to see her "start to the Wars," as brother Willie called it. She was mounted on a very tall horse, with her satchel, containing her wardrobe, looking al-most as large as she, strapped on securely to the horn of the saddle, and over all was raised a sun umbrella. Brother Willie tried to make her ride on the saddle bags too, but she refused most positively. I think if an artist had been present, he could not have wished for a better picture of the "little old woman who went to market, her eggs for to sell," so many long years ago.

13. This letter from Sheffey's sister Elizabeth to Josie Sheffey is included to give further insight on family affairs at home during wartime.

14. A native of Wytheville, James Cooley was a civilian until his April 1864 enlistment in the 4th Virginia Reserves. Jeffrey C. Weaver, *Reserves: The Virginia Regimental Histories Series* (Lynchburg, Va., 2002), 393.

I suppose Lucy [Spiller] and Nannie [Radford] have gone to the springs. I was a good deal disappointed when I found I had to give up my trip entirely. But as my throat seemed to be perfectly well and my general health very good, and there are so many reasons why I should not leave home at this time, I concluded to put it off until a more convenient season. My love to Lucy when you write, and tell her that I hope she will have a very pleasant time. I shall expect a full account when I next see her. Did Capt. Fulton[15] accompany them? If he did, I know they will have a perfectly charming time.

Ma leaves us tomorrow evening to pay a short visit to Grandpa [John Preston]. Pa will accompany her and we shall be very lonely by ourselves. Will you not write to some of us during their absence? This is such a miserable scrawl that I am ashamed to send it, but really it is so oppressively hot that I cannot write a cool, sensible, letter. As for the blots, I can almost say it "blotted itself." All of us are very well except Ma, who for the last few days has been afflicted as Lieut. Cannon was during his stay in our city.[16]

I suppose you heard that Col. McMahon had been "honorably acquitted" of every charge brought against him and ordered to take command of his Regiment again.[17] The Court adjourned on Friday. Col. McMahon received his orders on Sunday evening and left for his regiment at daylight Tuesday morning.

All join in much love to you and the family. Send John back if you think there is any necessity.

Affectionately,
Lizzie M. Sheffey

15. Capt. John Hall Fulton of the 4th Virginia Infantry lost a leg at the May 1863 battle of Chancellorsville. On August 1, 1863, he was discharged from Confederate service. Robertson, *4th Virginia Infantry*, 51.

16. Organizational records show no Lieutenant Cannon serving in any Virginia unit. The officer mentioned by Elizabeth Sheffey was therefore from another state and passing through Marion when he became ill.

17. Although the soldiers in the 63d Virginia Infantry thought well of Col. John J. McMahon's kindness, some troops and most superior officers criticized his lax way of commanding. On September 13, 1863, exactly a month after Elizabeth Sheffey's letter, McMahon was relieved from command for his "refusal to enforce military discipline." Jeffrey C. Weaver, *63rd Virginia Infantry* (Lynchburg, Va., 1991), 12–13, 22, 25, 36.

Marion, Va., AUG 29, 1863

My dear wife,

My father with his company went to New River Bridge yesterday.[18] If I thought the Yankees would come there, I would go myself, but I have no idea that they will get as far. There are said to be about a thousand men at the Bridge. Two-thousand are said to have come up from Lynchburg yesterday to Salem, & thence crossed over towards Lewisburg. The 21st and Clark's Battalion left Orange C[ourt] H[ouse] several days since for Covington in Alleghany.[19]

My eye is about as well as it was when I left you. I have followed your injunctions except as to the salts. I forgot them this morning. I will remember them tomorrow.

The 63rd is at Knoxville.[20] Col. Peters' Regiment and a battery of artillery, McClung's, are alone left to defend the Saltworks.

Since writing the above, news by the train has come of a defeat of the Yankees at Lewisburg. Our loss 250. Yankees loss 500.[21] The home guard will

18. Starting August 5 from Winchester, Union general William Woods Averell and thirteen hundred troopers conducted a month-long raid through West Virginia. The major engagement was an August 26 action at White Sulphur Springs near Lewisburg. This offensive put all of southwestern Virginia on military alert. James White Sheffey, Preston's father, was a member of the Smyth County Patrol Guards, in the main composed of men over the conscription age limit of forty-five. George S. Venable, mentioned several times in the Sheffey letters, was also a member of this unit. Jeffrey C. Weaver, *The Virginia Home Guards* (Lynchburg, Va., 1996), 126–27, 132–33. The New River Bridge was at Central Depot (Radford).

19. Col. William E. Peters's 21st Virginia Cavalry was already stationed near the New River Bridge. The 30th Battalion of Virginia Sharpshooters, under Lt. Col. John Lyle Clarke, moved toward West Virginia in the third week of August. Averell had no intention of confronting so many Confederates. Following the White Sulphur Springs engagement, the Union general turned north and returned to his lines. Olson, *21st Virginia Cavalry,* 5–6; Michael West, *30th Battalion Virginia Sharpshooters* (Lynchburg, Va., 1995), 52; *Official Records,* 29, pt. 1:33–38.

20. The 63d Virginia Infantry was organized in 1862 of men primarily from the six southwestern Virginia counties of Carroll, Grayson, Montgomery, Smyth, Washington, and Wythe.

21. Sheffey refers to the August 26 battle at White Sulphur Springs. Union casualties were 26 killed, 129 wounded, and 67 missing. Confederate losses were 20 killed, 129 wounded, and 18 missing. Stutler, *West Virginia in the Civil War,* 242–46. For the role of the 8th Virginia Cavalry in the action, see *Official Records,* 29, pt. 1:56, 57, 62. Fielding Cornett of Company C of the regiment estimated Southern losses at 200 and Union casualties at 600. "They made ten different charges upon our lines," he wrote his sweetheart, "and would get [with]in ten steps of our men but were repulsed every time." Fielding R. Cornett to Rosamond Hale, Sept. 5, 1863, Fielding Raphne Cornett Papers, University of Virginia, Charlottesville.

return from the Bridge tomorrow. 1500 men from Lynchburg have already gone back. I can hear nothing from my company and am very uneasy about them.

I will probably come back to Wytheville before Tuesday. That, however, will depend upon the news I may receive in the interim. I have finished Cosette, having found a copy here. It lacks much of being a "complete novel." Indeed Fantine and Cosette are neither of them, as they are represented to be, "complete novels in themselves." "Les Miserables" would have been more appropriately called "Jean Valjean in five parts."[22]

The news by the train this evening is only rumor. As yet I presume we will get more reliable information tomorrow.

All are well here but Lizzie. She is quite unwell. Mary also has some affection of the eye, but I think it is not very serious. She told Col. Moore[23] when he was afraid the house here would not hold all its guests, "that it was like an omnibus, and would always have room in it for one more," since which witticism, her eye has been very much affected. Indeed I was anxious about her general health when I hear it.

Lucy, I hope, has reached home safely. There will be quite a family reunion.

The girls, Ellen, Lizzie and Mary, will probably come to Wytheville on Saturday next to the dedication. I have delivered the message of yourself and Mrs. Spiller. I am afraid your house also will have to be like Mary's omnibus on that occasion.

Love to all and a kiss for yourself.

All send love. Mary has quite a crow to pick with you for not coming with me. The excuse that you had to prepare for this dedication and the Springs won't "go down" at all. I will be able, however, to make it all right in a few days.

22. In Victor Hugo's novel *Les Miserables,* Cosette was the daughter of Fantine and the adopted daughter of Jean Valjean.

23. Alfred Cleon Moore was the first colonel of the 29th Virginia Infantry. In April 1863 he resigned his commission because of advanced age and declining health. He then became an officer in the Wythe County reserves.

Adair's,[24] *Greenbrier Co., Va.*
SEPT. 21ST, 1863

My darling wife,

I have reached this point after several days of very hard riding only to find the regiment marching in the direction from which I have come.[25] The Regiment is ordered to report immediately to Col. McCausland at Princeton.[26] I think we will be sent to Saltville. You will direct your letters to Dublin & to McCausland's Brigade until you hear further from me. We will stay at Pickaway Plains[27] to-night and will get to the Narrows day after tomorrow.

My eye is doing very well. It is even in better condition than when I left Wytheville. Your mother's salve is quite a panacea.

There is quite an excitement in Greenbrier and Monroe on account of several armies of ghosts that have been seen and some strange noises that have been heard by different persons. These tales are very romantic, equal to those tales of the spectral Moors with which Irving embellished the pages of the Alhambra.[28] A man of undoubted veracity named Dwyer[29] says he will swear that he and three young ladies saw many men dressed in white uniforms, some walking on the ground and some walking in the air, pass the turnpike road in this county near [David S.] Skagg's & going northward. The same appearance was seen by many others and is well authenticated.

Many people think it is intended as a sign that the Yankees are about to return northward and leave us to rest in peace. But they be not Joseph's nor Daniel's that they should interpret truly, the visions of those who have the second sight.[30] Others still more superstitious think them the ghosts of the

24. Irish-born Robert Adair had a larger-than-usual farm in Greenbrier County.

25. On September 23, Federals reported the 8th Virginia Cavalry as being in the Sinking Creek region of eastern West Virginia. *Official Records,* 29, pt. 2:226.

26. For the orders attendant to the regiment's transfer to McCausland's command, see ibid., 733–34, 737.

27. Pickaway is on the road connecting Lewisburg and Union.

28. The Alhambra, built by Moorish kings in the thirteenth century, was a citadel and palace at Granada, Spain. Washington Irving visited it often when he was attaché at the American legation in Madrid. Irving later wrote a well-received volume of sketches and .tales entitled *Legends of the Alhambra* (1813).

29. The 1860 Greenbrier County census lists thirty-two-year-old John Dwyer as a trader. Since his name appears just above some stagecoach drivers, he was probably a traveling salesman in the region.

30. Joseph was a biblical hero in the book of Genesis. His interpretation of people's dreams brought him rank and honor. Daniel was another Old Testament man of courage and famed for interpreting a dream by Nebuchadnezzar and the Handwriting on the Wall.

slain, and others who are inclined to make fun of these serious matters say that the realms of Satan are filled so full of Yankees that he can accommodate no more, and many therefore are doomed to walk the Earth in the unrest of the wicked.

I think as I cannot doubt that such appearances have been seen, that they may be traceable to some natural causes. We have had a great many fogs this year and the air is constantly hazy. These spectres may have been created by some refraction on this peculiar atmosphere, as the mirage of the desert, or the spectre of the Hartz Mountains are produced.

The most incredible and unaccountable story is that of a woman and her daughters who live on Indian Creek in Monroe and who say they heard noises, like the beating of drums and the clashing of sabers, that they went towards the noise and it receded from them, that they then started toward a man's house, so that they were afraid to go [to] the house. They then called to the man of the house, but he also heard the noise and was afraid to go to them, but at last brought out his gun and fired it in the direction of the sound, after which it was heard no more. This I think is a great Munchausen yarn.[31] But enough on the spectre subject.

I hope you are very well. You must be very good, and take exercise and wear warm stockings, and not mope with that old handkerchief tied over your head. The Yankees, I understand, are at Bristol.[32] You must keep out of their way if they come to Wytheville. I will be very uneasy about you. Love to all. May God bless and guard you my dear, dear wife is my fervent prayer.

> *Camp in Abb's Valley, Tazewell Co., Va.*
> SEPT. 26TH, 1863

My darling Wife,

I wrote to you from Greenbrier several days ago—which letter was mailed at the Narrows and I suppose has been received. I curiously write you a short note this morning. We have been on horseback until yesterday, since I left Wytheville.

---

31. In 1785 Rudolf Erich Raspe published a collection of burlesque stories under the title *Baron Munchausen's Narrative of His Marvellous Travels and Campaigns in Russia.* The book's high-spirited satire caused it to go through numerous editions.

32. In mid-August heavy Union forces under Maj. Gens. William S. Rosecrans and Ambrose E. Burnside began a prolonged offensive to seize Chattanooga and occupy East Tennessee. Federal cavalry fanned out as far north as the Virginia state line. For the September 19 action at Bristol, see *Official Records*, 29, pt. 2:579, 592, 645.

My eye has stood the dust and sun wonderfully, but the discharge from it is constant. I do not think it advisable to delay the operation of tubing it until Dr. Crockett's return from Richmond.[33] I have therefore written to Dr. Hunter,[34] the Confederate surgeon of this department, and I expect to go to Giles C[ourt] H[ouse] for the purpose of having the operation performed as soon as I hear from him. You must not be uneasy about me as I will take the best possible care of myself, and if I go to Giles CH, I will come home from that place.

I am now within fifty-five or sixty miles from Wytheville, but our letters go around by Princeton, Pearisburg and Dublin.

I was offered the position of Provost Officer at Tazewell CH for the winter but declined it. I may regret that I did so before the winter is over, but as long as I am unfit for duty, they are compelled to let me go wherever I choose anyhow.

I have not heard from you since I left Wytheville and am getting somewhat anxious. Please write as soon as you can. I am very foolish about you, and am terribly disappointed when the mails come in without bringing me letters from you. When you do not receive letters regularly from me, you may know either that my letters have miscarried, or that I am upon some march where I can have no chance to write.

No news here except the news of Bragg's great fight in Tennessee.[35] If that is as successful as reported, it will pull us right side up again. The loss of Maj. Gen. Wood[36] is a great loss to the Confederacy and will be generously deplored. Many other gallant officers have, I doubt not, been killed.

Men of the Border Rangers pitched into a squad of Union men and Yan-

33. The term "tubing" referred to placement of a drainage tube into the corner of the eye to assist in the evacuation of an abscess. It was a painful and dangerous procedure that required a skillful physician. Robert Crockett, mentioned in the same sentence, practiced medicine in Wytheville for almost four decades.

34. John A. Hunter had been surgeon of the 27th Virginia Infantry. He served at a number of military hospitals before his appointment as medical director of the Army of Southwest Virginia.

35. A Union general called the September 18–20 fighting at Chickamauga "a mad, irregular battle, very much resembling guerrilla warfare on a vast scale." Gen. Braxton Bragg should have won a clear-cut victory, but his corps commanders failed repeatedly to obey attack orders. The battle produced 34,500 casualties and accomplished nothing tactically.

36. At Chickamauga Brig. Gen. Sterling Alexander Martin Wood led a brigade in Maj. Gen. Patrick Cleburne's division. Cleburne omitted any mention of Wood in his official report of the engagement; Wood promptly resigned from the army and returned home to Alabama.

kees recently on the edge of Wyoming, captured one, killed one, wounded one and captured several horses. The Yankees will suffer if they come up here now, unless they succeed in surprising us, which I think they cannot do, though our horses are ranging through a boundary of four thousand acres.

Abb's Valley is quite celebrated in the history of Tazewell, and of Va. Am at the residence of the [James] Moore family, who were all massacred here by the Indians except two who were carried off and kept in captivity for a long while. It is named, I suppose, from a man who discovered it or settled in it at an early period, though some of my men have suggested that it derived its name from the fact that the people regarded their education complete when they had learned their "A, b, abs." It is a narrow, rugged valley but the land is fertile, and the blue grass pastures are generally very fine.

The upper or western end is a sort of basin, and the spring branches all start towards the center, though they soon sink. Out of the lower end runs one of the forks of Bluestone, which empties into New River a short distance above Pack's Ferry.

Our Regiment will be very probably wintered in Tazewell, which will be pleasant as I can thus be near to you and can at least have the satisfaction of knowing that I am between you and the enemy. The Tazewell people, I am told, petitioned for us. I for one am much obliged to them.

I was much amused on the trip to Greenbrier by some of John's original ideas. One day I asked him to explain to me the operation of the telegraph, and in what manner the messages were transmitted upon the wires. He said that it was one of the deep things to him, and he didn't know whether he exactly understood it. He had thought a good deal about it and had concluded that the writing was caused by a kind of jar of the wires. He, of course, had no reference to Leyden jars. I asked him how he thought the jar was caused. He said he didn't know unless it was done by putting some sort of aquafortis upon the ends of the wires.

Among many of the curiosities of which I have recently heard is a family of Congo negroes near Cold Knob in Greenbrier. They go entirely naked, and if clothing is put upon them, they tear it off directly. They speak the Congo language and do not understand English at all. Their heads are perfectly flat, and they are generally hideous specimens of humanity. Every morning at sunrise they go out upon the hills, and with shrieks and yells and much uncouth gesticulation, worship the rising sun. They were brought over by a slave trader but are now free, I believe. Some of our men have seen them, and they must be a very considerable curiosity from the accounts they give of them.[37]

Much speculation was rife in Greenbrier upon the ghost subject, about which I have already written to you. I think the appearances there can be most reasonably accounted for upon the principles of refraction, though Kelly Bennett,[38] who is quite a scientific man, and is also a believer in "signs and wonders," has set them down to the credit of the supernatural. Among the ten thousand spectral soldiers who were seen there, none were going southward; the universal direction was northward. This is a peculiarity for which I cannot account.

Among the many marvelous things I have recently heard is the tale of an old man named Adam, from whose house I wrote my last letter to you. I hear the ghost subject has reached that of spiritual rappings. He said that for a long time he did not believe in them at all, but at last concluded he would try an experiment. So he and five other persons seated themselves around a small table and placed their hands upon it. After about a half-hour, the table began to move. They took their hands off and the table walked across the floor without any one touching it. He asked it many questions which it answered satisfactorily by rapping. A hat was lying upon the floor. He told the table to go to the hat and put one foot upon it, which it did, no one being near to it. He then threw himself upon the table, and though he is a large man, it moved with his weight upon it. This is perfectly incredible, yet he is a man of good character, and his talk was corroborated by two ladies who were present when he told me, and who said they were witnesses of the experiment. Hume's argument that it is easier for three persons to lie than for such a thing to be so, would, I think, be applicable here.[39]

If this be so, there is in nature some powerful, all-pervading principle or fluid as yet undiscovered, which is akin to electricity and yet very different from it. It is the principle which connects the brain of the mesmerist with

37. This is the most bizarre report in the entire collection of Sheffey letters. No such African tribe inhabited Greenbrier County. Further, one authority has stated, "a family of any naked humans would have trouble surviving the winter in the wilds near Cold Knob." James E. Talbert, archivist, Greenbrier Historical Society, to editor, Aug. 9, 2002.

38. The 1860 Wythe County census lists Kelley Bennett as a nineteen-year-old student. No record exists of his serving in the Confederate army.

39. David Hume was an eighteenth-century Scottish thinker whose philosophical skepticism restricted human knowledge to the experience of ideas and impressions. The best expression of Humanism is *Philosophical Essays Concerning Human Understanding* (1748).

that of the person under his influence, and gives the will of the one power over that of the other. It is the principle which links the mind of the clairvoyant with the far distant scenes through which he travels in his dreaming condition. It is the principle which gives the will of a man power over his own limbs, enabling him to move them as he chooses, and in the same manner, when he can extend the current beyond his own body, into another animate or inanimate object gives him power to move that also as he chooses. It is the principle which moved the inanimate chaos when God said, "Let there be Light" and which, under the influence of the Supreme Will, set the shapeless masses into order, until "the morning stars sang together and all the sons of God shouted for joy."[40]

Like the vital principle which is still more mysterious, it may forever be concealed from the finite comprehension of man, but it will exist nevertheless, and the work of its creation under the mere exertion of the will of the supreme architect will go on and the sons of men will continue to be startled by the strange workings of this unseen & unknown principle, which emanates from the mind of God and of man as the electrical fluid emanates from the jar of the chemist & the zinc & copper vessels of the telegraph operator.

If man possessed this secret, he also could create. He also could say to matter "do this" and it would do it, just as the medium compels the table under his influence to act, or to answer strange ideas. This is a strange subject. I will not weary you longer with them. When I commenced writing, I thought I would be brief, but I have written you a long and prosy letter for which you must forgive me. I do so love to write to you, my darling, that *that* should be a sufficient excuse.

Marion, SEPT. 26TH 1863[41]

My dear sister,

The excitement of the past few weeks would have prevented any writing to my "sweetheart," were I blessed with such an article, but still I feel that I have been remiss in my duty to you. I know you will give me absolution for my sin of omission, though I will readily submit to any punishment you may inflict upon me.

40. This quotation is from Job 38:7.

41. Here again one of Sheffey's sisters provides an excellent picture of the unstable home front during the war.

Last week was one of the most intense anxiety and excitement; anxiety for Brother Willie, Trigg, Jimmie[42] and other friends in Tennessee, and excitement about the near approach of the Yankees, who as usual *disappointed* us. Refugees flying through as if the enemy was in immediate pursuit, negroes, cattle, horses, hogs and sheep going through in perfect droves, really made me feel a little green, for we thought it very probable that we would be favored with a visit from our Yankee friends, but we are beginning to settle down into our usual quiet and feeling of security.

Mr. and Mrs. Leftwich[43] were still here, when Uncle Walter [Preston], Uncle Frank [Preston] and Aunt Fannie Preston came, driven off from Washington County by the approach of the enemy. We had a very pleasant visit from Mr. and Mrs. L[eftwich]. And I was sorry our genial enjoyment of their society was so often interrupted. They will have to make us another visit when there is no fear of the Yankees coming in, if such a time ever arrives. Uncle Walter and Aunt Fannie are refugees from Arkansas, where they lost all their property. I have no idea of how long they will stay with us, but as they are dependent upon their friends for a home, I suppose they will remain sometime. Sue White[44] is also with us, a refugee from Abingdon. We tease her a great deal about running away from home, and she vows that this is her last trip as "Miss Refugee." Uncle Frank brought his and Grand Pa's [Henry L. Sheffey's] negroes and cattle up here to keep them out of danger.

Tell Lucy [Spiller] that we had the pleasure of a visit from Major N[ounnan] a day or two ago, and that I think the pleasant impression made at the springs was mutual. He thinks Miss Lucy is one of the liveliest and most agreeable young ladies, always and forever excepting Miss Carter, that he has met with for a long time. He left here for Wytheville, and I presume has given himself the pleasure of a call ere this.

I hope Mrs. [Robinson] Stuart has entirely recovered from her attack. We were so sorry that she hadn't stopped here that evening, as I imagine this would have been a more comfortable place to be sick at than Glade Spring. Pa is still at the Salt Works with his Home Guards and we are becoming very

42. Col. Williams Peters and Trigg Sheffey were in the 21st Virginia Cavalry, while James W. Sheffey was a lieutenant in the 63d Virginia Infantry. These three soldiers had been part of a detachment involved in skirmishes at Blountsville and Carter's Depot, Tennessee. See Olson, *21st Virginia Cavalry*, 6–7.

43. Isaac J. Leftwich, a prominent Wytheville attorney, banker, and businessman, was married to the former Nancy Ward.

44. No such person is listed in the 1860 census for Washington County.

anxious for his return.[45] I fear so much exposure will have a serious effect upon his health.

Please write to us about brother—we haven't heard one word from him since he left here. We are very anxious about his eye. I have skipped from one subject to another with such rapidity that I fear you will be bewildered. Tell Frank [Spiller] that we were all angry with him for not stopping to get his breakfast yesterday morning. All send a great deal of love to you, your mother and sisters. Write very soon.

Your loving Ellen

Brother Willie was well when we heard from him last, which was before any fighting was done.[46]

Camp Bowen in Abb's Valley
Tazewell Co., Va., SEPT. 30TH, 1863

My darling wife,

Your sweet letter of the 25th inst. was received day before yesterday. I would have answered it yesterday if I had been at leisure. My eye is much better than it has been since it was first attacked. Unless I should be so unfortunate as to take cold, I will get along with it wonderfully well, very much better indeed than I could possibly have anticipated. I have not yet heard from Dr. Hunter. The sooner I have the stile (or style, I do not know the orthography) inserted, the better,[47] as I cannot get well without, if I am to trust the opinion of the learned disciples of Galen in this Regiment, and they are doubtless correct.

We have little news here. Col. Henry Bowen was attacked and beaten in Buchanan a few days ago.[48] We sent two companies to his assistance. The

45. The threat of Union cavalry raids on the works at Saltville kept the whole region in a state of anxiety. James White Sheffey's influence with the Wythe County Home Guards can be seen in *Official Records,* 29, pt. 2:787, 826.

46. During September 1863, Colonel Peters's 21st Virginia Cavalry participated in a number of skirmishes with Federal horsemen in the Bristol area. In one of those actions, Peters received a wound that forced him to retire from military service. Olson, *21st Virginia Cavalry,* 7.

47. A style, often called a stylet, was a slender probe or wire used to assist in drainage of an eye abscess. Oftentimes it was inserted through the tubing (see note 33) to probe more deeply into the infected area.

48. Sheffey was totally incorrect here. Col. Henry S. Bowen and his 22d Virginia Cavalry were then on patrol duty in East Tennessee. The regiment took part in no major engagement of note in September, but it lost 2 men wounded and 2 captured in that period. Jeffrey C. Weaver, *22nd Virginia Cavalry* (Lynchburg, Va., 1991), 17–19.

enemy number 130. Our regiment has been divided into squadrons. I am "Captain Commanding," First Squadron. We will soon be scattered over Tazewell County. Some of us will go to the West End. I hope I shall be sent either to the [Wyoming County, West Virginia,] Ct. House or to Liberty, as at either place I would not be more than twenty or thirty miles from Union.

Sgt. E. H. Ward came in [from] Wythe today, bringing me the pistol which caused Rob [Hammett] so much trouble, and the brush I forgot when I left Wytheville. I wish you would settle for mending the pistol. Poor Rob, I do not think he ought to have it to pay for it.

Whenever you need money, you must not hesitate to apply to me for it, or to my father with whom I left a thousand dollars when I left Marion.

I have a great deal to do before I can leave my company. I will, however, take advantage of every opportunity to get to see you. It is very, very dull here. Indeed, you have ruined a model soldier. But I will do my duty as well as the best, if it is irksome.

In the meantime, you must take very good care of yourself and must not go off into cold rooms by yourself until you are nearly "frozen." And indeed, you must dress your feet more warmly. If I could only be with you this winter, you would learn how delightful an institution woolen stockings are, and what a humbug King Cotton is. I doubt not you would think me very tyrannical, but I could stumble upon the spur of the moment.

I will write to you again in a very few days and will keep you advised of everything that turns up of importance.

Your letters are my comforters here as elsewhere. You could not write a dull one if you were to try. You must write very often but not in a cold room for if you were to get sick, I should be very miserable.

I have not heard from Marion since I left Wytheville except through men who have come from there. But I have not had time to write, and of course would not expect them to do so.

Camp near Tiffanys,[49] *Tazewell Co., Va.*
OCTOBER 9TH, 1863

My darling wife,

Your sweet letters of the 3rd and 4th have been received, one by mail and the other by Lieut. [Andrew F.] St. John, who came in today. I ought to have written to you several days since but we have been moving, and whenever we

49. Charles Fitzgerald Tiffany was "an active and influential citizen" who had "a splendid estate in the Bluestone Valley of Tazewell County." Pendleton, *Tazewell County,* 515, 626.

stopped, I have been so busy that I have scarcely had time to "turn around three times and say Jack Robinson."[50]

I hope you have enjoyed the conference very much. From the specimens of the Methodist brethren we occasionally listen to in this country, I doubt not you have heard much eloquence of a very extraordinary character.

I had a visit yesterday from my Uncle Robert, whom you have never seen but of whom you have doubtless heard. He is the father of the two boys, Trigg and James Sheffey, whom you have seen. He is one of the most singularly eccentric men I have ever known, but if there were, I think he is the one. He told me with much gusto of his marriage last January and of his perfect happiness. He said that just the kind of lady he has prayed for, he had succeeded in getting. He sends his love to you. He has been preaching in Tazewell for some weeks. He does not belong to the conference, but goes about preaching on his own hook, and is never satisfied until he gets up a tremendous shout.[51] He is then in his element. I have not seen him for several years until yesterday. He makes appointments from Craig to Russell [Counties] and is constantly going from one place to another.

I rallied him a good deal upon the fried chicken he was supplied with, and gave him a horrible description of our camp life, after which I invited him to sup with me. He fortunately declined the invitation. We had eaten dinner, and there was not a piece of meat or bread as big as a dollar in the camp chest. I went without supper myself, as I generally do, in camp.

I have been very busy recently writing up my rolls & accounts. It is heavy work and will take me several days yet. As soon as I get them completed, I will apply for a sick leave and come to you. I do not like to leave my company in the present unsettled state of the Regt. But my anxiety to see you and to have this eye cured will overrule all such consideration.

I am very glad you are in such fine health. If you are always so, I shall be always perfectly content.

I think you are mistaken about my father's promotion. I cannot learn that

---

50. This phrase means "immediately." Its origins are obscure, but it was in use as early as the eighteenth century.

51. A county historian repeated a popular story of Rev. Robert Sheffey encountering two whiskey stills: "He asked the Lord to destroy Harmon's by letting a tree fall on it which was done. An old dead tree struck by lightning fell on the still house, caught on fire and the whole thing burned up. Uncle Bob asked the Lord to destroy the still house on White Oak Branch and suggested that it might be an easy way to send a flood and wipe it out. The rains descended, the stream rose to heights never reached before, and when it subsided there was no still house." Wilson, *Smyth County History*, 359–60.

the homeguards in Smyth have yet been organized into a battalion, though it may be so. My father is, however, the ranking Captain and as such commands the County forces.[52]

I regret very much to hear of Mrs. Tartar's death.[53] Tartar is doubtless almost heartbroken; and my father will miss a housekeeper at the Wythe place very much.

It is now sundown, and as I cannot write in the dusk and have no candles, I must close. I will write to you again in a few days. As soon as my company affairs will permit me to leave them, I will come to Wytheville, unless my superiors refuse me a leave of absence, which under the circumstances they will scarcely do. Let me know when Dr. Crockett gets home. Two or three weeks may elapse before I come, as I would like very much to have my company paid off before I leave it, but I may come sooner. We are now near Springville & near the road leading from Princeton to Tazewell C.H. It is about ten or fifteen miles to Jeffersonville.

Best love to all, and to you I would send my whole heart if I could without injury to my health. But I will bring it very soon.

Camp Davis, 7½ Miles from Abingdon
OCTOBER 19TH, 1863

My Darling Wife,

We have been traveling so much that I have had no opportunity for some time to write to you. As I am sending a man to Abingdon this morning and have a minute or two to write, I will do so to let you know where and how I am. My eye is still in status quo. I do not suffer much from it. Cannot leave the command until the Yankees are driven from our front, which we hope to accomplish very soon. They have retreated to some point beyond Blountville [Tennessee], and we expect to make our advance in a few days.

Our Regt. now belongs to Genl. Wm. E. Jones' Brigade.[54] You can therefore direct your letters to Abingdon, 8th Va. Cavalry, Genl. Wm. E. Jones

52. Five days after this letter, Sheffey's father received orders to proceed quickly with the Smyth County Home Guard to Glade Spring and a possible Union raid. *Official Records*, 29, pt. 2:787.

53. According to the 1860 Wythe County census, James W. Tarter was a thirty-five-year-old carpenter with a twenty-three-year-old wife, Eliza, and one child.

54. Unknown to Sheffey, Brig. Gen. J. E. B. "Jeb" Stuart was trying to get the 8th Virginia Cavalry transferred to the Army of Northern Virginia. The War Department issued orders to that effect on October 8, 1863. Departmental commander Samuel Jones got the directive suspended, but on October 23 Stuart again requested that the 8th and the 14th Virginia Cavalry become part of the his cavalry corps. General Lee endorsed the request: "I fear that as

Brigade. We have [Gen. Montgomery D.] Corse's Brigade, William E. Jones & Wharton's; Majr. Gen. Jones & Brig. Genl. Crittenden[55] are also at Abingdon. Saw Frank Findlay[56] at Abingdon yesterday. We will possibly remain at this camp for a week as it will perhaps require that time to complete the organization of our Cavalry Brigades. Witcher & the Yankees had a considerable skirmish not long since at my grandfather's [Henry L. Sheffey].[57] The county is said to be much desolated.

I will write to you tomorrow or the next day. I must close now. The news from Lee is glorious.[58] Bragg also is said to be fighting[59] & Vallandigham is reported to have been elected Gov. of Ohio.[60]

Goodbye, my darling. Take good care of yourself and may God in his mercy watch over you.

---

soon as the order is issued it will give rise to a report of an advance [in southwestern Virginia] by the enemy, and the operation of the order be again suspended." Jones predictably protested. On November 4 Lee closed the matter with the gruff statement: "I still think that General Jones has more cavalry than is needed or can be used in his department advantageously. If it is kept to the decision of each general whether he will spare any troops when they are needed elsewhere, our armies will be scattered instead of concentrated, and we will be at the mercy of the enemy at all points." *Official Records,* 29, pt. 2:778, 800–1, 805, 807–8, 820; 30, pt. 4:239–42.

55. Maj. Gen. George B. Crittenden, whose brother Thomas was a major general in the Union army, had resigned his commission in October 1862 after being censured for drunkenness. Throughout most of September 1863, Crittenden was a colonel in charge of all Confederate cavalry in southwestern Virginia. Ibid., 30, pt. 2:607.

56. Abingdon's Frank Smith Findlay had been a member of the 1st Virginia Cavalry and courier for Jeb Stuart before becoming a captain in the 4th Virginia State Line. A wound from the December 1862 battle at Big Sandy River ended Findlay's military career. Robert J. Driver Jr., *1st Virginia Cavalry* (Lynchburg, Va., 1991), 173.

57. On October 18 Col. Vincent Addison Witcher and his 34th Virginia Cavalry Battalion repulsed a Federal attack at Blountville, Tennessee. Six days later near Zollicoffer, Witcher's troops attacked the rear guard of the 8th Tennessee Cavalry (U.S.) and inflicted 61 casualties. Cole, *34th Cavalry Battalion,* 59–60.

58. The October 14 battle at Bristoe Station was for Lee a tactical defeat that cost him 1,400 men. But the Confederate assaults temporarily severed the Orange and Alexandria Railroad and forced the Amy of the Potomac to retire forty miles.

59. Bragg was in fact fighting—with his insubordinate generals rather than with the Union army. A visit to the western army by Pres. Jefferson Davis did nothing to curb the dissension. The Army of Tennessee moved slowly to besiege nearby Chattanooga, but that offensive ended in disaster within a month.

60. Ohio congressman Clement Vallandigham was leader of the Peace Democrats in the North. Arrested in May 1863 for "expressing treasonable sympathy," he was banished to the South. Vallandigham was living in Windsor, Ontario, at the time of Sheffey's letter.

{ CHAPTER 8 }

INTO THE SHENANDOAH VALLEY

It was in the third year of the Civil War that Pres Sheffey saw his first major battle. For two months early in 1864, he was judge advocate on a departmental court martial that met in Lee and Scott Counties. Boredom was the overriding emotion; but as Sheffey admits, at least he was out of the winter weather. Isolated in the far southwestern corner of Virginia, the captain concludes to his satisfaction that the Civil War would end within several months.

Sheffey apparently spent most of May 1864 near his home and his wife. A five-week gap exists in his letters around that month.

The 8th Virginia Cavalry then became part of the Confederate defense of the vital Shenandoah Valley. Sheffey and his regiment were too late to be in the June 5 battle of Piedmont, where the Southern cavalry was routed and its commander, Brig. Gen. "Grumble" Jones, was killed. Yet the southwestern Virginians were engaged in fighting at Lynchburg and Hanging Rock, Virginia; Leetown, West Virginia; and Frederick, Maryland. Then, on August 7, Sheffey and a large number of his troopers were captured in a surprise Union attack at Moorefield, West Virginia.

For Sheffey, his field service had come to an end.

> *Hd. Qrs. Genl. Ct. Martial*
> *Jones Brigade, Lee Co., Va.*
> FEBY. 25TH, 1864

My darling Wife,

Though I have been very busy today, I cannot let another night pass without writing a few lines to you. Ere this reaches you, you will have heard of our gallant fight at Wyerman's Mills in this county within five miles of Cumberland Gap, in which we killed, wounded and captured over 270 Yankees.[1]

---

1. At dawn on February 25, 1864, Gen. "Grumble" Jones's brigade made a surprise attack on a Federal encampment near Gibson's and Wyerman's Mills. Most of the Union troops were in the 11th Tennessee Cavalry (U.S.). In the brief action the Federals were routed. The 11th Tennessee lost 13 killed and its colonel, Reuben A. Davis, was wounded and captured. The Confederates also secured 255 prisoners, one hundred horses, hundreds of small arms, and the en-

I was unfortunately at the time in command of a squadron in Hancock Co., Tenn., on picket & consequently was not permitted to participate in the honor of this brilliant little victory. Col. Peters' horse was shot by two balls, but he providentially escaped. He seems to bear a charmed life. The brave Capt. was killed by his side.[2] Three men (privates and sergeants) of the 8th were killed, and one of Witcher's men.[3] Our Brigade is invincible by anything like an equal force. The force of Yankees attacked at Wyerman's was about 500.

I am now on very laborious duty as Judge Advocate of a General Ct. Martial, whose duration from the amt. of business already in my hands will, I think, be almost interminable. We are at present at the house of Mr. Robt. Bales[4] in Powell's Valley, about 18 miles from Cumberland Gap. Col. Peters is President of the Court. The order is from Genl. [James] Longstreet, and it will doubtless be long before we are relieved from this disagreeable duty. It has one advantage, however, it takes us out of the wind and smoke.

I have written twice to you since I have been in Lee and you cannot imagine how anxiously I have looked for a letter from you. But I have never received a line from any of the dear ones at home. The Marion people, however, are excusable, as I have yet had time . . . [rest of letter missing]

Marion, MARCH 7TH, 1864[5]

My dear sister,

My poor dashing brother seems from the line of his letter to be in a "peck of troubles." Really it would be too bad, would it not, after all his pride in the gallant 8th for it to be disbanded just at the time when it could win for itself undying glory?[6] I regret so much that Gen. Jenkins was unable to get

---

tire camp equipage of the Federals—all at a cost of 3 killed and 7 wounded. *Official Records,* 31, pt. 1:411–15.

2. Charles E. Burks was captain of Company B, 21st Virginia Cavalry, when he was killed while leading his company in action. "He was a most gallant and meritorious officer," Colonel Peters reported. Ibid., 414–15.

3. Casualties of the 8th Virginia Cavalry at Wyerman's Mills were Jesse Meeks and Andersonville Frazier killed and James M. Shelton wounded; none was from Sheffey's company. Dickinson, *8th Virginia Cavalry,* 46.

4. The 1860 census shows that Robert M. Bales owned a large farm in Lee County. His family included a wife, Eliza W., and four children.

5. This is a letter from Sheffey's sister Ellen to Josephine Spiller Sheffey.

6. Apparently a rumor was circulating in Smyth County that members of the 8th Virginia Cavalry were not going to reenlist at the end of their three-year terms. In fact nine of the ten

the regiment back into his own command. Had he succeeded in his efforts, the men would have gladly remained in the South, fighting for the cause with which they have already identified themselves. They adore Jenkins and would follow him to the death, were they permitted to return to him.

I believe it is the only regiment I have heard of which has refused to re-enlist, and it must be exceedingly mortifying to brother. Dear boy! My heart aches to think that he has to endure so many hardships and privations and my wrath against the Yankees, the cause of all the suffering in our beautiful land, daily waxes greater, until I fear it will absorb all the better feelings of my nature. I wrote him a few days ago in as cheering a strain as I could and will write again in a day or two, though I fear many of our letters never reach their destination. We have felt quite anxious since the last fight for we have heard nothing directly from "our boys." From the papers we learn that brother Willie [Peters] had his horse shot from under him, but sister Mag hasn't received a letter from him yet.

Col. Bowen's regiment [22d Virginia Cavalry] moved yesterday from Pa's farm to Mr. Bear's farm,[7] about a mile west of town. We have one or two very pleasant acquaintances in the command, and have enjoyed frequent calls. Lieut. Kent,[8] Lucy's old sweetheart, is here drilling them and has taken tea with us two or three times. He seems to delight in recalling reminiscences of the past, in which Lucy figures extensively. He says that his extreme jealousy of Charles Boyd,[9] after the hiding scrape, almost deranged him, and he concluded that rather than lose his wits, he would abandon the field in Charlie's favor. Ask Lucy if she didn't help him to this conclusion!

I am going to take a ride with him the first pretty day. I am to have the honor of riding Capt. Stuart's[10] fine horse. You know Quartermaster's horses are always *Splendid!*

---

companies promptly reenlisted. Company E, the Border Rangers, at first refused, but after sixty-day furloughs, its soldiers signed up for another tour. Dickinson, *8th Virginia Cavalry,* 47.

7. Joseph Bear was also a Marion merchant. A picture of his home, which served as Col. Henry Bowen's headquarters, is in Armstrong, *Smyth County,* 2:140.

8. Joseph Ferdinand Kent had been a major in the 4th Virginia Infantry. He was then commander of the Wythe County Home Guard. Robertson, *4th Virginia Infantry,* 59. The object of his attention was Lucy Ann Spiller.

9. Charles R. Boyd had also served in the Wythe Guards of the 4th Virginia Infantry. Promoted to lieutenant in July 1861, Boyd then transferred to the C.S. Engineers. Ibid., 41.

10. Brother of the famous Confederate cavalry chief, William Alexander Stuart was a prominent Wytheville figure. He was then managing family affairs and was in charge of the salt works at Saltville.

Col. Johnnie has been absent for ten days or more and Mary [Sheffey] has been disconsolate. The news of Major [A. F.] Cook's departure, however, turned her thoughts into a new channel, and she is alternately grieving over that and John M. Preston's marriage.[11] His wound was a most fortunate one and I dare say he blessed the Yankee who gave it to him, as it hastened the consummation of his bliss. He brought his bride, formerly [Miss] Cochran of Charlottesville,[12] to Abingdon but had gone back to C[harlottesville]. John M. is still on crutches and suffers a good deal with his wound.

Sister Mag [Margaret Sheffey Peters] says that you must not trouble yourself any more about the cloth. Just leave it at the tailor's until he is able to make it up. I enclose the receipt for the money paid for the cloth you bought.

It is getting late and I must bid you good night. All send a great deal of love to you. Mrs. [Susan Crockett] Spiller and Lucy write often to dear brother and keep him cheered up. As ever my darling,

Your loving Nellie

Headquarters, Genl. Ct. Martial
Camp, Brig. Genl. Jones Brigade
MARCH 11TH, 1864

My darling Wife,

I received a few days ago a dear letter from you dated, I believe, on the 29th ult. I ought to have answered it immediately, but have been writing so incessantly that I could not.

Today we finished the twelfth case before this Court. We have not yet begun with the officers, but there are several, I regret to say, against whom charges have been preferred. The work upon me is very laborious but I stand it wonderfully. My eye, however, is not quite so well as it was on account of the quantity of writing I have had to do. But I am under shelter, and not exposed therefore to the March winds.

11. John Montgomery Preston of Smyth County had served as a captain in the 48th Virginia Infantry. He was wounded in the neck at Gettysburg. Four months later he received a severe thigh injury at Payne's Farm. Preston was a patient at the Emory & Henry College Hospital until his 1865 assignment to the Bureau of Conscription. One writer termed him "a lovable and beautiful character whose life was a benediction to the community." John D. Chapla, *48th Virginia Infantry* (Lynchburg, Va., 1989), 147; Wilson, *Smyth County History,* 126.

12. On February 3, 1864, John M. Preston married Mary Preston Lewis Cochran of Charlottesville. Jim Presgraves, ed., *Smyth County Families and History* (Pulaski, Va., 1974), 36.

Col. Peters, Col. Cook & Lieut. Alderson[13] are the Court, and Mr. Charles Calhoun,[14] of Lynchburg, who has been my Clerk thus far, are staying at the same house with me. So that we manage to wear the dreary time away. The days are weeks—the weeks seem long as years, which keep me away from my Darling. But they will wear away.

I have received two letters from you since I have been in Lee [County], and this is the 5th I have written. But I fear most of them have failed to reach their destination.

Genl. [William E.] Jones started on an expedition into Harlan Co., Ky., to overhaul a train of Yankee packmules.[15] He would not let the Court go with him, much to our regret. But perhaps it is best, as there is so much work for us to do that I fear we will not get to go on any expedition for a month or two.

I hope my father has long ere this recovered entirely. I was very uneasy about him for awhile. I have not written to Marion at all, as Col. Peters and John are both here with me, and they are constantly sending letters to their Jerasha's[16] which keep them posted as to me.

I have written today until my hand is tired and am now writing on my knee by the flickering light of a very indifferent dipped candle. So that you must excuse this scribbling.

Your mother and Lucy, I hope, are well. Have Lucy's senators come a-wooing yet? Tell her she must not make any final arrangements without my knowledge and consent. But she must not say nay to a Senator, for the Conscript Fathers have done well.[17] We are at the house of a Union man named

13. Thomas Coleman Alderson had seen brief service as a lieutenant in the 8th Virginia Cavalry before transferring in November 1862 to the 14th Virginia Cavalry. He ended the war in the 36th Virginia Cavalry Battalion. In the postwar period Alderson was director of the West Virginia State Penitentiary. Robert J. Driver Jr., *14th Virginia Cavalry* (Lynchburg, Va., 1988), 96.

14. A member of the 21st Virginia Cavalry, Charles A. Calhoun would be appointed a captain in the spring of 1864. But chronic diarrhea forced him to leave the army in September of that year. Olson, *21st Virginia Cavalry*, 62.

15. Any such expedition by Jones was short lived. On the day of Sheffey's letter, departmental commander Lt. Gen. James Longstreet ordered Jones to move his brigade to Abingdon and cover all approaches to that town. *Official Records,* 32, pt. 3:613.

16. "Jerssha" (or "Gerasa") was a slang expression for an elderly woman.

17. "Conscript Fathers" refers to Confederate legislators who had voted for the National Conscription Act of April 1862, the first involuntary enlistment of men into military service in American history.

Marks[18] who ran off to Kentucky, but it is now the home of a southern soldier named McDonald.

I wrote to you that the 8th had reenlisted. The Border Companies have been sent home on a Sixty days furlough. I have bidden them farewell, and fear we will see some of them no more, as I doubt whether all of them intend to return.[19]

We cannot stay here very much longer. A large number of the horses of the command have been fed entirely upon wheat for some time.

The Currency Bill[20] will occasion me some loss, as I have three or four One Hundred Dollar Bills which I cannot get off my hands, and there is no way to get them home except by mail, and in that way they would be almost certainly lost. Well, it is a good bill and I will give & endure.

My candle is dying out, and I must wind up this epistle. It is a very uninteresting one but is from me, and I know it will be welcome. I bear this separation from you with less stoicism than any previous one. It is a sad prospect before me. But I do not think the war can possibly last many months longer. It will continue through the summer, but I do not now think that it will be a very hot campaign. We are masters of the position & the Yankees know it. When Peace shall shower her blessings on our heads, Oh how happy we will be!

Love to all. Goodbye and may God ever bless and preserve my darling.

Hd. Qrs., Genl. Ct. Martial
for Jones Brigade
MARCH 16TH, 1864

My darling Wife,

I received a day or two since from you a sweet letter enclosing the paper upon which I am writing for which I herewith return my thanks. You have

18. The 1860 census for Lee County lists no one named Marks residing in the area. A dozen Marcum families were inhabitants, though. Sheffey many have misunderstood the surname.

19. For more on why the Border Rangers (Company E) would not reenlist and how they collectively changed their minds, see "War-Time Reminiscences of James D. Sedinger," 71.

20. In an attempt to curb galloping inflation and to reduce the Confederacy's huge debt, the C.S. Congress on February 17, 1864, passed the Currency Act. It called for the issuance of new treasury notes and a phasing out of the old ones over a sixty-day period. The old bills could either be used to purchase twenty-year treasury bonds or else exchanged for new notes at a 3:2 ratio. The Currency Act, like all financial matters in the Confederacy, failed to stabilize the Southern economy.

been very good to write to me so often. This is the 6th or 7th letter I have written to you since I have been in Lee. I hope you have ere this received them all. It is difficult to get letters through from here, but if you do not receive them regularly, you still know that I am always thinking of you and grieving that I am so far away from my darling.

My labors as Judge Advocate have been very onerous, but I think I have done the work well. I shall rejoice, however, when I am recalled to my company. A Judge Advocate sees the dark side of human nature, and the constant contemplation of a gloomy picture is far from agreeable. I shall have to act too in some instances as prosecutor of some of my own friends, or at least of some whose friends and relatives are mine. But a Judge Advocate is also to some extent counsel for an accused party. And that enables him to see that justice is done. At best, it is an onerous and thankless position, and I shall be more grateful if I can so perform its duties as to meet the approbation of my superiors.

It is probable that the Brigade will soon leave Lee County and go back to some point in Scott [County], but I do not know. Forage is becoming very scarce here. One Battalion (the 27th) has been sent to Russell [County] CH, and it is possible that others may be sent there also.[21] But we know little of the projected movements.

Col. Peters is still with the court. He is becoming very uneasy lest he should not get to go home this spring! As for me, I trust to get home sometime, but must perforce be content to bide my time. I am as homesick already as if I had been away from you for twelve months, but if I were in the Col.'s predicament I should go crazy!

You must write to me ever so often. If I were to get a letter from you today, I would look for another tomorrow as anxiously as if I had not received one for a month.

Lieut. Alderson is sitting opposite to me writing to his sweetheart. How infinitely better a good wife like you is than any sweetheart! To all the men both great and small I have but one word of advice to give and that is "Marry." Away from you, I am indeed the most miserable of mortals, but with you I am the happiest, and the few days of true happiness to man in this life amply repay him for his sorrows and sufferings. If there were no wars,

---

21. The wear and tear on cavalry mounts at this time was severe. In the 37th Virginia Cavalry Battalion of Jones's brigade, 197 men were without horses. Scott, *36th and 37th Virginia Battalions Cavalry*, 59.

this could be a glorious world—but we would not, probably, appreciate the lights if there came no shadows. The most genial sunshine is ofttimes that which comes breaking through gloomy clouds, and the brightest days are those which succeed the tempest.

Some day this storm will blow over and this night pass away, and this "winter of our discontent be made glorious summer"[22] in the sunlight of peace. Then will we indeed know how properly to appreciate the inestimable blessings and the enviable happiness which will be ours. Like the stormy petrel, I could be at home among the billows and breakers if I could have my mate always with me, but at all times the life of those who are mateless and homeless must be miserable in the extreme. To love and be loved again is of itself a happiness. But this room is becoming too crowded to admit my continuing this strain. I shall look for a letter again from you in a day or two.

You can easily perceive from the emptiness of this epistle that I have no news. Col. Peters says you must send a better envelope & better sheet of paper the next time. It was very lucky, for I have long been out of letter paper and on the borrowing list. The Col. is a great scamp, and you must not mind his little jokes.

Tell Lucy she must not get so very literary all at once. Ask her who was the Father of History, and if she answers that correctly ask her who was the father of Zebedee's children? That will stump her as it did Miss Sallie Vanmeter.[23]

Love to all. Goodbye.

Millers' Camp of Jones Brigade, Lee Co., Va.
MARCH 23RD, 1864

My darling Wife,

Your letters of the 11th, 15th & 17th have been received. I have also received recently from you a letter dated on the 3rd which must have visited Johnson's Hd. Quarters in its rounds.[24] You are very good to write so frequently. I wish

---

22. This slightly altered quotation is from Shakespeare's *King Richard III.*

23. Two sisters, Sally and Mary Van Meter, taught at a private school for small children in their Main Street home in Marion. Wilson, *Smyth County History,* 158.

24. Sheffey's sarcastic reference was to Gen. Joseph E. Johnston, commander of the Army of Tennessee, with headquarters hundreds of miles away at Dalton, Georgia.

I could write as often, but I have such constant work to do from morning early till late at night that it is only by snatches that I can write to my darling.

I received your letter with the wholesome advice from Dr. Robert Crockett, and if my eye were in as bad a condition as he thinks, I would follow it. But it is much better than it was when I left home, a proof of which is that I write night after night, which I would certainly not do if it were greatly to the injury of your especial pets. I think when the winter passes away, my eye will get entirely well. If it becomes inflamed, I shall follow your Uncle Robert's advice.

There is no danger of my resigning. The law providing for the retirement of disabled officers and soldiers will in any event obviate the necessity of my resigning. It is my duty to stick to my post as a soldier as long as I am able to do so, however disagreeable, and it will be a matter of pride to both of us if I can boast after the war that I stuck to it from the beginning to the end.

I have done more work during the last 25 days than any two officers in the Brigade, and my eyes are in better condition now than when I commenced it. It might have been different had I been exposed to the smoke and wind in camp. But we will not be returned to our commands for some time yet, as we have about a hundred untried cases on our hands. We have completed 26 cases but charges come in faster than we can try them. We will be returned to duty without command in case of a fight or an expedition, but will resume our work trying these charges afterwards.

I have every hope that the war will end in the next fall or winter. Whether the oncoming campaign is a severe one or not, I think it can lead to no other conclusion. Such a hope will enable us to endure our present separation with more fortitude. If the war does not end by next winter and my eyes then are still diseased, I shall apply for retirement, at least until completely recovered, but I think they will be entirely well by that time. My separation from you becomes daily more irksome to me, but we can do nothing but think of and write to each other and let the dreary time wear away. I employ myself with the utmost assiduity to kill dull care. When I go back to camp, my loneliness will be awful.

The gentleman who criticized the "Dream of Aljamon" so severely must have had an intimate acquaintance with Ossian, as there is not a sentence in that humble production which in any way resembles anything in that poet.[25]

25. Ossian was a legendary third-century Gallic warrior who became a poet in his old age. Fifteen hundred years later Scot writer James MacPherson pirated a long portion of Ossian's

It is worse than Mrs. Leftwich's criticism of Rachel of Rama.[26] So many persons have accused me of a want of originality that I have been occasionally much puzzled to know whether or not I was indeed a plagiarist, but I have come to the conclusion—I think a just one—that the critics stultify themselves, not I.

We will ere long move back to the east of Jonesville on account of forage. Col. Davis, the Yankee commander captured at Wyerman's Mill, recovered from his wounds and left two days [ago] in defiance of his written parole of honor.[27] Such are the Yankees. We have lost two pickets recently besides that "all is quiet along" this valley.

The decisions of this court in some cases will soon be published. When they are, I will write you about them. A good many officers are under arrest. As yet but one has been tried by the court.

But it is bedtime and I am writing in Mr. Miller's bedroom. Therefore I must close. Write soon and frequently. My best love to your Ma & Lucy. May God in his infinite goodness and mercy continue to guard from all harm my darling is ever the prayer of your devoted husband.

> *Office, Judge Advocate of Genl. Ct. Martial for Brig.*
> *Genl. W. E. Jones Brigade, Stickleyville, Lee Co., Va.*
> MARCH 28TH, 1864

My darling wife,

Your letter of the 26th inst. has just reached me and I hasten to answer it. I am still engaged, as you have perceived from the manner in which I have dated, in the everlasting labors of Judge Advocate of this interminable Court. I have been at it already long enough to gain for myself numerous titles. By some I am called "Judge." By others, who have an idea that I fill an office something similar to that of a Provost Marshal, I am called *General Court Marshall.*" I received a note from a captain not long since who displayed his ignorance by combining both titles. He addressed me as "Capt. J. P. Sheffey, Judge Advocate and General Court Marshall."

---

writings. The author of "Dream of Aljamon" was Sheffey himself, for throughout this paragraph he writes about quality in a literary work.

26. Jeremiah 31:15–17 contains the story of Rachel of Ramah weeping for her children and being comforted by God.

27. After his release from capture, Col. Reuben Davis returned to duty with his 11th Tennessee Cavalry (U.S.). Sheffey interpreted this as a violation of Davis's parole and unacceptable conduct by a gentleman.

You must get rid of the mopes or I will take to writing to you every day to the great detriment of the business of the Court. One of the deserters sentenced by the Court will, I understand, be shot next Friday in [the] presence of the Brigade.[28] I do not think I will witness it. Desertion is becoming a very dangerous experiment. I hope sincerely a check may be put to this bane of the army, and that a long period may elapse before such severity will again be necessary in our Brigade.

Col. Peters is a great deal bluer than you represent yourself to be. He says he will vindicate himself to you in a separate epistle. He sighs constantly like a fellow when first smitten by Cupid's ruthless dart, and says he intends to go home if he has to run off. But that he will not do. I do not think he will get an opportunity to go at all.

The Court has completed twenty nine cases. So you see we have not been idle. I will not lose anything by the currency bill, I hope. I sent $400 to my father, and my expenses are about $30 to $50 per week. This is caused, however, by the quantity of paper I have had to purchase, and will not hereafter be so great.

I have concluded to follow Dr. Crockett's advice and took out the stilette several days ago. You must not think that I am suffering with my eye, for I am not. Though not well, it is in better condition than it has been since it was first affected.

In this beautiful Spring weather, you must not allow yourself to get blue. You must take a great deal of exercise and be very happy. The hours are "tedious and tasteless" to me also, but they are much more so when I think that you are making yourself miserable.

I have pondered long and anxiously over the interrogatories propounded by Mlle. Lucie, and am prepared to answer them as they would have been answered by one of the seven sages of Greece.[29] In the first place, we are informed somewhere in sacred history, that the mother of Zebedee's children was the wife of Zebedee. In the second place, a soldier is most tired in the month of April for that is immediately after the cold and cheerless March is

28. Grayson County's John H. Jones deserted three times from the 30th Virginia Sharpshooters Battalion. After his third apprehension, he was sentenced to death. On April 15, 1864, the execution took place at Abingdon. West, *30th Battalion Sharpshooters*, 74, 277.

29. Here Sheffey twists mythology. The "seven sages of Greece" is a synonym for the "Seven Wise Masters," a collection of Oriental tales. The septet did not have extraordinary knowledge, rather they were advisers who told long stories to an Eastern ruler to show the evils of hasty punishment.

ended, and in the third place, I don't believe a miller always wears a white hat for I have frequently seen them bareheaded. But if it be really true, there are several reasons why it is so. In the first place, being a great rascal, he naturally desires to conceal his occupation, and a black hat in such a business is a great tell-tale. In the second place, he is totally unable to wear a black hat, for he no sooner puts one on than it becomes white. In the third place, he wears a white hat for the same reason that colliers and blacksmiths always wear black ones, viz, to save the expense of purchasing a hat brush. And in the fourth place, if these are not the reasons, what are they?

Talking about whereabouts, I have so much writing to do that I cannot find time to write to you as often as I could wish, and if I were to write to Marion, I could not write to you so frequently. That is a good excuse, and another is that there is no one here to keep you posted but myself. Whereas Col. Peters and John both send letters to Marion at the rate of two or three a week. They both use my paper too, and it would soon exhaust my supply of stationery if I were to furnish another correspondent to Marion. They must rest assured of my ceaseless affection for them, and ought not to stop writing to me because I have not the time to write to them.

Write to me very frequently, my darling. I will write to you as often as possible.

Dr. Robert Crockett's bill was a low one. I expected much heavier charges to be made. I am much obliged to him for his kindness and only regret that the operation performed by him was not as successful as he himself wished. I hope soon to hear from you. I cannot get along without frequent letters from you.

Our Brigade is falling back slowly on account of scarcity of forage. I have no idea where we will go to. Some think that our summer campaign will be in Gen. Breckinridge's Dept.[30] But I cannot tell. This country will not hereafter support us even in the summer. We leave a desert behind us for the Yanks to regale their appetites upon. May thousands of them drop by the wayside athirst and ahungered even unto death, is my fervent prayer. The campaign will be brief and bloody. It is my fervent hope and confident belief that the enemy will be defeated at all points by the next Autumn. God grant it and speed the day of our restoration to our homes and our darlings. Longstreet

30. On February 25, 1864, the more affable and efficient Maj. Gen. John C. Breckinridge succeeded Maj. Gen. Samuel Jones as head of the Western Department of Virginia. But Breckinridge did not assume his new duties until May.

is advancing, it is said, and the enemy has fallen back to Strawberry Plains.[31] It is our misfortune that our advance must be made through a desert where there is almost no living thing. But heroic toil and bravery, energy and endurance will overcome all obstacles.

Goodbye and may God bless and protect you, my dear, dear wife.

Pattonsville, Scott Co., Va.
APRIL 7TH, 1864

My darling Wife,

Your letter of the 1st inst. was received yesterday evening. Since I wrote last, our court adjourned sine die, and we all returned to our commands. We had not properly ensconced ourselves in camp before an order came appointing another court, of which I am Judge Advocate and Col. Peters President. I am glad we gave satisfaction. The court convened today and proceeded to the trial of Capt. C. B. Duncan,[32] 37th Battn. Va. Cav. This evening the court adjourned to meet Saturday morning, since tomorrow is general fast day. It is probable we will move back tomorrow to Estilville. We are gradually getting back towards Abingdon. I think we will be in Washington County in less than two weeks, and I hope soon to get a glimpse of my darling. If I can get to Abingdon, will you not come down? But I need not make calculations as it is yet undecided where we are going. Being on that court, it will be impossible for me to come either to Wytheville or Marion. But if the Brigade should happen to camp near Abingdon, the Court will sit there and I know you will think it a pleasure trip to run down and see how well I am.

I sincerely regret that Lucy stumped me on the miller question. It is as dead as the question of identity between an elephant and a brick-bat. But it is not quite original, for I have heard it before, and I doubt not I have paid

31. Longstreet was not making any advance toward Strawberry Plains, Tennessee. From his headquarters at Bristol, the general wrote Lee early in April of trying to get a supply of horses: "It was my intention to use them by mounting some of my infantry to drive out beef-cattle from Kentucky. We have been in such distress for want of forage for the last two weeks that our mules are hardly in condition for such a trip." *Official Records*, 32, pt. 3:737.

32. Quartermaster Charles B. Duncan of Franklin County was acquitted of all charges and continued on duty to the end of the war. Scott, *36th and 37th Virginia Battalions Cavalry*, 85. It should be noted that at the time of these courts-martial, an inspector reported Jones's brigade to be woefully deficient in military knowledge, drill, and discipline. *Official Records*, 32, pt. 3:842–43.

her well in her own coin. I have given her so many to solve that she won't have time to think up any severe interrogatories soon.

I am glad Frank has been at home. He will do a great deal of good in getting you out of the mopes. I hope you have laid aside its three cornered hankerchief. Golden I know very well. There were two of them in the Border Rangers and both, I think, were transferred to the navy.[33] I am not certain about the orthography of the name but think it is Golden. It may be, as you spell it, Gouldin, but I have seen it spelled the other way by members of the Regiment. Where Frank could have come across him, I can't imagine.

The scarcity in this country is alarming. Some people are moving towards Abingdon, and others I think to save themselves from starvation will go to Kentucky.[34]

Genl. Jones has reduced the people to three bushels of corn per head. We all here are waiting anxiously to hear what will be done by the armies before Richmond. We have come to the conclusion that there will be little fighting out here. A good victory in the east would, I think, put a quietus upon the war. But no one knows. It is to be hoped that something will be done to bring it to a speedy and honorable close.

I hope soon to hear from you again. I would write to you every day if I had the paper, but I have to be miserly in that particular. For the last five days I have had no chance to write, being in camp between rain and mud all the time. The weather has been horrible. The mud in many places is almost bottomless.

I will write again in a few days. Write as often as you can. Best love to all. Tell Lucy she mustn't fall in love with Golden's (or Gouldin's) piano playing and singing.

I am glad that the charges against Will Hammett[35] & Col. Edmondson,[36]

33. William E. Golden was a physician who served as a private in the Border Rangers. Charles M. Golden enlisted in the same company in June 1861 but transferred seven months later to the C.S. Navy. Dickinson, *8th Virginia Cavalry*, 85.

34. Yet conditions at this time in Abingdon too, particularly with respect to the scarcity of food, were alarming. See Lewis Preston Summers, *History of Southwest Virginia, 1746–1786, Washington County, 1777–1870* (Richmond, Va., 1903), 531–33.

35. William R. Hammet of Montgomery County was a captain in the 25th Virginia Cavalry. Twice in 1864 he faced a court-martial. In March 1865 Col. Montgomery Hopkins endorsed the captain's transfer to another regiment. If he remained longer with the 25th Virginia, Hopkins stated, Hammet might be killed. No explanation exists for such an unusual statement. Dobbie E. Lambert, *25th Virginia Cavalry* (Lynchburg, Va., 1994), 116.

36. In December 1863, following the loss of an arm at Chancellorsville, Col. James K. Edmondson of the 27th Virginia Infantry resigned his command. He immediately became provost

which were before the last court, will not come before this. Do not, however, speak of there being charges against them. From all I can learn, the charges against Edmonson will come to nought. And if the facts in the charges are proved against him, I think that the worst punishment which can be inflicted in the case will be a reprimand. I would like to be his counsel. I am glad I will not have to act as his prosecutor. I would not have done it, however.

I have been in a neighborhood recently where the people acknowledge negro equality to its fullest extent. This is in Hancock Co., Tn. This white woman & black woman came to a Crosside preaching together as if they were bosom friends and companions.

But I must not cross those lines any more or you will not be able to read them. Goodbye

> *Camp 8th Va. Cavalry, at Wilson Buchanan's*[37]
> *Rich Valley, Smyth Co., Va.*
> MAY 1, 1864

My darling Wife,

I would have written to you several days since, but the bad weather (for you are aware we are shelterless), and the difficulty of procuring paper have prevented [it]. I have borrowed this [sheet] and will employ a portion of this beautiful Sabbath May evening writing to my May Queen. You were once justly styled Queen of Love and Beauty, and as the merry month among whose flowers you "went a Maying" long ago comes round again, the royal title is again, I think, perfectly a propos.

I have found kinsfolk here in abundance, and have been kept from suffering for something to eat through their kindness. My thanks are due to your cousin, Mrs. Wilson Buchanan, for my supper last night and dinner to-day. Our command has treated them very badly. We have our horses upon their meadows, very unnecessarily too, I think, and last night their turkeys were taken, notwithstanding the firing of a pistol upon the thieves by one of the young ladies.

---

marshal of Lexington and served in that post for the remainder of the war. Reidenbaugh, *27th Virginia Infantry*, 91, 142.

37. Wilson Buchanan was probably the largest landowner in the Seven Mile Ford area of Smyth County. He and his wife, Eliza, had six children, all of whom were living at home in 1860.

For several days after coming back to the command, I was in command of the Regt. On the 27th we moved towards Abingdon. Passed through Abingdon on the 28th and came back to Rich Valley yesterday. The Yankees, of course, retreated as soon as our Brigade started towards them. I have not been to Saltville. My father was there yesterday, engaged in some business connected with the transfer of the property and rights of Stuart, Buchanan & Co. to Clarkson.[38] Clarkson seems to be very cordially disliked by the people of this valley. I hope he may be thwarted in some of his schemes.

I met Col. Peters in Abingdon. He had returned to the command for his witnesses. He is perfectly confident of his acquittal, but is still much enraged at this outrageous treatment. The charges against him were preferred by a Col. Win. Barbour of [the] 28th Regt. N.C. Troops[39] and were for receiving, entertaining and enlisting a deserter. Col. Barbour had better keep out of his way. Col. Peters was told in Richmond that the charges would be withdrawn upon his statement, but he very properly declined this. He asks them no favors. Going and coming, he could not stop at home being under arrest, but he would not ask the privilege of doing so, I think very properly.

Averell is reported to be in the Kanawha Valley and 400 Yankees, it is said, are at Lewisburg.[40] If he will only come, we will try to give him a salutation that he will not ever forget.

I will write to you again if I can get the paper in a very few days. I have no way to carry anything, and dislike to beg or borrow.

The men all around me are drawing their rations with the usual amount of grumbling. Their everlasting discontent sickens me. Goodbye, and may God bless my darling.

38. John N. Clarkson was superintendent of the salt works at Saltville. A native of Albemarle County, he was a forty-five-year-old schoolteacher when the war began. By the end of 1864, suspicions apparently existed of Clarkson gaining personally from the sale of salt to the government. *Official Records,* ser. 4, 3:925.

39. Thirty-year-old William Morgan Barbour was an attorney who commanded the 37th (not 28th) North Carolina Infantry. He suffered a leg injury at Spotsylvania in May 1864 and was mortally wounded at Petersburg four months later.

40. Federal general George Crook's division of twenty-one hundred men was preparing to conduct a heavy raid into southwestern Virginia. From Charleston, Crook embarked with four objectives: to seize the supply depot at Dublin, to destroy the facilities at Saltville, to cut the railroad bridge across the New River at Central Depot, and to destroy as much of the Virginia and Tennessee Railroad as possible. The battles of Cloyds Mountain (May 9) and Wytheville (May 10) would be the major engagements in this partially successful offensive. Brig. Gen. William W. Averell commanded the cavalry brigade in Crook's division.

Camp 8th Va. Cavalry, Tazewell Co., Va.
MAY 6TH, 1864

My darling wife,

As I am about to send one of my men to Marion, I write you a short note to let you know that I have not forgotten you. We are constantly moving and as we have no baggage except what we can carry with our horses, it is almost impossible to find an opportunity to write.

Our horses are starving and though we are accomplishing nothing, we are doing hard service. We have neither grass nor grain in this country, and there are more than 2000 horses. The Yankees are preparing in Ka[nawha] Valley for a big raid with 6 or 7000 cavalry. We will try to be ready for them. The 16th Regt. was sent yesterday to capture a squad of 200 at Logan C[ourt] H[ouse].[41]

I received your letter, [and] am glad to hear that Mag is doing well. My best love to her and the baby.[42] It bears a distinguished name. I have consulted the stars and cast his horoscope as the Astrologer did for Harry Bertram[43] and predict great things. There is talk in Col. [Peters's] Regt. about firing a salute in honor of the event.

Was at Mr. Stuart's once while in the Rich Valley. Ellie is very anxious for you to come to see her.[44] She is very well. The portrait so much spoken of, though a fine painting, is not much like you or her either. Both of you are better looking than it is.

Miss Bell invited me to her wedding, which she said Madam Rumor had appointed for the day after I was there, but as like Tony Weller[45] when he applied for his license, she didn't know who the fellow was. I didn't go.

I hope you are still at Marion. Please keep me posted as to your movements, for as we wander about, I may come to see you when you least expect

41. Most of the 16th Virginia Cavalry was then on duty in Mercer County and would shortly join Col. William H. French's mounted brigade in southwestern Virginia. *Official Records,* 37, pt. 1:62–63.

42. The new child of Colonel and Mrs. Peters was named James White Sheffey Peters.

43. Harry Bertram was the hero of Sir Walter Scott's 1815 novel, *Guy Mannering,* an adventurous tale set at the time of King George III.

44. Elvira Spiller, Josephine's sister, married Alexander Brown. After his death she wed William A. Stuart, brother of the famed cavalry leader Jeb Stuart.

45. Weller, Mr. Pickwick's coachman in *The Pickwick Papers,* was known for his propensity for marrying widows.

it. As soon as we get back to the Rich Valley, I will come to Marion if you are there and I can get off. No passes are now granted for more than six miles except by [the] Brigade Commander. My best love to all.

> *Camp 8th Va. Cavalry near*
> *Waynesboro, Augusta Co., Va.*
> JUNE 9, 1864

My darling wife,

You have doubtless been anxious about me since I left you and I regret that no opportunity has been afforded me of relieving your anxiety.

Our Brigade did not reach Augusta [County] in time for the fight at Fishersville in which Genl. Jones was killed.[46] I had two men among the dismounted men in the fight, of whom one is missing.[47] Our loss was very heavy in that fight and our defeat complete.

The reverse is a severe one. Eighty dismounted men of our Regt. were in the fight of whom 40 were killed or captured. Capt. Win. Saunders, as you have perhaps heard, was killed.[48] Col. Browne[49] and Josiah Davis[50] of [the] 45th fell into the hands of the enemy; the former was wounded, some say killed. It is said that Maj. Davis is also wounded.[51]

46. The Shenandoah Valley was weakly defended when Maj. Gen. David Hunter and a sizable Union force began a southward march toward Lexington. A makeshift band of Confederates under Brig. Gen. William E. Jones rushed to the scene from southwestern Virginia. On June 5 at the village of Piedmont, five miles northeast of Staunton, the opposing hosts collided. Jones was outnumbered but managed to fight well until Federals overran the Confederate lines. While trying to rally his men, Jones was killed. One-quarter of his men became casualties. Union losses were 380 soldiers. Scott C. Patchan, *The Forgotten Fury: The Battle of Piedmont, Va.* (Fredericksburg, Va., 1996), 216, 223.

47. Smyth County native Peter Hayton was the Smyth Dragoons trooper captured at Piedmont. He was a prisoner at Camp Chase, Ohio, and Point Lookout, Maryland, until the end of the war. Dickinson, *8th Virginia Cavalry*, 88.

48. William Campbell Sanders, who led a Wythe County company in the 45th Virginia Infantry, received a bullet wound near the heart. He was taken to a nearby home, where the mistress forced "nearly half a pint of whiskey in him, which produced a reaction and revived him." Sanders later was treasurer of Wythe County. Scott, *45th Virginia Infantry*, 42.

49. Col. William Henry Browne died from a severe wound in the thigh. Patchan, *Battle of Piedmont*, 177.

50. Pvt. Josiah Davis underwent incarceration at Camp Morton, Indiana. He received a parole in March 1865 only to die a month later. Scott, *45th Virginia Infantry*, 88.

51. Wytheville's Capt. Alexander Mathews Davis spent the remainder of the war at Johnson's Island, Ohio. Ibid.

One hundred and sixty of the 45th escaped out of 500.[52] The loss in the 60th is still more severe. The 36th also suffered very much.[53] Our men fought bravely and inflicted a severe loss upon the enemy. The enemy buried, it is said, 550 men. Our number in the fight was 3800. The enemy had about 8000. It is reported that our men captured at that fight have been paroled.[54]

Yesterday we were in line of battle from 12 o'clock 'till night—during a portion of which time, there was some firing between our skirmishers and those of the enemy with no loss on our side. One Yankee reported killed & one captured. The enemy retreated towards Staunton. We expected a severe encounter—but the enemy was not willing to risk it. Averell, Hunter & Crook are now together at Staunton, and between Staunton and Greenville. Their force is probably about 15,000 men. The success of Genl. Lee will in a few days enable us to make a suitable settlement with these gentlemen.[55]

I reached the command about 4 miles west of Salem on the evening of the next day after I left you. But the alarm sounds.

Same JUNE 10TH, 1864

My writing was interrupted at this point by an alarm caused by an approach of the enemy similar to that of yesterday. We were thrown into line of battle, but the enemy retreated without even a skirmish. It is probable that they fear an attack and send out reconnoitering parties daily to guard against surprise.

We are receiving reinforcements now, and though the force of the enemy is very strong, we will soon be able to match them.

A prisoner was wounded in the head and captured yesterday, who stated that the enemy was moving down the valley from Staunton towards New Market. But this is not true.

I hope you have recovered entirely from your sickness. You seemed so

52. Losses at Piedmont in the 45th Virginia Infantry were 14 killed, 21 wounded, and 325 captured. Patchan, *Battle of Piedmont*, 224.

53. The 60th Virginia had 114 casualties; the 36th Virginia, 177. Ibid.

54. The report was false. Most of the captured Confederates were held in Northern prisoner-of-war camps for the rest of the war.

55. Sheffey's optimism came from Lee's stunning June 3 victory over Lt. Gen. Ulysses S. Grant at Cold Harbor. Yet the determined Union commander soon made a swift move across the James River and against the city of Petersburg. A ten-month besiegement of Lee's army and the Confederate capital ensued.

much better when I left there. I have not been very successful. You must take good care of yourself, my darling. I can go cheerfully through all the hardships and perils if I know that you are well and are not distressing yourself unnecessarily.

Address your letters to Staunton, Va. I will write soon again and often. Love to all. I hope Frank is recovering his hearing. He ought not to think of returning to the army until that is restored, if it can be avoided. Kindest regards to Mr. and Mrs. I. J. Leftwich. Please write to my mother at Marion— and let her know that I am well, and where I am.

Camp 8th Va. Cavalry, near Brownsburg, Rockbridge Co., Va.
JUNE 27TH, 1864

My dear dear darling wife,

Many long and weary days and nights of danger, fatigue, suspense and anxiety have intervened since I heard from you.[56] The wall the enemy put between us seems to have been as impassable as that of Tartaros.[57]

I wrote to you last at Waynesboro. Since I left Waynesboro, I have passed through the most arduous campaign of the war. The cavalry has been a great portion of the time fighting and skirmishing with a vastly superior force. The result has been little else than disaster to us. For 25 successive days since we left Wytheville, our horses have been under saddle.

At the Quaker Church near Lynchburg,[58] the cavalry was badly whipped but there were only about 2000 of us pitted against the whole force of the enemy. The whole disaster there was the fault of the commanding Genl., Imboden.[59] My company suffered no loss in that fight. We were exposed to a

56. A good itinerary of the movements of the 8th Virginia Cavalry during this period is in Mary Hoge Bruce, ed., *A Journal of John Milton Hoge* (privately printed, 1951), 15–19.

57. In classical mythology Tartaros was the lowest region of existence, located as far beneath Hades as Hades was beneath the earth.

58. Sheffey refers to the June 17 cavalry action preceding Hunter's assault on Lynchburg the following day.

59. Two Confederate mounted units were engaged in the June 17 action: Brig. Gen. John McCausland's brigade and Brig. Gen. John D. Imboden's small remnant of cavalry left from the fight at Piedmont. Near Lynchburg Imboden made an impetuous probe against advancing Federals, who promptly counterattacked and routed the Confederates. General Breckinridge, the Southern commander, wired Richmond: "The cavalry, under Imboden, doing less than nothing. If a good general officer cannot be sent at once for them, they will go to ruin." Thomas Lewis, *The Shenandoah in Flames: The Valley Campaign of 1864* (Alexandria, Va., 1987), 59.

heavy fire when we retreated. We were upon the left of the line. The right suffered most severely and was the first to give way. The enemy was whipped the next day by the infantry at Lynchburg. We were posted upon the right of the line, and our fighting amounted to little else than light skirmishing, though there was a considerable artillery duel immediately in front of our position.

The enemy commenced his retreat that night, 18th inst., much to our chagrin, as we would have annihilated his army. We pursued rapidly, and on the 23rd the cavalry overtook his columns near Salem.[60] While Jones's Brigade[61] skirmished with a body of cavalry and artillery on the rock road east of Salem, McCausland with his brigade attacked the artillery of the enemy in a defile and gap about five miles NE of Salem and captured eleven pieces. After driving the enemy from his position on the rock road, we moved rapidly with [the] support of McCausland.

My company was thrown forward in advance of the whole command. Totally unsupported, I was attacked in a defile by a large body of the enemy; and my company, thrown into inextricable confusion, saved itself by flight. Eight of my men remained with me. I moved back about 150 yards, and they and I dismounted, and with about twenty five of McCausland's men, drove the enemy again under cover. But in a few minutes he came upon us in still heavier force and drove us from our position.

We then found ourselves almost completely surrounded. I had sent my horse and the horses of the men who had dismounted with me to the rear, and they had run into a Regt. of Yankee Cavalry. Two of the horses were captured and three of my men—Sergt. W. P. James and Privates B[enjamin] Aker & R. P. Copenhaver.[62] My saddle-bags were lost off the saddle, and with all my clothing fell into [the] hands of the enemy. Consequently I haven't even a change. But my horse though, turned loose by the horseholders, made his way out.

60. The action at Salem (or Hanging Rock, as it is more familiarly known) occurred on June 21 rather than the date Sheffey gives. One segment of Confederate cavalry assailed the rear of the retreating Union column. At the same time, McCausland's troopers overran a line of enemy artillery; four cannon were seized and six disabled. Confederate general Jubal Early reported, "The enemy moved so rapidly that I could not attack him before he got to the mountains, though I marched over twenty miles a day." *Official Records,* 37, pt. 1:101, 160.

61. After Jones's death at Piedmont, Brig. Gen. John C. Vaughn succeeded to command of his brigade.

62. All three soldiers spent the remainder of the war as prisoners at Camp Chase, Ohio. For a comment on prison life by Benjamin Aker, see Armstrong, *Smyth County,* 2:145.

We were saved by Steve Halsey,[63] who came to our support with the 21st Regt. and drove back the enemy. A kind Providence has again spared me for your sake, I suppose, certainly not for my own.

We are now moving rapidly towards the Potomac.[64] Our prospects are bright and brightening, but the time of my absence from you is very wearisome. God grant that the time may soon come when there will be no more need for our separation.

I am well, and will get clothing at Staunton. You must not be uneasy about me. Don't believe any reports you may hear—unless they are good or well authenticated. I have been several times in the last 10 days reported killed, captured, wounded and missing. But I am still well and unhurt. Saw Jay Hanson[65] near Liberty. He looked well. I didn't have time to stop and talk with him. Saw Sam Sayers[66] near the Hollins Institute in Botetourt. Will Spiller[67] was in Lynchburg, but I didn't get to see him. Heard from him, however, and he was well. Love to all.

Camp at Sheperdstown, Jefferson Co., Va.
JULY 4TH, 1864

My darling wife,

I wrote a brief note to you this morning which I handed to Mrs. Roedel.[68] I have at a late hour this evening learned that she did not start for Wytheville this morning as she expected—but will set out again. As I have a few minutes before dark, I write again.

I wrote to you last from a camp between Salem and Staunton about the 25th or 26th ult. We came up with Mulligan's force yesterday at Leetown, in

63. Maj. Stephen Peters Halsey was a nephew of Col. W. E. Peters. Wounded twice in the fighting at Lynchburg and a third time in a skirmish at Woodstock, Halsey remained with his regiment to its surrender at Appomattox. Olson, *21st Virginia Cavalry*, 68.

64. Having cleared the Shenandoah Valley of Union troops, Early's Confederate army began marching down the Valley on a raid that would reach the outskirts of Washington, D.C., and create near panic among most of its inhabitants.

65. Probably Thomas Jefferson Hanson, a Smyth County native then serving in the 51st Virginia Infantry. Davis, *51st Virginia Infantry*, 63; Kegley, *Wythe County*, 412.

66. Wytheville's Samuel Rush Sayers was surgeon of the 4th Virginia Infantry.

67. William Hickman Spiller at the time was a cadet at VMI and a veteran of the May 1864 battle of New Market. Richard M. McMurry, *Virginia Military Institute Alumni in the Civil War* (Lynchburg, Va., 1999), 208.

68. Josephine Roedel was the wife of Lutheran minister William D. Roedel in Wytheville.

this Co[unty].[69] His force consisted of four Regiments of infantry, twelve hundred cavalry and a battery of four pieces of artillery, in all four thousand two hundred men. Our and [Capt. Thomas E.] Jackson's Battery of artillery [were] in all about a thousand or twelve hundred.

We fought them from sunrise till dusk—and drove them about five miles. Our loss will perhaps reach fifty in killed and wounded. The enemy acknowledged a loss of 60 killed besides wounded and prisoners.[70] Three of my men were wounded—Privat[es] R. H. Repass of Wythe, J. H. Copenhaver of Smyth, [and] J. G. Sanders of Franklin.[71] They have been sent back to Winchester. None of my men were killed. The enemy has crossed the Potomac, and we will cross tomorrow near Martinsburg. McCausland captured 225 prisoners.[72]

It is too dark to write more. Col. Peters is well. John Ross is well. I wish I had time to write you forty pages. Our Brigade is now known as B. T. Johnson's Cavalry Brigade, (Ransom's Division, Army [of] Northern Virginia). Write to me & don't forget to specify the Co., Regt., Brigade, Division, &c. Millions of kisses for yourself and an infinite amount of love to all.

Camp near Charlestown, Jefferson County
JULY 18, 1864

My darling wife,

[Undecipherable] . . . since I left Wytheville . . . tells me you [had] written and sent several others. I suppose they are lying in some office at Staunton or Winchester. I cannot complain of the mails, however, since we have not

69. In a June 28 reorganization, Early placed Marylander Bradley T. Johnson in command of Jones's old cavalry brigade. General Johnson termed his new unit "eight hundred half-armed and badly disciplined mountaineers from Southwest Virginia who would fight like veterans when they pleased." *Southern Historical Society Papers* 30 (1902): 217. On July 3 at Leetown (near Martinsburg), Johnson's brigade ran into a sizable Union force under Col. James A. Mulligan of the 23d Illinois Infantry. Sporadic fighting lasted throughout the day as Mulligan held off the Confederates until Maj. Gen. Franz Sigel's main army could evacuate Martinsburg.

70. For references to the Leetown fight, see *Official Records*, 37, pt. 1:18, 21, 57; George E. Pond, *The Shenandoah Valley in 1864* (New York, 1883), 48; and *Southern Historical Society Papers* 30 (1902): 216–17.

71. R. F. Repass, James Henry Copenhaver, and James Garland Sanders all survived their wounds.

72. For McCausland's feats at this time, see Jubal A. Early, *Autobiographical Sketch and Narrative of the War between the States* (Philadelphia, 1912), 383–84.

been in communications with anybody but Yankees for some time. I hope to hear from you frequently now since our Army has recrossed into Virginia.

We fought the fight at Leetown, with regard to which I wrote you by Mrs. Roedel, on the 3rd inst. On the 4th our Brigade marched to Shepherdstown, McCausland and Imboden & the infantry following by way of Martinsburg. On the 5th we crossed the river at Shepherdstown and occupied Sharpsburg, crossed Antietam [Creek], passed Reedysville and Boonsboro and camped near Boonsboro, upon the battle ground of South Mountain.[73]

McCausland moved to our left and occupied Hagerstown, where [on] the 6th a shell was thrown into our Regt. by the enemy which killed and wounded eleven men.[74] This blow would have fallen upon my company, but providentially for us this Regt. had been reversed and the left was in front. Had my company been in its usual position on the march, the shell would have fallen into the midst of it. The shell exploded on Co. B, which usually marches in the rear of the Regt. After some slight skirmishing, the enemy retreated.

On the 7th we attacked him at Frederick City.[75] The 8th, 37th, and 21st [Virginia Cavalry] were thrown to the front on foot, and we had heavy skirmishing until night. One of my men was killed here by a shot through the brain,[76] and another slightly wounded by a piece of shell. The enemy were too strong for us, and we fell back at night to await the coming of our infantry.

The enemy pursued and the skirmishing commenced again the next morning and continued throughout the day, when the Yankees drew off. During the day I was to charge on foot upon a body of the enemy who appeared upon our left. We drove them in utter rout. The enemy gained no advantage and the next morning [July 9], when the infantry moved upon them, they had fallen back to Monocacy Junction, 3 miles from Frederick.

73. The September 14, 1862, battle of South Mountain, Maryland, was a prelude to the ferocious contest along Antietam Creek three days later.

74. James Sedinger of the 8th Virginia Cavalry dated the exploding-shell incident to July 8 and thought that fourteen members of the regiment were casualties. "War-Time Reminiscences of James D. Sedinger," 71.

75. A good Union account of this action is in Abner Hard, *History of the Eighth Cavalry Regiment, Illinois Volunteers, during the Great Rebellion* (Aurora, Ill., 1868), 196–97.

76. In the light action of July 7, Daniel Walker of Company A was killed. He was from Washington County and had enlisted in the army only seven months earlier. Dickinson, *8th Virginia Cavalry*, 113.

Here, after a considerable battle, they were completely routed.[77] We were not in this.

In the morning after the 9th, our Brigade moved off to the left of Frederick and into [the] heart of Maryland.[78] A more beautiful country never gladdened the eye of man. The horn of plenty had been outpoured upon the fields, and the land seemed burthened with its wealth of golden grain. But the people, the people, the villainous Dutch with their outlandish lingo![79] What a pity that they should hold so fair a land! They are nice farmers, however, and have made this portion of Maryland almost a garden. Still, it is to be lamented that this country does not belong to Southern Sympathizers.

When we left the valley in which Frederick City is situated, we soon found plenty of friends—and provisions were abundantly supplied. We passed through Liberty, Unionville, New Windsor—where there is a railroad—to Westminster—where we also struck a railroad—and burned six bridges across Gunpowder River at and north of Cockeysville on the Balto. & Phila. R. R. We then struck southwest near the Relay House and Ellicotts Mill. . . . [Rest of letter is missing.]

> *Moorefield, Hardy Co., Va.*
> AUGUST 25TH, 1864

My dear Sister,

You have doubtless ere this heard of my own and the misfortune of Preston—on the 7th inst. in an engagement near this place.[80] I received a very

77. The fighting at Monocacy lasted all day. Union soldiers under Maj. Gen. Lew Wallace held back the Confederates and bought time for reinforcement of the defenses around Washington. When Early arrived on the outskirts of the Northern capital on July 11, he found the city too strongly protected to be attacked.

78. For the movements of the 8th Virginia Cavalry and Johnson's brigade, see *Southern Historical Society Papers* 30 (1902): 216–18.

79. Western Maryland had been heavily settled by German immigrants, whom outsiders came to regard as "dumb Dutchmen" too thickheaded and slow to be of great use to society.

80. Confederate cavalry swept into the North and on July 30 burned Chambersburg, Pennsylvania. The brigades of McCausland and Johnson then retired to a camp near Moorefield, West Virginia. Feeling safe, Southern commanders became lax in their vigilance. Federal cavalry staged a surprise early morning attack on August 7 and routed the entire Confederate force. Union troops captured 420 men (including thirty-eight officers), four hundred horses, and most of the Confederate equipment in what was a devastating defeat for Southern cavalry. While McCausland and Johnson angrily blamed one another for the debacle, General Lee took quick action—on August 11 Johnson was relieved of his command. *Official Records*, 43, pt. 1:3, 5–7, 551, 734; "War-Time Reminiscences of James D. Sedinger," 73.

severe wound in the breast[81] and Pres was made prisoner. I am grateful to be able to say that I am improving and hope soon to move homeward. I hope you will stand our misfortune in the capture of your dear husband with all fortitude. I saw him after his capture and the Federal Colonel Powell[82] assured me that he should be well treated on account of the kindness shown him by your mother when he was a prisoner and wounded at her house. I learn that Pres alone of the prisoners was allowed to ride.[83] He was sent to Camp Chase, Ohio.

I have already written to my brother residing in New York,[84] informing him that Pres is a prisoner and requesting him to provide him with everything necessary to his comfort. This I know he will do. You have, my dear Josie, great reason to be thankful that it is as well as it is with Pres. He is a prisoner, it is true, but then he is perfectly well and was never in such fine health. Moreover, in the full and faithful performance of his duty as a soldier, he was relieved by his captivity from the peril and exposure of the terrible campaign in which we have been engaged in the valley. I will tomorrow write to him and suggest a way by which we can hear from him regularly.

I cannot write more at present. Tis the first time I have written since I was wounded, and I write now flat on my back. I have telegraphed my dear Maggie regularly or by every opportunity as to my condition, and hope she has received my dispatches. Remember me kindly to your mother and family and believe me

Very truly & affectionately
Your brother,
Wm. E. Peters

81. First Union reports of the Moorefield action listed William Peters as mortally wounded. *Official.Records*, 43, pt. 1:726, 734.

82. Col. William H. Powell then commanded a Union cavalry brigade. He returned the kindnesses of Sheffey's mother-in-law by personally intervening to ensure that the captain was well treated by his captors. Powell's congratulatory order to his men for the August 7 victory is in ibid., 735–36.

83. This oblique reference likely means that Pres Sheffey rode a horse the thirty miles from Moorefield to the railroad siding at New Creek, West Virginia. From there the four hundred Confederate prisoners moved by rail to Wheeling and thence to Camp Chase at Columbus.

84. The 1860 census for Campbell County, Virginia, shows Don T. C. Peters as a forty-eight-year-old broker with personal assets of $123,000.

CHAPTER 9

PRISON AND PEACE

For the next six months, Sheffey's address was Camp Chase Military Prison, Ohio. Established in the late spring of 1861 as a training camp for Ohio recruits, the installation outside Columbus was named for the former abolitionist governor who served as Abraham Lincoln's secretary of the Treasury. Authorities soon converted Camp Chase into a holding facility for political prisoners. In April 1862 it became a prison for captured Confederates and remained as such for the remainder of the war.

Camp Chase was an enclosed-barracks type of prison in which stockade walls were placed around existing structures. Eleven acres were divided by sixteen-foot plank walls into three sections, known as Prisons 1, 2, and 3. Prison 1, where Pres Sheffey was housed, was an acre in size and held two hundred officers. The other two divisions each consisted of five acres and could accommodate as many as four thousand enlisted men apiece. Camp Chase's peak population came in January 1865, when more than nine thousand prisoners of war were incarcerated there.

Small shacks or shanties sixteen by twenty-four feet in size housed the inmates, with twelve to fifteen men in each. Narrow streets ran through the clusters of buildings. While food rations and other amenities were comparatively better at Camp Chase than at other major Northern prisons, the environment suffered from poor sanitation and attendant sickness. Drainage inside the compound was all but nonexistent. Latrines were merely open excavations.[1]

Unknown to Sheffey, his father approached the highest levels of government in an effort to gain Pres's release from prison. On November 21, 1864, the elder Sheffey wrote an old acquaintance, Confederate secretary of war James A. Seddon, "I have never troubled you before with any application for myself or family and now a painful sense of delicacy is only overcome by the

---

1. Lonnie R. Speer, *Portals to Hell: Military Prisons of the Civil War* (Mechanicsburg, Pa., 1997), 46–47, 80–82, 37–38. The only lengthy studies of the Ohio prison are William H. Knauss, *The Story of Camp Chase* (Nashville, 1906; reprinted: Columbus, Ohio, 1990); and John H. King's highly opinionated *Three Hundred Days in a Yankee Prison* (Atlanta, 1904).

strongest conviction of parental duty." Sheffey asked for help in securing the parole or exchange of his only son.[2]

His father's letter may have been a factor in Sheffey obtaining an early release from prison. In any event he was already in Marion preparing a home for himself and his wife (still in Wytheville) when the Civil War ended. Yet the couple's future in the defeated South seemed tenuous at best.

Prison No. 1, Camp Chase, Ohio

James W. Sheffey, Esq.
Moorefield, [W.]Va.[3]

My dear father,
Your letter of the 27th ultimo was received today. I am rejoiced to hear that Col. Peters is improving. I have been treated with much kindness since my capture. Ned Halsey sent me $571 and said I could get anything I needed from him. Weaver Schoolfield did the same. So I shall not suffer except from confinement.

The prospect for a speedy exchange is rather slim, and it is almost too much for my philosophy to contemplate with complacency a long imprisonment and absence from home. The news from Col. Peters will go far towards making me contented for awhile, for I feared when I left him that he was mortally wounded.

I wrote to Josie from Moorefield. I have also written to her by Flag of Truce via Fortress Monroe.[4] Write to me frequently, also to Mr. Don T. C. Peters, Astor House, Corner [of] Spring & Crosby Streets, New York. Love to Maggie & the baby, and to all the dear ones when you see them or write. Kindest regards to Col. Peters, also to Ellen & John.

2. James W. Sheffey to James A. Seddon, Nov. 21, 1864, Letters Received by the Confederate Adjutant and Inspector General, 1861–65, RG109, National Archives, M474.

3. Sheffey's father had gone to Moorefield to arrange for the transfer home of his wounded son-in-law, Colonel Peters. Servants John and Ellen Ross accompanied the elder Sheffey on the 550-mile round trip between Marion and Moorefield.

4. Neither letter reached Josephine Sheffey.

Prison No. 1, Camp Chase, Ohio
SEPTEMBER 25TH, 1864

Miss Hannah Gibson,
Care [of] Wm. S. Purgett,[5]
New River Creek Station, Balto. & Ohio Rail Road.

Miss Gibson,

Will you please do me the favor to communicate to my friends that I am well and anxious to hear from them. I have written two letters directed to the care of Mr. D. Gibson,[6] your father, I presume. I suppose they have not reached their destination. Your letter to your friend, Mr. S . . . ,[7] in which you mention that you had seen my sister, was received with a portion of it torn off. I have not seen Mr. S . . . but received a note from him.

Please tell my sister that I have written three letters to my wife by Flag of Truce via Fortress Monroe. Tell her that I have recd. money from Ned Halsey & Wm. W. Schoolfield, & some clothing from another friend, A. H. Dorr of New York, that I preserve my health in spite of the confinement and my anxiety, by keeping myself constantly employed—that I am with a party of jolly fellows who would not die if they were in irons, that we are well-treated and spend the time with chess, drafts, backgammon, quoit-pitching, reading & a debating society where eloquence is "dispersed with" to an alarming extent.[8]

5. The 1860 census for Hampshire County shows William S. Purgett as a twenty-eight-year-old farmer with a large family and limited means. He served in the 13th Virginia Infantry for a month before deserting. In the postwar years Purgett became a member of the county's first board of education. David F. Riggs, *13th Virginia Infantry* (Lynchburg, Va., 1988), 136; Hu Maxwell and H. L. Swisher, *History of Hampshire County, West Virginia* (Morgantown, W.Va., 1897), 292.

6. David Gibson was a prominent Hampshire County merchant, farmer, and benefactor. Among his four children was a daughter, Hannah. Maxwell and Swisher, *History of Hampshire County*, 707–8.

7. Sheffey, uncertain of the man's name, identified him by a capital letter and dots.

8. This pleasant description of life at Camp Chase runs strongly counter to most accounts primarily because Sheffey was in the officer's section. Crowding, sickness, filth, meager food, a smallpox epidemic, and exposure to the elements took a heavy toll in Prisons 2 and 3. In all, twenty-six hundred prisoners of war died at Camp Chase. Included among the fatalities were seventeen members of Sheffey's regiment. Inmates labeled the prison's cemetery the City of the Dead. Speer, *Portals to Hell*, 81–82, 167, 304, 324.

Our exercises, however, in the society are very interesting, as there are many officers here who are not only good speakers but men of fine information. Several of us have procured lawbooks and are reviewing that grand science called by Sir Wm. Blackstone[9] "the perfect of reasoning"—an old friend of ours but not likely to inspire contempt by familiarity. There was a time when some of us perhaps fancied that we were in a fair way to become Burkes or Erskines or Wirts;[10] but we have since passed like the petrels thro. storms & tumults until we find that like necessity, we know no law.[11] If you will hand or send this to my sister, you will confer a favor upon both her & myself.

Prison No 1, Camp Chase, Ohio
NOVEMBER 9TH, 1864

My dear Wife,
A considerable time has elapsed since I received a letter from you. The weary time drags very slowly away at best, but when many days elapse without bringing me a letter from you, it becomes still more intolerable.

The presidential election in [the] US is now over. Of course we who are shut up here know nothing about the result. We had an election for fun in Prison 1, and cast 41 votes for Lincoln and 42 for McClellan.[12] The fears which troubled us some time ago with regard to the small pox have all died away.[13] Lieut. Pollock after being reported dead, has returned to us.[14]

My arm is improving.[15] I handed to a friend of mine who went on ex-

9. For centuries Blackstone's *Commentaries* were fundamental to any study of English law.

10. Edmund Burke, Thomas Erskine, and William Wirt were leading statesmen and orators of their time.

11. Saint Augustine stated in *Soliloquiorum, Animae ad Deum:* "Necessity has no law."

12. More than 4,170,000 people actually voted in the 1864 presidential election, which Abraham Lincoln won by a 500,000-vote majority over Democratic candidate George B. McClellan. Lincoln's electoral count was a whopping 212–21.

13. The last six months of 1864 witnessed a smallpox epidemic that caused most of the nearly three thousand deaths at Camp Chase. See Knauss, *Camp Chase,* 257–58.

14. Davis Statton Pollock of the 4th Virginia Infantry was imprisoned three times during the Civil War. His third capture came at the battle of Cedar Creek on October 19, 1864. After his June 1865 release, Pollock returned home to Pulaski County and lived until 1934. Robertson, *4th Virginia Infantry,* 68.

15. Sheffey had received a relatively crude vaccination for smallpox and was suffering the consequences.

change a copy of a poem which I had been amusing myself in writing, entitled "The Reign of Peace."[16] He will perhaps give it to our friend, F. H. Alfriend of S. Lit. Mess.[17] I wish you would write to Alfriend not to have it published.

Reading here wearies. Writing is a better amusement since it occupies the mind more closely. We have a good many books, but the mess-rooms are so noisy and crowded that we cannot get much satisfaction from them.

I ought to write to Marion, but being limited to two letters per week, and compelled to write a good many letters to friends in the North, I hope the dear ones at Marion will regard my letters to you as intended for them also. I received a letter from [Maj. James N.] Nounnan a few days ago. Love to all.

Prison No 1, Camp Chase, Ohio
NOVEMBER 30TH, 1864

My dear Wife,

Many weeks have elapsed since I received a letter from you. Have written twice to you since your last. I presume you have written and that your letters have been delayed or lost. Do not write more than one page and be careful about putting anything contraband in them. They will then be more apt to reach their destination.

I have been quite uneasy not having heard [anything] since the Saltville affair.[18] I received a letter a few days ago from Sister Elle written at Saltville in September, and postmarked at St. Louis, Mo. The letter was a few days after you left Saltville.

Nearly four months have now passed since my capture and very dreary months they have been. I have, however, read a great deal and will employ

16. This lengthy and sometimes tedious poem concentrated on the blessings of peace. The unpublished work is in the John Preston Sheffey Papers, Virginia Tech University, Blacksburg.

17. Frank Heath Alfriend was then editor of the *Southern Literary Messenger.*

18. On October 2, 1864, thirty-six hundred Union cavalry under Maj. Gen. Stephen Burbridge raided Saltville. Confederate general John S. Williams and hodgepodge force of twenty-eight hundred men were able to repulse the probe; the Federals retreated back to their Kentucky base. Among the wounded left behind were at least one hundred members of the 5th U.S. Colored Cavalry. Evidence is strong that Confederate general Felix H. Robertson ordered his men to murder the black soldiers. What exactly transpired in the "Saltville Massacre" remains controversial. See William Marvel, "The Battle of Saltville: Massacre or Myth?" *Blue & Gray Magazine* 8 (Aug. 1991): 10–19, 46–54; and Thomas D. Mays, *The Saltville Massacre* (Fort Worth, 1995), 42–68.

the time as advantageously as possible. I wrote to you some time ago to write to F. H. Alfriend, Richmond, not to allow my poem "The Reign of Peace" to be published. Hope you received that letter.

Mr. Nathan Look[19] from Smyth was here a few days ago. Was not admitted. I have an old copy of Caesar here sent to me with some other books by Albert H. Dorr, N.Y., and when I tire of Blackstone, I amuse myself with what Lord Bacon called the "universal language."[20] I can fortunately read it easily without a lexicon. My own health in particular, as well as the general health of the prison, is good. Not having heard from you for so long, however, I am getting very blue. My vaccinated arm is improving and will, I think, soon be well. Col. Dave Edmundson is said to be in prison at Washington City. Letters have been received from him here. Love to all our dear ones at Wytheville & at Marion. Col. Graham[21] and Lt. St. John & Adjt. Burns[22] are well.

May God ever bless and guard my beloved wife is ever the prayer of your devoted husband.

Prison No 1, Camp Chase, Ohio
DECEMBER 28TH, 1864

My dear Wife,

I have not heard from you for a long time, though I know you have written. I have written to you frequently but fear that my letters during the last two months, like yours, have failed to reach their destination. We are allowed to receive three papers now in the prison. The news fills us with anxiety. As that from SW Va. interests me more particularly, I hope some of you will contrive to get a letter to me which will relieve my apprehension as to your condition.[23]

19. Nathan L. Look was a native New Yorker residing in Tazewell County at the time of the 1860 census. During the Civil War, he and his wife had a home on the west side of Marion. Look's profession is unknown. Armstrong, *Smyth County*, 2:155.

20. English philosopher and essayist Francis Bacon was referring to Latin.

21. David Pierce Graham served as major of the 51st Virginia Infantry until his 1864 transfer to the staff of Brig. Gen. Gabriel Wharton. Graham later became a prominent miner and iron manufacturer in Bluefield, West Virginia. Krick, *Lee's Colonels*, 140.

22. Capt. Andrew F. St. John of the 8th Virginia Cavalry and Adj. Allen Crockett Burns of the 45th Virginia Infantry both survived imprisonment. Dickinson, *8th Virginia Cavalry*, 109; Scott, *45th Virginia Infantry*, 82.

23. Sheffey had reason to be concerned. Just before Christmas, Maj. Gen. George Stoneman and four thousand mounted Federal troops galloped into southwestern Virginia. The Union

With regard to our monetary affairs, the prospect of considerable loss to us, I fear, is imminent. The notes in your possession ought to be converted into some other kind of property. Please consult my father with regard to it.

The amount due from me to John Ross at the date of my capture was $291.66 2/3. J. H. Ashlin[24] of Smyth Co. has my note for $100.00 payable in currency; I wrote to my father with regard to this and he has perhaps arranged it. If not, it stands against me. Please ask my father to arrange these matters for me. My bay horse had better be sold. I have no other liabilities.

I am quite well, but suffer much anxiety with regard to you and ours. Love to your mother and family and to the family at Marion. Kindest regards to the servants.

Prison No. 1, Camp Chase, Ohio
JANUARY 25TH, 1865

My dear wife,

Your letter of 27th ult. received, also Mary's of Oct. 22nd. The latter must have made quite a sojourn at Richmond or Old Point. I fear none of my letters by Flag of Truce reach you. We receive very few here by that route, and all those a month or more after date. Your letter has me of much anxiety. I had indeed learned from a Col. Coats[25] of [the] U.S. Army that my father's property escaped destruction, which news was further confirmed by a letter from my Uncle ENS [E. N. Sheffey] at Greeneville, Tennessee. But your letter gives me the first certain information since the raid of affairs at Wytheville, and I was very fearful that your mother's house had been destroyed. Com-

---

targets remained the same: to destroy the salt works at Saltville, the lead mines near Wytheville, and as much of the Virginia and Tennessee Railroad as possible. Stoneman's command advanced northward from Bristol. At Marion on December 17–18, about one thousand Confederate cavalry under Brig. Gens. John C. Vaughn and Basil W. Duke held back the Federal advance for a day. When the Federals did occupy Marion, they burned an important covered bridge, destroyed an iron foundry, and wrecked the local newspaper office. A number of private homes were wantonly looted before Stoneman's troopers headed for Wytheville. *Official Records,* 45, pt. 1:813, 815–17, 820, 833; Basil W. Duke, *Morgan's Cavalry* (New York, 1909), 425–31; Armstrong, *Smyth County,* 2:150–57.

24. The 1860 census for Smyth County lists James H. Ashlin as a thirty-two-year-old laborer with no personal assets.

25. This was in all probability Benjamin Franklin Coates, who was a colonel of the 91st Ohio Infantry.

pared with others, we have indeed been fortunate, and have much reason to
be thankful.

My own unfortunate imprisonment (for few worse misfortunes than capture can befall a soldier) is of little moment compared with the welfare of
those I love. It can be easily borne as long as I have good news from home,
country and friends. The news we generally get now is, however, horribly
bad, and fills us with anxiety.

My health is very good. But my homesickness does not get better as I grow
older. Already chronic, none but those renowned physicians; Patience and
Fortitude, can manage it. Our spirits rise & fall like stocks on Wall Street.
One day the Bulls announce immediate exchange, another day, the Bears cir-
culate rumors to the contrary which, like "hope deferred, make the heart
sick."[26] An exchange according to the papers is now going on, but it is not
general, and at this out-of-the-way prison we stand a slender chance.[27]

Lt. St. John, Col. Graham & Adjt. Burns are well. We have plenty of books
and in spite of smoke and cold, we manage to enjoy ourselves at times. I have
read 7 books of Caesar, 3 books of Blackstones, and a history of the Girond
by Lamartine,[28] etc., and an infinite number of novels. Without books, I
think I should "shuffle off this mortal coil."[29] But there's a time for all things.
I'll defer that to the last. We have candles & newspapers. You must all keep
your hearts beating high and write to me often.[30]

26. "Hope deferred maketh the heart sick." Proverbs 13:12.

27. During 1863–64, the exchange of prisoners by the opposing sides collapsed because of
disagreements over how captured black soldiers were to be treated as well as Lt. Gen. U. S.
Grant's opposition to releasing Confederate prisoners of war. Authorities continued negotiat-
ing, and in January 1865 the cartel resumed. Several thousand prisoners per week were released
thereafter through the end of the war. Sheffey was among the early parolees.

28. Alphonso Marie Louis de Lamartine was a prolific nineteenth-century French poet,
writer, and statesman. One of his works was a history of the Gironde, the middle-class political
party during the French Revolution.

29. In one of Shakespeare's most famous orations, Hamlet exclaims: "To sleep, perchance
to dream: ay, there's the rub; / For in that sleep of death what dreams may come, / When we
have shuffled off this mortal coil, / Must give us pause."

30. The remainder of Sheffey's Confederate service is hazy. Efforts were made in mid-
February 1865 to exchange him for a captured Union captain, and on the seventeenth he was
moved to Point Lookout, Maryland, on the peninsula formed by the Chesapeake Bay and the
Potomac River. Sheffey apparently was paroled immediately, for no record exists of his being
incarcerated there. In all likelihood he was back in Marion by the time of Appomattox and
the end of the war. National Archives, "Selected Records of the War Department Relating to

Marion, Va., JUNE 30TH, 1865

My dear wife,

As Capt. Moore[31] is going up to Wytheville this morning, I take advantage of the opportunity to write to you. Col. Clarkson[32] has vacated our house here, and paid up the remainder of his rent, twenty three dollars & something. So that we now have 67 or 68 dollars. Oh, we are getting along admirable.

I am going to work to fit up the premises so as to make you as comfortable as possible. I have borrowed good furniture for one room until next summer from Mrs. Look. I will buy you two neat bed-steads and 7 or 8 cane-bottomed chairs this morning. I will have more difficulty about a cooking stove but will succeed, I think. I shall also provide a capable maid of all work. One woman can easily do all the work about our establishment. Nellie [Ellen White Sheffey] will live with us if you desire it.

As to eatables, we will have no lack for them. We must look forward therefore with heart and hope to the future, trusting that God will strengthen us to override all obstacles and triumph over all difficulties. Our lot will not be so hard a one as that of most other people, and if we only pull together heartily, ever strengthening each other's hands, we will soon have every comfort around us.

Capt. Moore is waiting and I must close. All send love. Ma says she will never have a piece of pie but she will send you half of it, and my father & the girls are delighted that we are coming to Marion. I forgot to add that Ma & Pa will give us a good deal of furniture.

Marion, Va., JULY 4TH, 1865

My dear Wife,

I did not expect when I came here to be absent from you so long, and fear I have occasioned you some anxiety. Several days must yet elapse before I

Confederate Prisoners of War, 1861–1865" (Washington, 1966), Microfilm Reel 23, 118–19; *Official Records,* ser. 2, 8:307.

31. This is probably Jackson Moore, the last captain of Company B of Col. William Peters's 21st Virginia Cavalry. Wallace, *Virginia Military Organizations,* 61.

32. The July 1865 property transfer between John N. Clarkson and James W. Sheffey is on file in the Clerk's Office, Circuit Court of Smyth County. Deputy Clerk Carole Wassum Rosenbaum to editor, Oct. 29, 2002.

can come to Wytheville, as I am trying to make your home that is to be as comfortable as possible than most of the houses of young people. The property has been terribly injured by my renters and others, but I will remove their footprints before I bring you to it.

A few days ago I thought I had succeeded in hiring a Negro woman who is an elegant cook, washer & ironer & maid of all work, but I understand today that she has concluded to leave the Country, so that I shall have to look round for some one else. I apprehend little difficulty in getting one to suit us, and one good servant will be sufficient for us for a while.

I have not yet secured a cooking stove but hope to get Col. Clarkson's when he leaves. I bargained with Mrs. Bear[33] for 6 cane bottomed chairs, a rocking chair & two bedsteads, all very neat for $21.50. I am to get them when she leaves, which she will do as soon as the cars run through. I think I will be able to make our house a pleasant home, notwithstanding its vicinage, and hope before many years have rolled away that we will have retrieved our losses and gathered every comfort and luxury around us. It is, at any rate, evident that we are at present unable to go to housekeeping anywhere else, and housekeeping is, I think, a necessity, for those who would succeed must settle. A rolling stone gathers no moss, nor do undecided people.

I look forward to the future with resolution and with hope. I do not need help, except the help of an occasional loving and encouraging word from you, to give me success, and God willing, I will yet gather around you every blessing of which I dreamed in the far away years of my boyhood. They seem far away when I look back over the gulf that flows between the now and then, in which so many have buried life, fortune, hope and happiness. God has favored us greatly, and if we are only true to ourselves, He will always help us. I have no desire on earth but to make you perfectly happy, and whenever I am satisfied that you are so, I shall be perfectly happy myself. Everything I do or devise is for that end, and I would not have thwarted a single wish of your heart could I have avoided it. But why should our happiness depend upon locality? We may have sunshine in our house and hearts whatever circumstance may surround us.

Had we, in our condition settled at Wytheville,[34] we would have had long

33. According to the 1860 census, Nancy Bear was the wife of Bavarian-born Joseph Bear, who had a mercantile store in Marion.

34. Josephine Sheffey wanted to continue living in her hometown, Wytheville. Her husband is explaining here why this is not practical.

to bear "the whips and scorns of outrageous fortune."[35] We had no home there and no money to buy one. Here we have a good house and a sure guarantee that we shall not want for bread, and not long, I hope, for anything else. When we get money enough to justify it, you may then select a home wherever you think you will be happiest. In the meantime, we will go to work and beautify the one into which *necessity* has impelled us, and whatever discomforts we may have, let us lay them at the door of the same stern old despot.

But again to more practical matters. Our kitchen you know was burned and we will have to do without one for a while. A carpenter offered today to build one for me & take his pay in professional services. He was in earnest. I think my friends will eventually enable me to pay for everything in that way. I have had a carpenter at work today upon the house, repairing the damage by the fire, and another building a paling around the yard. The repairs immediately necessary will not cost me more than ten or twenty dollars. The stable and woodhouse are still the best in the town, though much injured by plankburners. We have a cook-house that will answer for a while all the purposes of a kitchen. Our grapevines are burdened with fruit, and there are few apples. I will throw the three lots into one. My father will give us a good garden on the hill north of the stable.

We will have therefore a yard of three quarters of an acre, all fertile, for flowers and vines & fruit trees. There is no well on either of my lots, and we will have to get water at the well on the opposite side of the street until I can have one dug. I think I can get water on either of the lots at a depth of 25 to 39 feet. The garden has not been worked since it was planted by Col. Clarkson in the spring until I came here. I have worked it out myself. There are 9 or 10 rows of beets, 3 rows of parsnips, a few potatoes, 40 or 50 tomato vines, etc.; the cellar is the best in town.

How many myriads of miserables would fancy themselves as wealthy as the Rothschilds[36] if they had such a house. There is a dwelling with six large rooms, 2 closets, a cook-house, calf lot, cow-house, stable, yard of 3/4ths acre planted with grapevines, fruit trees, currants, gooseberries, roses, etc., lumberhouse, grainary, store-house and work-house—all this *in* esse—and a gar-

35. Sheffey combines two quotes from *Hamlet:* "Whether 'tis nobler in the mind to suffer / The slings and arrows of outrageous fortune" and "For who would bear the whips and scorns of time."

36. The Rothschilds were a family of internationally known German-Jewish financiers whose banking house went into business near the end of the eighteenth century.

den of an acre, and a well of 25 feet, and a neat kitchen and the elegant society of the Rs & the Ds, all F.F.V's[37] *in prospectu* besides a number of other things whereof this deponent saith not.

But I have been working hard all day and it is now late at night. It is possible that I may not be at Wytheville for 7 or 8 days. How this letter is to go I know not. But I will get some one to take it. All send love and none more than

Your devoted husband

Josie wanted to continue living in Wytheville. Sheffey insisted that their home be in Marion, where his father had offered him both a law practice and the white frame house Pres was repairing a half-block up Main Street from the Sheffey family residence. The former captain had little free capital, but he was able to furnish comfortably his and Josie's only home. There the couple would spend the rest of their lives.

In the summer of 1865 Sheffey sought to become a candidate for commonwealth attorney of Smyth County. Being a disenfranchised ex-Confederate ended this hope. He then resumed the family law practice, became the town's foremost attorney, and was widely hailed as Marion's most distinguished Civil War soldier. He and Josie had five daughters and two sons. The family became devoted members of Royal Oak Presbyterian Church; Pres served as an elder for three decades, while Josie enjoyed a long tenure as the church organist.

Captain Sheffey accepted appointment in 1895 as judge of the Seventeenth Judicial Circuit of Virginia. Three years later he took leave to serve a term in the Virginia legislature. The impressive judge with a drooping mustache remained on the bench until he stepped down in February 1904. A local editor said of Sheffey, "He left the bench with the respect and affection of the lawyers who had practiced before him, and all men who knew him, whether as a private citizen, as a lawyer, or as a judge, will bear willing testimony to his spotless integrity and to the nobility of his character."

An enjoyable retirement was short lived. On November 19, 1904, after several years of failing health, Josephine Spiller Sheffey died. The blow was undoubtedly severe for her husband—he lived but nine months longer. On August 26, 1905, sixty-seven-year-old John Preston Sheffey died at his home. Husband and wife are buried side by side in Round Hill Cemetery.

37. This was a reference to Republicans and Democrats who were in the elite First Families of Virginia.

Forty-four years earlier, Pres Sheffey had donned a Confederate army uniform. He had departed for war with the same feelings inherent in every patriotic American of every conflict: to defend home and family and to protect his society's way of life. Sheffey faced danger, disease, and death. He did so unflinchingly. The pride he felt in his last years was justified. He had been a good citizen as well as a good soldier.

INDEX